The Texas Revolution

A Day-by-Day Account

by Bob Boyd

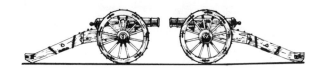

Edited by Soren W. Nielsen

**To my sons, Robert and David —
the blood of heroes flows through their veins.**

FOREWORD

The book that you hold in your hands is a compilation of articles which have appeared in the pages of the San Angelo Standard-Times between Sept. 29, 1985, and April 22, 1986.

Its publication is the result of requests by — and at times, the insistence of — some of our readers to consolidate the articles into book form.

The daily dispatches reproduced here, as well as the weekly profiles, have been a labor of love by City Editor and historical author Bob Boyd. We have been both pleased and proud of the results.

Many have asked why we undertook such a project, a question we even asked ourselves at times.

The decision to proceed with such an undertaking came following much discussion of what we could do as a newspaper to provide our readers with a meaningful commemoration of Texas' 150 years of statehood. These discussions were taking place long before the Sesquicentennial year began.

There were attempts to secure commercial sponsorship of the series, and modest attempts for limited syndication. There were no takers. And although it was a disappointment, it was understandable. We knew the significance of the project, but it was difficult to communicate this to others, especially when the West Texas economy was presenting issues to people that were far more important at the time.

But, the decision was made nonetheless to proceed with the project, and to committing considerable resources of time, money and newspaper space to it.

Only a little more than a year earlier our newspaper had celebrated its Centennial, an event which brought into clear focus for all of us the part that this newspaper had played in the history of West Texas. Our anniversary also reminded us of the passion and respect for history that our readers in West Texas have.

We have not regretted our decision. Bob Boyd's tenacious research and talented writing have brought to the pages of the Standard-Times an account of the Texas Revolution that should be read by every Texan, native or transplanted. It has been enhanced by the artwork of James Robertson, creative services manager of the newspaper, who also has a deep respect and love for Texas history.

It is because of the quality and significance of the project that the second decision was made — to compile the articles in book form and to offer it to other Texans and anyone else with an interest in Texas.

We think that you, like us, will be glad you have taken the time to read "The Texas Revolution: A Day-by-Day Account."

KEVIN J. BARRY
Publisher, Standard-Times
San Angelo, Texas

March 11, 1986

CONTENTS

Preface
and selected bibliography

In 1980 my wife, Jackie, took a trip to the Alamo with her aunt, Mrs. Nell Brocato of Columbus, Ga. During the drive to San Antonio, Mrs. Brocato told Jackie that she had recently learned that their family was related to the first man who stepped over the legendary line that William Barret Travis had drawn in the dirt with his sword.

At the Alamo, Jackie saw a painting of that dramatic scene. The first man over the line was Tapley Holland, the 24-year-old son of one of Stephen F. Austin's original colonists. There was something about the painting, something about the haunting, old stones of the Alamo chapel that touched Jackie. She was filled with a bittersweet feeling of pride and loss. I also became inspired.

I began to read everything I could about the Alamo, the Holland family and early Texas history.

In June 1983, I wrote an article for Infantry Magazine, the journal of U.S. Army Land Forces, the first discussion of the tactics used at the Alamo ever to appear in a military journal.

When the Standard-Times decided to publish a special Sesquicentennial project, we chose to employ a unique concept: In modern reporting style, publish a daily account of what happened 150 years ago, with each dispatch containing only what information would have been available at the location of the story on that particular day.

The writings can be viewed on two levels — first, as the history of the revolution presented as it would have been in a modern newspaper; second, as a more subtle look at the strengths and weaknesses of media coverage of wide-ranging event such as the Texas Revolution.

In using this method, it was necessary to draw conclusions on events and motivations not accepted by all historians. A reporter on the scene of an event cannot give a half-dozen versions of something he is supposed to have witnessed. In reaching these conclusions, I have weighed all the evidence available and tried to come down on the side of logic and common sense.

The publication of the dispatches started the Sunday before the first battle of the revolution and continued for seven months. In scope and commitment of resources, this project dwarfed any Sesquicentennial project by other newspapers in the state.

It was made possible because of the courage of the publisher, Kevin J. Barry, and the editor, Soren Nielsen, who were committing the resources to finish the job. I was given the time I needed. I was given a creative genius in his own field, artist Jim Robertson, to work with.

I don't think that many newspapers could have pulled off this project, because not many newspapers have the type of readership the Standard-Times has. San Angelo is one of those special cities where history is viewed with a passion. My support group included the people at Fort Concho, the staff of the newspaper, particularly Arlen Lohse, and my best friend and fellow Texas historian, Gus Clemens.

I am indebted in particular to two people at the newspaper. In addition to his role as editor, Nielsen found the time to be my personal editor for the

Texas Revolution project. I could not have found a better person for the job. Nielsen is a history lover who went far beyond merely copyreading to help me reconstruct confused constructions and prod me toward the type of writing I am capable of only under the guidance of a strong editor.

Suzanne Perry, the newspaper's librarian, helped me in many ways. She almost ruined her own reputation at Angelo State University by continually finding and checking out books I invariably kept overtime. She proved to be a proofreader of the old school, gracious enough to keep my absurd errors to herself. She also compiled the index for this book.

Clemens was a tower of strength, counseling me during my down periods and always urging me to take the path of moderation in my conclusions.

Jackie was much more than an understanding wife. She has a B.A. in history from the University of Texas and has always been a history lover. Our long discussions on Texas history helped me mold my own thoughts.

This work would not have been possible in the form it took without the 10-volume "Papers of the Texas Revolution" by John H. Jenkins. In a monumental achievement, Jenkins and Gen. Jay A. Matthews put together many of the important and obscure letters, reports and documents of the revolutionary period and presented them in day-to-day order. Whenever I was hung up on a date, I knew Jenkins would be able to bail me out. I cannot imagine a serious student of Texas history not reading and (if you can find a set) not owning this important contribution to Texas history.

A number of fairly obscure works proved invaluable, including such books as "The Texas Navy" by Jim Dan Hill, "The Bicentennial Commemorative History of Nacogdoches," "Presidio La Bahia" by Kathryn Stoner O'Connor, "The Forgotten Colony," by Rachel Bluntzer Hebert, and "Susanna Dickinson, Messenger of the Alamo," by C. Richard King. These books and many others that are in the hard-to-find category were the building blocks for the project.

The cement that held these blocks together was found mainly in the Eugene Barker Texas History Center at the University of Texas in Austin. It was there that I spent many hours reading the correspondence of the men and women who were making history. The Barker Center contains the "Austin Papers," which should be the starting place for serious research on the period. Barker's "The Life of Stephen F. Austin," which is a condensation of the large amount of material in the collection, is essential in understanding the colonization and revolutionary periods in Texas history.

A word to those who would follow my footsteps in studying Texas history: Read the primary sources. Immerse yourself in the correspondence of the people of the times. Go to the primary sources whenever possible, find the little-known books by men and women who were moved by a passion for history and by pride in their ancestors' accomplishments.

There are several standard works that provide a good overview of Texas history. The most readable is "Lone Star" by T.R. Fehrenbach, who also wrote a highly readable history of Mexico, "Fire and Blood." "Texas, A History," by Joe B. Frantz is probably the best of the general histories. The best mood builder of the general histories is "Great River, the Rio Grande in North American History," by Paul Horgan.

Three major books on the Alamo are "13 Days to Glory," by Lon Tinkle, "The Alamo," by John Myers Myers and "A Time to Stand," by Walter Lord.

The best work done on the Alamo, is the unpublished dissertation "A Critical Study of the Siege of the Alamo and of the Personnel of its Defenders," written in 1931 by Amelia Williams. This work is a milestone in Texas historiography.

Works on battles in the revolution other than the Alamo are harder to come by. "The Day of San Jacinto" by Frank Tolbert gives a good account of the battle and takes the reader through some of the more memorable events during the Runaway Scrape.

Among the secondary works that were important to this book are "The Texas Republic," by William Ranson Hogan, "The Texas Rangers," by Walter Prescott Webb, "The Raven, A Biography of Sam Houston," by Marquis James, "Sam Houston, the Great Designer," by Llerena B. Friend. "After San Jacinto" and "Attack and Counter-Attack" by Joseph Milton Nance are scholarly works of the 1836-42 period with many useful footnotes and references.

A must for any advanced student is the "Handbook of Texas," compiled by the Texas State Historical Association.

There are several remarkable autobiographies of participants available. Whenever possible, I attempted to weave quotes from these works into the daily dispatches. Thus, the reporter on the scene obtains quotes from Noah Smithwick after the battles of Gonzales and Concepcion and after fights between Rangers and Indians from Smithwick's autobiography, "The Evolution of a State."

Hermann Ehrenberg's "With Milam and Fannin" is used for quotes on successes in San Antonio and the disasters in Goliad. "With Santa Anna in Texas" by Jose Enrique De La Pena and "The Evacuation of Texas" by Gen. Vicente Filisola are among the writings of participants on the Mexican side that were essential in bringing subjectivity to the book.

The journalistic practice of attributing quotes to "sources" is used. Such references represent my best assessment of conditions and are used to encapsulate events and enhance readability.

The materials for study are voluminous. There are several good collections of official documents at the State Library and the General Land Office. There are large collections of manuscripts at several locations, including the Barker Center, the Alamo Library and the Austin Public Library.

A full bibliography on the materials which went into the preparation of this book is impractical. Once a serious student begins to dig into the period, the sources present themselves. One must balance certain writers against others as there are several schools of thought in Texas revolutionary history. Part of the fun of becoming a student of the period is being able to take part in the sometimes animated discussions of what did and what did not happen and why.

My research has convinced me that what happened in Texas in 1835-36 was a triumph of freedom and a reaffirmation that there is nothing more important to the human condition than personal liberty. The men and women of revolutionary Texas knew that, fought for it, died for it and are honored for it in this book.

BOB BOYD
San Angelo, Texas
March 8, 1986

September 29, 1835

SAN FELIPE — This Brazos River center of Anglo power in Texas is a powder keg of tension waiting for a spark.

The town of 500 is jammed with hundreds of armed men from Stephen F. Austin's colony and other parts of Anglo Texas.

News that many Mexican reinforcements are on their way to garrisons in Texas has effectively ended the dispute between the Peace Party and the radical War Party. While still disagreeing on whether to push for complete independence or to stay within the framework of the Mexican Constitution of 1824, leaders of both parties agree that any attempt to occupy and disarm Anglo Texas must be resisted.

Austin, once the most influential voice of moderation in the Peace Party, has been calling on the people of Texas to organize their militia.

"War is our only recourse," the one-time peace activist said Sept. 19 in a letter for general distribution.

Taking their cue from their grandfathers 60 years ago, Texans have been forming and operating committees of correspondence, similar to those set up before the American Revolution. Also called committees of safety, the groups represent different municipalities and rural districts. More than a dozen such groups are now operating.

There has been a notable increase in the activity of these committees as news of Mexico's plans to impose harsh new restrictions on the Anglo colonists have spread throughout the province.

A general consultation of representatives from throughout Texas is scheduled for Oct. 15 in San Felipe. Austin has called on each committee to send a representative to San Felipe in order to form a government-in-being until the consultation is convened.

Meanwhile, Don Lorenzo de Zavala, the Mexican liberal party leader who was forced to flee from Santa Anna, has been lobbying influential colonists to fight the man he calls a military dictator.

Zavala told an audience in Brazoria that "Texas is the only part of the Mexican nation not overrun by federal troops. It must organize itself for the preservation of constitutional government."

Zavala, a former governor of the state of Mexico and leader of the York Masonic political party, is one of five men in Texas that Mexican authorities want extradited. Also on the list are radical War Party activists William Travis, F.W. Johnson, Robert (Three-legged Willie) Robertson and Sam Williams.

Texas officials still trying to avert a war have complained that the order for the extradition of these men is not only unthinkable, but impossible.

As one aide of Austin said, "Even if we wanted to placate the Mexicans, our people would never let us turn their friends and neighbors over to Mexican justice."

The demands for the arrest have heightened the level of tension in Texas. Most observers agree that open warfare will result from the first Mexican attempt to exert military pressure on the colonists.

GONZALES — The Gonzales militia has been formed under Alcalde Andrew Ponton following the refusal of town authorities to turn over to a Mexican patrol a brass cannon.

A small Mexican cavalry patrol appeared on the banks of the Guadalupe River about a week ago requesting the six-pounder. Ponton stalled for time, requested more specific instructions from Mexican political authorities and sent messages to Anglo settlements asking for immediate reinforcements.

The 18 men of the Gonzales militia have removed all boats from the west side of the river and have hidden the ferry.

There are reports that as many as 200 Mexican troops are approaching the town from the west with orders to seize the cannon and any colonists who have resisted lawful orders.

MEXICO CITY — This capital is buzzing with rumors that President Antonio Lopez de Santa Anna will soon ask Congress to formally abolish the federal system of government in Mexico.

Such an action will effectively end the last guarantees of the Constitution of 1824 and turn the republic into a Centralist-controlled nation.

Centralist politicians say Santa Anna will, within a few days, abolish all state governments and turn the states into departments in a reorganized and centralized Mexican government.

Informed observers in this politically turbulent city point out that Santa Anna has been moving vigorously to curb powers of the states since he deposed the Federalist-leaning President Gomez Farias last year.

When Santa Anna, acting with the full backing of the Centralist-supporting clergy and large landowners, was opposed by Federalist leaders in northern states, he resorted to military action and retribution.

Federal troops crushed the militia of the state of Zacatecas. Towns in the prosperous state were sacked, several hundred prisoners were shot and martial law was imposed on the survivors.

When faced with opposition from Coahuila y Texas in April, the president marched on Monclova and arrested or put to flight all Federalist politicians.

The action in Monclova leaves only the subprovince of Texas out of the firm military control of the Santanista regime.

Mexican military sources say reinforcements are already streaming into that faction-torn and Anglo-dominated province.

Santa Anna is reported to be consulting with leading clerics and landowners about the financing of a large military expedition to Texas. The object of the expedition will be the elimination of Anglo influence from the province.

The Federalist leaders who contended for 12 years with the Centralists for control of the political destiny of this young nation are on the run or in hiding. The victory of the Centralists is also a victory for the Scottish Rite faction of the Masons. The York faction of the Masons had been dominated by liberals and federalists. Their defeat leaves the more conservative and Centralist-leaning Scottish Rite order in control.

Mexico has no political parties as such, and the Masonic orders have served that function since the early 1820s.

SAN ANTONIO — This normally sleepy town of 2,500 on the San Antonio River is alive with rumors of troops movements and colonial unrest.

The town's garrison is the largest concentration of Mexican military in Texas.

The troops seem edgy. Patrols have been increased and Anglo businessmen are being searched and questioned.

Military observers say that the commandant, Col. Domingo de Ugartechea, split his forces when he sent a company of more than 100 dragoons 60 miles east of here to the town of Gonzales to retrieve an unmounted cannon.

Mexican authorities refuse to discuss military matters, but observers say Ugartechea has been left with fewer than 400 troops to defend the most important post in Texas.

He is expecting 600 reinforcements with the arrival of Gen. Martin Perfecto de Cos, but is said to fear that a quick massing of Texans might put him at a disadvantage.

"I don't think we have anything to really worry about," one Mexican officer said. "The Texans have no military structure and are incapable of mounting a campaign. As soon as Gen. Cos gets here, we will teach them a lesson."

Some military sources believe there are more than 1,000 armed Texans on the move in the province and that hundreds of volunteers are expected to cross the Sabine River to help the revolutionaries if hostilities break out.

WASHINGTON, D.C. — Sources close to the White House said today that a top-level meeting was held by President Jackson to discuss the escalating crisis in Texas.

Attending the session were top aides and Secretary of State John Forsyth.

A report was given Jackson on a series of naval incidents early this month involving American merchant ships and Mexican naval vessels. Other topics discussed were the growing unrest among the Anglo settlers, the failure of American government attempts to purchase Texas from Mexico and Mexican troop movements within the province.

"We have to move slowly on Texas," one presidential aide said, adding that the nation would not support a war to protect the interests of slave-owners in Texas.

"What the Mexicans don't realize is that the Texas colonists are kith and kin. We cannot let them be slaughtered like the liberals of Zacatecas."

The liberals of the northern state of Zacatecas resisted orders from the central government to disarm the militia. Santa Anna led an army to crush the resistance and won a pitched battle May 10. After the victory, the Mexican president allowed his troops to plunder the state. Several hundred liberals were executed.

During the meeting, orders were drafted to Gen. E.P. Gaines in New Orleans to increase patrols along the Texas border on the Sabine River. Gaines additional orders are top secret.

September 30, 1835

MATAGORDA — A deserter from a Mexican warship has told authorities here that the vessel is loaded with military supplies to be used in a campaign in Texas.

The seaman is an Englishman who said he was a merchant sailor pressed into service by the Mexican Navy. He was serving on the brig Vera Cruzana, which appeared two weeks ago near this Gulf Coast port.

The ship dispatched a small boat to the Pilot's House. The Englishman was one of three crewmen manning the boat, which was commanded by an American mercenary named Cannon.

The Englishman escaped and made his way into this town of 300.

He told authorities here that the Vera Cruzana was bound for Copano Bay with a cargo of cannon, small arms, ammunition and iron hobbles.

He said more than 500 Mexican troops from Matamoras were expected to land at Copano Bay in a short time to form the nucleus of an army that was to move to Goliad and San Antonio.

The Vera Cruzana has sailed in the direction of Copano. The chairman of the local committee of safety, R.R. Royal, has sent an urgent message to San Felipe about the Vera Cruzana, also asking that reinforcements be sent to Matagorda.

"I expect if the enemy should find out how badly we are armed here, he may make an effort to pay us a visit," Royal said.

October 1, 1835

GONZALES — A steady stream of women and children is leaving this Guadalupe River settlement, while the men of the town prepare for a possible battle with the Mexican Army.

While noncombatants were heading east, scores of reinforcements were moving west into this center of Green DeWitt's colony.

Meanwhile, authorities here continue to use stalling tactics in an attempt to postpone an outbreak of violence until more help arrives from other Anglo settlements.

A company of more than 100 Mexican dragoons is camped four miles from here on the west side of the Guadalupe. They were sent to reinforce a smaller patrol that attempted to remove a six-pounder cannon from the militia.

Town Alcade Andrew Ponton has been organizing the settlement's militia of 18 men, while negotiations with the Mexicans are being carried out by his assistant, Joseph D. Clements.

Clements has been asking for clarifications and more time to deal with the request.

He sent a letter yesterday to the Mexican commander saying that he could not take action on the cannon in the absence of clearer political instructions from his superiors.

With the Mexicans' patience wearing thin, Clements added, "The said cannon is now in this town and if you force it from us, we must submit; we are weak and few in numbers, but will nevertheless contend for what we believe to be just principles."

He signed the letter with what has become the battle cry of the colonists' freedom movement — "God and Liberty."

Mexican military sources in the Guadalupe camp refuse to comment on the escalating crisis, but say that the dragoons will carry out their orders.

October 2, 1835

GONZALES — A Mexican cavalry company of more than 100 men was routed in a brisk but almost bloodless battle with 150 Texans today four miles east of this Guadalupe River settlement.

It marked the first time that shots had been fired in anger between Texans and Mexican soldiers since the current increase in tensions.

The fighting claimed only one life, a Mexican private. Neither side reported any seriously wounded men.

The hostilities resulted from an attempt by a small Mexican detachment to repossess a brass cannon from the Gonzales militia.

The six-pounder cannon was given to the settlement four years ago to help protect it from Indian attacks, according to Andrew Ponton, the town's alcade.

Mexican sources insisted the cannon was loaned to the Gonzales militia and, in view of the present unstable political conditions in the colony, it was thought prudent to retrieve it.

After the small detachment was rebuffed, Capt. Francisco Castaneda was dispatched from the garrison in San Antonio with a company of 100 dragoons.

Castaneda and Texan officers conferred yesterday. The Mexican officer urged the colonists to return the cannon.

"I am a republican, too, but I am a Mexican officer and must do my duty," Castaneda said.

The Texans urged Castaneda to join them in resisting what they termed the tyranny of Mexican President Antonio Lopez de Santa Anna.

Negotiations were broken off and on this fog-shrouded morning, Texans commanded by Col. John Moore formed a single battle line after crossing to the west bank of the Guadalupe.

In the middle of the line was the mounted six-pounder. A banner streamed over the cannon. It read, "Come and take it."

The Mexican troops hastily formed a firing line and each side exchanged several long-range volleys. When the Texans advanced, Castaneda ordered a withdrawal to San Antonio, which was effected without interference from the victorious Texans.

Castaneda defended his actions by saying that his commander-in-chief, Col. Domingo de Ugartechea, had ordered him to avoid provocations.

Texas reinforcements continue to pour into Gonzales and now number nearly 300. An additional several hundred men are under arms and are massing in San Felipe.

Military sources estimate the number of Mexican troops still in Texas to be 900 at San Antonio and 600 at Goliad. Most of the Goliad troops are reported to be on the march to reinforce the San Antonio garrison.

October 3, 1835

MEXICO CITY — The Santanista-controlled congress eliminated the last guarantees of the Constitution of 1824 here today, stripping state legislatures of their powers and returning full control of the country to the office of president.

Under the sweeping legislation, all state legislatures are ordered to cease exercising their legislative functions after electing five members who will act as a council to the governor.

The legislation marks the final victory of the conservative Centralist-Scottish York political party over the liberal Federalist-York party.

The two Masonic factions served as political parties during the contest between the liberals and conservatives.

The legislation is contained in five articles. Other parts of the bill include provisions for all judges and tribunals of the state to continue to administer justice until new judicial bodies are formed. All officers of the state are directed to continue their duties.

The legislation, which gives almost total power to President Antonio Lopez de Santa Anna, was signed by acting president Miguel Barragan. Santa Anna has taken the field as commanding general of the army and legally cannot assume the title of president until he relinquishes his military office.

Political observers point out, however, that the move makes Santa Anna a virtual dictator with almost unlimited powers. The Centralist-dominated congress is not expected to offer any opposition to the move, which is backed by most large landowners and the powerful elements of the Catholic Church.

Observers believe the legislation will hurt the Peace Party in Texas. Colonists attempting to head off a break between Centralist officials and the subprovince have based their arguments on the Constitution of 1824.

The return to Centralist rule is expected to strengthen the hand of the radical War Party in Texas.

October 4, 1835

SAN FELIPE — One of the most radical members of the War Party announced his intention today to run for a seat in the Oct. 15 consultation.

William Barret Travis, 27, said from a sickbed in San Felipe that he has authorized his name to be submitted as a candidate from Fort Settlement.

Travis is in this Brazos River center of Anglo power recovering from influenza. The illness kept him out of the recent fighting in Gonzales, much to his disgust.

"I have been quite sick with influenza, or I would have gone," Travis said in a letter announcing his candidacy. The letter was sent to Capt. Randal Jones of the Fort Settlement Committee of Safety.

Travis has been an activist in the most radical faction of the War Party for several years. Last summer he led an armed force against the Mexican garrison at the port of Anahuac. His actions were strongly criticized at the time by the majority of leading citizens in Texas.

Travis has emerged again as a political figure since the recent escalation of tension between Mexican authorities and the colonists. His name appeared on a list of agitators whom Mexican officials want Anglo leaders to hand over for trial.

The demand was rejected and Travis has been active in recent weeks recruiting colonists to the War Party.

"The situation is now critical and I will go to Gonzales as soon as possible," Travis said, adding that he expects to be at the Guadalupe River settlement within a week.

October 5, 1835

GOLIAD — A visibly upset Gen. Martin Perfecto de Cos today commanded speed in the movement of troops and supplies from Copano Bay to this Southwest Texas supply center.

Cos issued the orders after learning of a military action near the Guadalupe River town of Gonzales three days ago.

Details of the action are sketchy. Mexican military sources said a patrol from the San Antonio garrison apparently exchanged shots with a group of colonial militia. The Mexican troops retired toward San Antonio, apparently in good order.

Cos had hoped to head off action against the colonists until his moves to reinforce the garrison in San Antonio were completed.

He has up to 800 troops strung out from the port of Copano Bay to Goliad, with advance elements already on the 95-mile march from here to San Antonio.

Mexican military sources said almost all the troops and supplies will be moved out of Goliad within 24 hours. They said the action at Gonzales might benefit them since Texans massing at Gonzales will be in no position to interfere with the forces marching to San Antonio.

One aide to Cos hinted that the San Antonio commander, Col. Domingo de Ugartechea, might have instigated the move on Gonzales as a feint to ensure the safe arrival of the reinforcements.

"Ugartechea is a smart soldier. He has had more experience fighting Texans than any officer we have. It sounds like something he might do," the aide said.

October 6, 1835

NACOGDOCHES — Powerful Cherokee war chiefs near this East Texas town have warned their young men to stop discussing the possibility of a war with Texans, according to a report released here today.

In a speech for general distribution to the tribe, two chiefs, Bowles and Big Mush, told the tribe's warriors to tone down their warlike rhetoric.

William Goyens, a well-known black merchant and landowner from Nacogdoches, returned today from Cherokee territory and delivered a report and his translation of the speech.

According to Goyens, Bowles refuted rumors that Texans would soon seize their lands. He said common reports about Americans having hanged Cherokees in Arkansas were unfounded.

"There are enough good members of society among the Americans that they would not have taken any of our lives without a cause. We old chiefs had heard a different tale," Bowles said.

More than 6,000 Cherokees live on East Texas lands from west of Nacogdoches to the Neches River. The tribe can field a fighting force estimated at more than 800 warriors.

Nacogdoches officials, including Goyens, have been working behind the scenes to smooth relations between colonists and Cherokees. Officials fear that if fighting breaks out in West Texas between Texans and the Mexican Army, the Cherokees could threaten a second front.

Authorities believe Mexican agents have been trying to recruit Indians of several tribes, including Cherokees, to fight Texans.

October 7, 1835

SAN FELIPE — The creation of a post office department for Texas has been recommended by Stephen F. Austin.

Acting as chairman of the San Felipe Committee of Safety, Austin urged consideration of an official recommendation he drew up earlier this week.

"During the present interesting period of affairs of Texas, it is very evident that facility of communications between the different sections of the country is all important," Austin said.

Austin's recommendations include the establishment of a provisional post office department under the direction of former U.S. postal official, John Rice Jones.

Under Austin's plan, mail routes to the United States frontier by way of Harrisburg, Liberty and Nacogdoches would take top priority because of the need to communicate quickly with Americans during the current political and military crisis with Mexico.

Other routes would be established to Velasco, Matagorda, Washington, San Felipe, Bastrop, Gonzales and other locations.

The postal service would be expected to pay for itself through fees and contributions by colonists.

October 8, 1835

PHILADELPHIA, Pa. — A Mexican official has protested the capture of a warship by an American vessel.

In a letter addressed to Ashbury Dickins, the acting secretary of state, J.M. de Castillo Lanzas, the Mexican charge d'affaires at the Mexican legation here, demanded the immediate release of the ship Carreo de Mexico.

The armed schooner was captured by the San Felipe, an American ship operating out of Texas. The battle took place off Galveston Island last month. A prize crew from the San Felipe sailed the Mexican ship to New Orleans, where the crew and the ship are being detained by U.S. authorities.

Lanzas complained that the Mexican consul in New Orleans has been unable to obtain the release of the ship or crew and that legal proceedings now anticipated will hold the Carreo de Mexico out of action for several months.

Naval sources familiar with the situation said that the Texans' plan is to bog down the proceeding in legal technicalities. War supplies and volunteer troops should begin arriving soon in Texas ports. The absence of the Mexican warship at this critical time gives the Texans a chance to maintain control of their sea lanes.

"Having the Carreo de Mexico and her crew held in prize court is as good as disabling her," one naval source said, emphasizing that the remainder of the Mexican fleet is deployed in defensive positions around Matamoras and the Mexican Navy does not yet have enough ships to replace the Carreo de Mexico, leaving the Texas coast open to the colonists.

October 9, 1835

SAN ANTONIO — Gen. Martin Perfecto de Cos entered this center of Mexican influence in Texas today with more than 600 cavalry and infantry troops.

Cos immediately assumed command of the garrison from Col. Domingo de Ugartechea. Observers estimate the reinforcements, which have been trickling in from Goliad for several days, have increased the San Antonio army to about 1,200 men.

In an effort to bolster the morale of the troops, Cos told his officers that the forces at his disposal in the San Antonio area are the largest concentration of military power from the Mississippi River to the interior of Mexico. His artillery includes as many as 30 cannons.

Cos was reported to be angry at the outcome of a skirmish with Texas militia troops near Gonzales a week ago.

Sources close to Cos said he wanted to assume the initiative in his dealings with the colonists, but he has now been thrown into a defensive position.

Mexican intelligence officers estimate more than 500 Texans are massed in Gonzales with hundreds more on the move.

There is concern about the loyalty of the population of this town of 2,500. San Antonio has traditionally been a republican town and has supported Federalist politicians in the past. The current highly centralized government has only recently disavowed the Constitution of 1824. Prominent Mexican citizens of San Antonio are thought to be in correspondence with rebellious Anglo colonists.

"We need to keep a sizable force in San Antonio just to make sure of the loyalty of the population here. Cos will have to move cautiously. I'm afraid the Texans have the initiative," one military source said.

October 10, 1835

GOLIAD — The most formidable fortress in Texas was captured this morning in a surprise attack by a force of colonial troops.

A company of 47 men commanded by Capt. George M. Collinsworth slipped into the imposing fortress of La Bahia and overwhelmed a 28-man Mexican garrison.

One Mexican was killed and three wounded in the action, while one Texan sustained a slight wound. Twenty-four members of the garrison, including three officers, were captured.

In a report sent by courier today to the Council of War at Gonzales, Collinsworth described the action:

"I arrived here last night at 11 p.m. and marched into the fort by forcing the church doors, and after a small fight they surrendered.

"(The Mexicans) have dispatched couriers for troops to several points and I expect I shall need your aid."

Texas military sources said two companies from Brazoria are nearing Victoria and should reach Goliad within 24 hours.

Collinsworth reported the fortress was stocked with supplies for the anticipated Mexican invasion of Anglo Texas. Included in the material seized by the Texans were 300 muskets, several cannons, including a pair of nine-pounders, powder, lead, foodstuffs and $10,000.

Goliad has been considered the strongest fortification in the Mexican subprovince of Texas. It has reinforced walls which, at some points, are six feet thick, and well-designed parapets allow defenders to trap attacking forces in crossfire.

Gen. Martin Perfecto de Cos, the commander of Mexican forces in Texas, passed through Goliad several days ago with an army of more than 600 men.

Texas military sources said that Cos was counting on Goliad as a supply center and link to the Texas coastal port of Copano Bay.

October 11, 1835

NACOGDOCHES — Volunteers have begun pouring into this East Texas center of Anglo power in answer to an urgent plea from Sam Houston, a former governor of Tennessee.

Houston, acting as general in chief of the Department of Nacogdoches, issued a call Oct. 8 for volunteers to join the ranks of the militia. He urged that they arm themselves with good rifles and 100 rounds of ammunition.

Houston, a close friend of U.S. President Andrew Jackson, issued the call to arms in hopes of attracting fighting men from East Texas and from Anglo settlements across the Sabine River in Louisiana.

He promised liberal bounties of land to all men who take up arms in defense of the Mexican Constitution of 1824. In his plea for volunteers, Houston commented:

"The morning of glory is dawning upon us. The work of liberty has begun. Our actions are to become a part of the history of mankind. Patriotic millions will sympathize in our struggles while nations will admire our achievements.

"We must be united — subordinate to the laws and authorities which we avow and freedom will not withhold the seal of approbation. Rally around the standard of the Constitution.

"Let your valor proclaim to the world that liberty is your birthright. Our only ambition is the attainment of rational liberty — the freedom of religious opinion and just laws. To acquire these blessings, we solemnly pledge our persons, our property and our lives."

Authorities have released no figures on the number of men who have answered Houston's call, but observers said hundreds of men are believed to be heading toward Texas from Louisiana. At least 300 Texans from the Nacogdoches area are believed to be under arms. Several groups of armed men loosely formed into companies have already departed for San Felipe, where Stephen F. Austin has called for volunteers to rendezvous.

October 12, 1835

GONZALES — More than 300 Texans marched out of this Guadalupe River town today toward San Antonio.

The Army of the People, as the group has designated itself, stepped off smartly under the command of Col. Stephen F. Austin.

In the front ranks of the army was the "Old Cannon Flag," unveiled moments before the start of the battle of Gonzales 10 days ago.

It still bore its defiant inscription, "Come and Take It."

The cannon was pulled by two yokes of Longhorn steers. It was under the command of Capt. Almeron Dickinson, who renamed his force the "flying artillery."

Austin was elected by acclamation when he arrived here two days ago. Before he arrived, the force was in danger of disintegrating because of disputes over who should command.

Austin's position as the leading colonizer and most respected man in the province made him the logical choice to pull the factionalized forces together, according to a source close to the scene.

Austin took command reluctantly. He is in poor health after spending two years in a Mexican prison and has almost no military experience.

He is surrounded by men with various degrees of military expertise, however, and is expected to lean on their advice.

In a brisk series of orders before the march began, Austin appointed Warren D.C. Hall adjutant general and David B. McComb assistant adjutant general. Patrick Jack was appointed quartermaster. P.W. Grayson and William T. Austin were named aides.

Sources close to Austin said the commander sent urgent instructions to Anglo towns to send reinforcements, artillery and ammunition to bolster his force before beginning the march.

October 13, 1835

SAN FELIPE — Orders were received here today to parole the captured Mexican commander of the fortress at Goliad.

Col. Stephen F. Austin, supreme commander of all Texas forces, issued instructions to release from arrest Capt. Manuel Savariego.

Savariego commanded the fortress of La Bahia, which was seized by a raid of Texas troops four days ago.

Savariego and two other officers were taken to San Felipe after their surrender. Approximately 24 soldiers under their command have been disarmed and reportedly have been ordered to make their way by foot to the Rio Grande.

In his order from Texas Army headquarters on the Guadalupe River, Austin instructed the San Felipe Committee of Safety to release the Mexican officer and arrange for him to meet with Mexican liberal leader Lorenzo de Zavala.

In his letter to the committee, Austin wrote that Savariego said it is the general opinion among Mexicans that Texans have declared independence and that it is this opinion which is preventing more Mexicans from joining forces with the colonists.

Austin said he wanted Zavala to explain to Savariego that Texans were defending the Mexican Constitution of 1824 and are not seeking independence.

Savariego is to be released on a written parole of honor not to take up arms against the colonists until he is exchanged or war ceases.

The two officers captured with Savariego are expected to receive the same treatment, although Austin did not specify that in his order to the committee.

October 14, 1835

SAN ANTONIO — The commander of the Mexican Army in Texas issued a strongly worded statement to his troops here today, denouncing the actions of rebellious colonists and promising punishment for lawbreakers.

Gen. Martin Perfecto de Cos told his command of 1,200 men that he was delaying the start of a campaign against the rebels only until "such time as is necessary to concentrate all our forces."

Military sources said Cos was acting to quell a growing sense of uncertainty among his troops following news of the fall of La Bahia.

The powerful fortress in Goliad was seized five days ago by Texans, effectively isolating the San Antonio garrison by blocking the possibility of reinforcements.

"The veil which has long concealed the perfidious designs of the colonists is at length withdrawn. These ungrateful men have revolted against our government, and assumed the right to live as they like, without any subjection to the laws of the republic," Cos said.

The commander and brother-in-law of President Antonio Lopez de Santa Anna went on to say:

"They (the rebel colonists) are presumptuous enough to believe that the nation which has adopted them as her sons has no sufficient power to subdue them and compel them to share that obedience to which they have sworn.

Cos went on to warn his troops not to distrust the citizens of San Antonio because they have proven in the past to be patriots.

He promised the troops that a campaign against the rebels would begin soon.

"Soldiers, after fatigue comes repose. We shall obtain it covered with glory; this will be the inevitable result of your valor," he said.

October 15, 1835

NEW ORLEANS — A meeting of volunteers was held at a popular coffee house here tonight and more than 100 registered for service in the Texas Army.

Attending the meeting at the Arcade were prospective volunteers and men who had signed up for duty during an emotion-charged rally held two days ago.

Included among the volunteers are members of some of the most prominent families in the South.

The meeting today included plans for organizing two companies of about 60 men each to be known as the New Orleans Greys. The committee organizing the expedition promised to furnish all arms and ammunition. The committee also furnished smart-looking gray uniforms for the volunteers.

One company of volunteers will make its way toward Texas overland, crossing the Sabine River and passing through Nacogdoches. The second company will go by sea, arriving at the port of Matagorda.

Similar meetings are being organized in other cities in the United States, including Mobile, Charleston, Jackson, Philadelphia and New York City.

One volunteer explained his reasons for going to Texas:

"My cousins and their families are there. They are threatened by a military despot. I am going to help my kin. People in my family don't duck a fight and always help their own."

October 16, 1835

SAN FELIPE — The general consultation, scheduled to begin here today, has been reset for Nov. 1 at Washington-on-the-Brazos.

Fewer than 30 of more than 80 delegates had assembled in this Brazos River capital of Stephen F. Austin's original colony yesterday.

Because of confusion and rumor, nearly half the remaining delegates assembled in Washington-on-the-Brazos, under the impression the meeting had been moved there.

Many other delegates are serving in the Army of the People, now moving on San Antonio from Gonzales.

The effective government during this period continues to be the Permanent Council, consisting of the San Felipe Committee of Safety and one delegate each from a dozen other committees of safety.

That government will continue in place, with the addition of any general consultation delegate who wishes to join in the deliberations.

The new group will be called the General Council.

Most delegates indicated they would go immediately to the Army of the People, which is reported to be in the vicinity of Salado Creek, about 15 miles from San Antonio.

Austin is in the command of the Army of the People, which is reported to have grown from 300 to more than 600 in the four days it has been on the march from Gonzales to San Antonio.

Gen. Martin Perfecto de Cos has a force of more than 1,000 soldiers in San Antonio, but has thus far refused to battle the advancing Texans. He is reported by military sources here to be barracading key intersections in the town of 2,500 and preparing for a siege.

October 17, 1835

SAN FELIPE — A resolution creating a corps of rangers to protect the frontier against Indian raids was presented to the Permanent Council here today.

Representative Daniel Parker offered the resolution, which was forwarded to a committee of five members for consideration.

Acting quickly, the committee approved later in the day a plan for a "Ranging Company of Riflemen."

The company, which is being called the Texas Rangers, has been in the planning stages for some time. Representatives from exposed frontier regions have been insisting that the council address the security needs of their areas as well as the needs of the Texas Army now approaching San Antonio.

Under the plan submitted by the committee, Silas M. Parker is authorized to employ and direct the activities of 25 Rangers, "whose business shall be to range and guard the frontiers between the Brazos and Trinity rivers."

Garrison Greenwood is to establish 10 Rangers on the east side of the Trinity. D.B. Frayar and 25 Rangers are to patrol the country between the Brazos and Colorado.

The commanders of the Ranger detachments are to be designated superintendents, not captains.

The committee recommended that superintendents of the Rangers operating between the Colorado and Brazos and between the Brazos and Trinity should rendezvous at the Waco village on the Brazos. The company operating east of the Trinity should have its headquarters at a settlement on Buffalo Bayou.

Observers said the recommendations of the committee are expected to be passed without opposition and steps are already being taken to recruit and arm the Rangers.

Compensation for the Rangers is still under discussion, but most observers believe they will be paid about 50 cents a day.

October 18, 1835

SAN FELIPE — A 12-year-old boy pulled his 6-year-old brother from the jaws of a huge alligator here today after battling the beast with a Bowie knife.

John Falenash saved his young brother from an alligator that had grabbed the youngster while he was wading in a pond on the family's farm about 15 miles north of this Brazos River settlement.

The boys are the sons of Charles Falenash, one of the earliest settlers in Austin's colony. Falenash, like most of the men in the Brazos River valley, is serving with the Army of the People, which is preparing to lay siege to San Antonio.

In his absence, 12-year-old John has taken over the father's duties and was helping his mother bale the cotton crop when he heard the cries of his brother.

According to witnesses, John ran to the pond and spotted the alligator with its jaws clamped around his brother's leg.

Knowing the alligator would make for deep water, John wasted no time in trying to summon aid, but drew his knife and rushed to the rescue.

John explained that he knew the eyes were the only vulnerable points in an alligator's head, so he directed his blows accordingly. He slashed both the creature's eyes before it released its hold. Then, seizing his brother by the arm, John broke for the bank.

The youngster was shaken by the experience, but suffered only superficial wounds.

Alligator attacks are a constant menace in most parts of Texas, according to officials in this de facto capital of the province.

The creatures, some being 20 feet in length, roam the waters and swamps from the Sabine to the Nueces rivers. They are particularly numerous in the Trinity River valley. Some travelers have reported man-eating alligators up to 25 feet in length.

October 19, 1835

SAN ANTONIO — Military sources in this center of Mexican power in the troubled province of Texas reported today that a large group of native Texas-Mexicans had joined a rebellious force of colonists.

The stunning news that Juan Seguin and Placido Benavides, two of the most influential Texas-Mexicans in the municipality of Bexar, had joined the rebels has jolted the 2,500 inhabitants of this subprovincial capital and the officers of the garrison.

Seguin and Benavides reportedly rode into the camp of the Army of the People, a mostly Anglo force of more than 600 men camped about 15 miles west of town on the banks of Salado Creek.

The two men brought with them a force of about 65 Texas-Mexicans. Seguin and Benavides were immediately embraced by the commander of the Texan forces, Col. Stephen F. Austin, who stressed that the colonists were fighting to preserve the Mexican Constitution of 1824 and not fighting the Mexican nation.

The Seguin and Benavides families have long supported a federalist system of government for Texas. When President Antonio Lopez de Santa Anna abolished the provisions of the federalist constitution earlier this month, Seguin, Benavides and other federalist supporters decided to throw in their lot with the quickly massing Texas forces.

Military sources in San Antonio said that the commander of the garrison, Gen. Martin Perfecto de Cos, is attempting to halt any more defections of Texas-Mexicans by stressing that this is a racial war between Anglos and Mexicans and not a constitutional struggle.

Cos has also restricted all movement out of San Antonio. Anyone attempting to leave San Antonio must have a passport issued by military authorities.

Cos has begun fortifying the town, barricading key intersections, Military and Main plazas and the Alamo.

October 20, 1835

SANTA ANA de TAMAULIPAS, Mexico — The commander of an elite infantry battalion issued a tough statement to his troops and inhabitants of this Northern Mexico town, denouncing the actions of Anglo colonists in Texas and promising swift retribution.

Col. Gregorio Gomez, commander of the 600-man Tres Villas battalion told his veteran troops that recent actions have proven to all good Mexicans that Anglo colonists are carrying on illegal actions.

In a speech later released as a circular to the town residents, Gomez referred to the colonists as hypocrites and said:

"These traitors, these unnatural guests, in return for the liberty and favors shown them by our country, are attempting now to plunge a murderous knife into her bosom.

"The crisis in which the republic is now involved has favored their plans. They have openly declared the rebellion and attempted no less than dismembering that rich part of our territory, where they have been received with such liberal hospitality.

"By the last official accounts, we have learned that they have already begun to act. The weak garrison stationed at Bahia del Espiritu Santo, has been captured by the rebels, who have taken military possession of the place. What will be the consequence of such wanton proceedings, if not the complete annihilation of these usurpers?

"Is there a Mexican who would not be fired with indignation at beholding the national honor and integrity of our territory violated by a gang of lawless foreigners? Foreigners the Anglo colonists certainly are by birth and principles and by their treacherous conduct, they have forfeited all the privileges and immunities granted to them by our too generous country.

"A thousand curses on the Mexican who should be dastardly enough to join in that murderous and anti-national plot. His name should be branded with infamy and his crime never forgotten by his people.

"Let us then appeal to arms; let us rally round the government and with the native bravery of Mexicans, let us rush on these gangs of perfidious foreigners. Let us dispel them and avenge the country's honor."

Military observers say Gomez will probably soon have a chance to turn his words into action. His battalion is one of the crack units of the Mexican Army and was bloodied and victorious in the recent campaigns in Zacatecas and Coahuila against federalist militia.

The Tres Villas battalion is expected to take part in a military operation planned for Texas in the next several months.

Observers also point out that Gomez's words were a veiled threat to the people of this northern state to put aside their federalist leanings and support the government in the present emergency.

October 21, 1835

GOLIAD — A deserter from the San Antonio garrison today told the commander of the Texas forces here that many Mexican troops are ready to desert and join forces with the rebellious colonists.

In a letter dispatched today from this South Texas stronghold, Capt. Philip Dimmit reported to Gen. Stephen F. Austin that a deserter from the Mexican forces in San Antonio reported that morale is low and confusion exists among the troops in the town of 2,500.

The Mexican soldier said he deserted from San Antonio eight days ago and was traveling to Monterrey when he heard of the Texans' seizure of La Bahia fortress in this town of 800.

He reported that the size of the garrison was much weaker than Texas intelligence officers have estimated.

Texas officers have estimated that San Antonio is held by up to 1,200 soldiers, but the deserter said only 700 are in the garrison. Texas military sources say that many of the Mexican units are at half-strength and that may account for the difference.

Approximately 600 men commanded by Austin are camped less than 15 miles from San Antonio and are expected to launch an attack upon the town when they receive reinforcements and artillery.

"He says there are only 300 infantry and 400 cavalry there — one half of them former convicts — that Gen. (Martin Perfecto de) Cos was making no preparation whatever for defense, in the way of fortifying — that there were two cannon on the western side of town near the church and two in the Alamo," Dimmit reported.

Dimmit reported the deserter said that Mexican officers and infantry want a fight, but that the cavalry does not.

"When the men were sent to Gonzales after the cannon, they were paid only 3 pesos each and drew only a little corn," Dimmit reported.

Texas military sources here believe some parts of the deserter's story. It is known that a strong republican sentiment exists among the cavalry units, which are the elite part of the Mexican Army in Texas.

"It makes sense that they might want to throw in with us. We are fighting for the Constitution of 1824. It's their constitution as well as ours," one Texas officer explained.

October 22, 1835

GOLIAD — Just 24 hours after reporting that Mexican strength in Texas has been overestimated, the commander of this strategic post has warned of large enemy reinforcements and predicted that his position will soon come under attack.

Capt. Philip Dimmit appeared in good spirits after a deserter yesterday told him there were only 700 Mexican soldiers in San Antonio.

Today, Texas scouts told Dimmit that the San Antonio commander, Gen. Martin Perfecto de Cos, would soon receive 500 reinforcements and that the total number of troops under his command would swell to 1,700.

Dimmit ordered immediate preparations for the defense of the imposing fortress of La Bahia and sent out urgent appeals for reinforcements.

One of Dimmit's staff officers explained that the commander is convinced that Cos will put top priority on retaking Goliad while remaining in a defensive position in San Antonio.

In a letter addressed to Texas inhabitants residing east of the Guadalupe River, Dimmit commented:

"The hour has come when your country requires the service of every man in it. Information received through an unquestionable channel leaves not the least doubt of the movement of a very considerable force on this place from the south.

"We can only muster 50 men at this post. Our men have been fatigued from the hour we entered this fort to the present in mounting guard, repairing arms, making cartridges, putting the works in a defensible condition, mounting artillery and patrolling the country.

"If attacked by the force which we are now threatened with aided by heavy artillery I do not believe less than 200 men can hope to make a successful defense. Let all therefore who love their country, all who value their homes, now rally and unite and let them hurry to this post of danger.

Dimmit has told his officers that he expects Cos to send at least 500 men to attack Goliad. The veteran commander was surprised at the news that Cos has apparently been reinforced by a force which marched overland, probably from Laredo. However, any more reinforcements will have to come by sea and whoever holds La Bahia blocks the possibility of reinforcement of San Antonio from troops landed at Copano Bay. Dimmit is keeping a small detachment at that port, but it would not be able to defend the landing areas against a determined assault, according to military sources here.

October 23, 1835

ARMY HEADQUARTERS ON SALADO CREEK — Activity at the Texas military camp here quickened as Gen. Stephen F. Austin issued a string of orders while preparing to move the army.

This camp is 10 miles south of San Antonio. There are more than 600 men here, many growing impatient for action.

The army is facing a force of Mexican troops in San Antonio estimated at between 800 and 1,200 men under the command of Gen. Martin Perfecto de Cos.

Cos has made no attempt to offer battle to the rebellious colonists. He has concentrated his forces at key intersections of the town of 2,500 and at the Alamo, an abandoned mission that has been used as a fort off and on for many years.

In orders issued in staccato-like fashion, Austin ordered Col. Jim Bowie to take command of the first division of the first battalion and to proceed to the missions of San Juan Espada and San Jose "for the purpose of gaining information in regard to the present condition of those placed — the supplies of corn there and the disposition of the inhabitants."

Austin ordered Bowie to take possession of one of the missions if he deems it expedient.

Austin then ordered Capt. James Fannin and his company to join Bowie's forces and proceed with Bowie to the missions. The combined forces moving on the missions is approximately 100 men.

Military sources here said that Austin is eager to find a spot closer to San Antonio for the Texan army to camp. Both missions are less than three miles from the center of town and will allow the Texans to effectively put San Antonio under siege.

Several officers have been urging Austin to lay siege to San Antonio. They point out that there are few provisions in the town of 2,500 and that the Mexican Army will soon find itself out of food if supplies from outlying rancheros are cut off.

Austin also ordered officials at Goliad to dispatch here 100 barrels of flour, six boxes of sugar, six sacks of coffee, two barrels of wine and one of rum, seven kegs of powder and 300 pounds of tobacco.

In addition, Austin informed the commander of the Texans at Goliad that he could expect no reinforcements from the main army. He explained that a tight siege of San Antonio will so occupy Cos that he does not believe the Mexicans will risk diverting any troops for an attack on Goliad. He did urge the Goliad commander, Capt. Philip Dimmit to recruit men from the coastal plains settlements to meet manpower requirements and urged him to maintain strong patrols to ensure against a surprise attack.

October 24, 1835

VERACRUZ, Mexico — The ruler of Mexico today learned of the opening of hostilities in Texas and reacted by issuing a string of orders to key aides.

Major Gen. Antonio Lopez de Santa Anna, President of Mexico, was vacationing at his hacienda at Manga de Clavo near this Gulf Coast port when a courier delivered a report from military officers in Texas.

Santa Anna reported to his staff that the situation in the Anglo-dominated sub-province had deteriorated to a crisis.

According to the report, armed colonists near the town of Gonzales had fired on a Mexican patrol sent on a lawful mission to retrieve a cannon.

Other reports included rumors of armed Anglos massing at several points and one confusing report of an attack on the key Mexican fortress of La Bahia in Goliad. Santa Anna was particularly concerned about this report because if Goliad falls, the road from Copano Bay to San Antonio will be blocked and the forces of Gen. Martin Perfecto de Cos will be isolated.

Mexican staff officers discounted rumors that La Bahia had fallen, pointing out that the fort is the strongest in Texas and that Cos must have left an adequate force to guard it.

"After all," one aide asked, "who are we dealing with? A bunch of farmers and merchants who have no military organization and no chance to stand up to a professional army."

Santa Anna did not appear to be as optimistic as his aides. The Mexican dictator ordered his minister of war and marine, Jose Maria Tornel, to make an immediate report of the Texas situation to the Mexican National Congress meeting in Mexico City.

Santa Anna issued a series of orders for troop movements and began discussions with financial advisors on the raising of funds needed to carry on a war in Texas.

October 25, 1835

ARMY HEADQUARTERS ON SALADO CREEK — A man banished from Texas in 1831 has been found serving in the Army of the People, but officials say no action will be taken against him.

Noah Smithwick, a mechanic and blacksmith, was banished by officials in San Felipe. The banishment decree included not only Stephen F. Austin's colony but also all of Texas, although some legal experts serving with the army think officials overstepped their authority with the province-wide banishment.

Officials from San Felipe now serving in the army said any man who could fire a rifle was welcome to join the army and that Smithwick was especially needed because of his skill in repairing arms. They said they had no intention of enforcing the 4-year-old banishment.

Smithwick explained his differences with authorities this way:

"As bad as many of the San Felipeans were, I was presumably the worst of the lot. I was banished from the colony in a Star Chamber proceeding in which I was not allowed to participate.

"The indictment against me charged me with being 'a dangerous person, having treated their authority with comtempt.' To the latter part of the charge I enter no defense, for I certainly felt the contempt."

Smithwick explained that a friend of his got into an argument with the alcalde of Gonzales and killed the official in a fair fight. Knowing that he would not get impartial treatment after killing an alcalde, he fled to San Felipe, but was arrested and put into chains.

Smithwick admitted that he supplied his friend with a file to free himself and a rifle, food and a horse to make good his escape.

"Instead of getting out of the way, however, he lay around in the hills, stealing into the house of his brother-in-law to find out if his case was decided," Smithwick commented.

Smithwick explained that when the authorities learned of his hiding place, they surrounded him and shot him dead when he attempted to escape.

"Unfortunately for me, he had the rifle I had given him. It was a rather noted weapon, being all of my own make and the first rifled gun made in the colonies."

Smithwick added that when a militia squad under Capt. Abner Kuykendall came to serve the banishment papers, he told them not to make such a big deal about it.

"Considering the character of the place (San Felipe) it was about the best thing they had ever done for me," Smithwick said.

The blacksmith said he lived in the Red Lands between Louisiana and Texas for several months before returning to Texas and settling in Nacogdoches.

October 26, 1835

SAN FELIPE — The General Council of Texas today issued an appeal to citizens of the United States to help in the struggle against Mexican military domination.

R.R. Royall, the president of the council, issued the resolution. It was unanimously adopted by the de-facto government body of the rebellious Mexican subprovince of Texas.

The resolution, which is addressed to the "Citizens of the United States of the North," details reasons Texans have taken up arms against the Mexican Army.

"Our citizens were invited to settle Texas by a government of a federal republican character, having for its model that of the government of the United States of the North. Under that invitation and that promise of protection to our lives, persons and property, thousands emigrated here and have subdued a vast and extended wilderness," the resolution states.

The document claims that because Mexico abandoned the federalist form of government, Texans are no longer subject to orders from the central government and will not submit to a military occupation.

"What number of mercenary soldiers will invade our country we know not, but this much we do know, that the whole force of the nation that can possibly be spared will be sent to Texas and we believe we have to fight superior numbers. But one sentiment animates every bosom and everyone is determined on victory or death.

"Citizens of the United States of the North, we are but one people. Our fathers, side by side, fought the battles of the revolution. We, side by side, fought the battles of the war of 1812. We were born under the same government — taught the same political creed, and we have wandered where danger and tyranny threaten us. You are united to us by all the sacred ties that can bind one people to another," the resolution states.

The document urges Americans to come to the assistance of Texas and promises large bounties of free land for volunteers.

The resolution states that the course of Texas has been set and cannot be reversed.

"The cause of Texas is plainly marked out. She will drive every Mexican soldier beyond her limits, or the people of Texas will leave before San Antonio the bones of their bodies. We will secure on a firm and solid basis our constitutional rights and privileges or we will leave Texas a howling wilderness," the resolution states.

Political observers in San Felipe said the resolution was one of a series of steps Texas leaders are planning in an attempt to obtain enough supplies and volunteers from the United States to meet a major invasion by Mexico.

October 27, 1835

WASHINGTON, D.C. — Federal and state officials were warned today by the administration to enforce laws that prohibit citizens from aiding in the domestic disputes of other nations.

Secretary of State John Forsyth sent dispatches to Henry Carleton, the U.S. attorney for the eastern district of Louisiana, and to the state's governor, Edward D. White.

The dispatches, which were shown to reporters, warned the officials that the escalating situation in Texas called for increased alertness on their part to make sure that no U.S. citizens become involved in the dispute.

In his dispatch to Carleton, Forsyth wrote:

"In the too probable event of a contest between the different portions of the Mexican empire in the quarter adjoining the United States, some of our citizens may, from their connection with the settlers there, and from their love of enterprise and desire of change, be induced to forget their duty to their own government and its obligation to foreign powers.

"It is the fixed determination of the president to faithfully discharge so far as his power extends, all the obligations of the government and that obligation especially that requires that we shall abstain under every temptation, from intermeddling with the domestic disputes of other nations.

"You are therefore earnestly enjoined to be especially attentive to all movements of a hostile character, contemplated or attempted, within your district and to prosecute without discrimination all violators of those laws of the United States which have been enacted to preserve peace with foreign powers and to fulfill the obligations of our treaties with them."

Political observers said that President Andrew Jackson is determined to maintain at least the appearance of neutrality in any conflict between Anglo settlers and the Mexican Army.

The observers point out, however, that there is little U.S. officials can do to prevent Americans from aiding the Texans. Hundreds of volunteers and thousands of dollars' worth of military supplies have already been sent to Texas.

October 28, 1835

MISSION CONCEPCION — A detachment of 90 Texans today routed a 400-man Mexican assault force near the abandoned mission of Concepcion, less than two miles from San Antonio.

More than 50 Mexicans were killed and an unknown number wounded during the three-hour battle. One Texan was killed and one slightly wounded in the action.

The Mexican force, including cavalry, infantry and two pieces of artillery, had surrounded the party of Texans during an early morning fog.

The Texans had camped beside the San Antonio River. The detachment, which was commanded by Col. Jim Bowie, had been sent to examine the mission and surrounding territory preparatory to the main Texas force moving its base of operations to Concepcion.

The Texans were divided into two companies, one commanded by Capt. James Fannin and the second by Capt. Robert Coleman.

When the fog lifted to reveal Mexican troops deployed for an attack, Bowie ordered his men to take up position in a U-shaped hollow of the river. The position offered the men natural breastworks.

Protected by six-foot banks, the Texans withstood an artillery bombardment without casualties. Some Texans could be seen eating pecans which the Mexican grape shot had knocked down from the large trees lining the riverbank.

The Mexicans charged three times. The Texans broke each charge with accurate rifle fire by platoons. One platoon would fire while another reloaded, so that there was never a pause in the Texans' deadly shooting.

Every Mexican artillery gunner was shot down by the Texans, who were mainly armed with Kentucky long rifles — deadly at 300 yards in the hands of experts. The Mexicans fired more rapidly and wildly, their British-made muskets effective at less than 100 yards.

After the third charge was broken, the Mexicans retired in disorder. The Mexican cavalry, which had been posted on the opposite bank of the river to prevent escape by the Texans, withdrew without seeing action.

The Texans captured one six-pounder cannon. The Mexicans were able to retrieve the other cannon.

The battle marks the first time that a large number of men have been killed since the rebellion began. Previous engagements had resulted in only two Mexican deaths.

October 29, 1835

MISSION CONCEPCION — The first death of a Texan in the rebellion was a needless tragedy, according to an eyewitness.

Richard Andrews of LaVaca was the only Texan killed in the Battle of Concepcion, which raged here yesterday leaving at least 60 Mexican soldiers dead and a number wounded.

The battle broke out when a force of 90 Texans under command of Col. Jim Bowie was surrounded by a 400 Mexican troops. Bowie ordered his force to take cover in a hollow of the San Antonio River which afforded natural breastworks.

Andrews was attached to a company commanded by Capt. Robert Coleman. Another member of that company, Noah Smithwick, described what happened in the action.

"We were protected by a six-foot embankment. Our force was divided into two companies, one commanded by (Capt. James) Fannin and one by Coleman. Each company occupied an arm of a U-shaped bend.

"Col. Bowie kept yelling, 'Keep under cover, boys, and reserve your fire. We haven't a man to spare.' And if he would have been obeyed, we wouldn't have lost a man."

According to Smithwick, the charging Mexican infantry concentrated on Fannin's position. Bowie responded by ordering a portion of Coleman's company to reinforce Fannin.

Smithwick reported that some of Coleman's men became so eager to get into the fight that they mounted the bank and cut across, exposing themselves to the fire of the whole Mexican assault force.

"The first man I saw as I got there was Dick Andrews, lying as he had fallen, great drops of sweat gathering on his white-drawn face, his life blood gushing from a hole in the left side, just below his ribs," Smithwick recalled.

Smithwick ran to Andrews' aid and cried out, "Dick, are you hurt?"

"Yes, Smith, I'm killed, lay me down," Smithwick recalled the dying man's last words.

Smithwick said he propped up the dying man's head, grabbed his rifle and began firing, because the Mexicans were continuing to advance upon the Texans' position.

"He was alive when I left him. He lived long enough to know we had won a great victory. We buried him under a big pecan tree," Smithwick commented.

Military sources confirmed that Andrews was the first Texan killed in the month-old war.

October 30, 1835

MEXICO CITY — The Mexican National Congress today declared that a state of war exists in the subprovince of Texas.

In a noisy and emotion-filled session, the delegates were told by Jose Maria Tornel, minister of war and marine, that Mexican blood had been shed by Anglo "bandits and adverturers" in Texas.

Tornel had been instructed by President Antonio Lopez de Santa Anna, to advise Congress of the latest developments in Texas and of plans for dealing with the rebellion.

Tornel briefly described incidents at Gonzales and Goliad where fighting took place early this month.

In Gonzales, one Mexican soldier was killed when 150 Texans fired on a company of 100 dragoons who had been dispatched to retrieve a cannon loaned to the citizens for protection against Indians.

Tornel informed the delegates that a week later, a small garrison in the fortress of La Bahia in Goliad was surprised and overwhelmed by a large force of Texans. One Mexican was killed in that incident and about 20 taken prisoner. Their fate remains unknown.

The Congress immediately began deliberations on how to raise funds for a campaign in Texas.

One source close to Congress said most of the funds would probably be raised through contributions from the Catholic Church.

Tornel told the cheering delegates that Santa Anna would personally lead a large army into Texas to chastise the Anglos.

"This will be a war of racial extermination. Anglos will be driven from Texas and all who have taken up arms against the mother country will pay the highest penalty," Tornel said.

October 31, 1835

MISSION CONCEPCION — A high-ranking Texas officer today dispatched a messenger to the commander of the besieged Mexican army in San Antonio, demanding his immediate surrender.

Col. Jim Bowie released the text of a message he sent to Gen. Martin Perfecto de Cos.

Bowie commands about 300 troops occupying Mission Concepcion, south of San Antonio. A slightly larger force under Gen. Stephen F. Austin occupies positions north of the town.

The Texans have a Mexican force of more than 800 men under a gradually tightening siege.

Bowie wrote to Cos that the two Texas forces are prepared to act in unison and that further hostilities will result in large loss of Mexican lives.

Bowie reminded Cos that four days ago 92 Texans defeated a much larger Mexican force at the Battle of Concepcion and added that it is with great difficulty that he is able to restrain his troops from further fighting.

"I am induced by the most friendly and humane considerations for my Mexican fellow-citizens to open a communication with you in order to close the war and unnecessary spilling of blood," Bowie wrote.

Texas military sources said that a council of war will soon meet to vote on whether to attack San Antonio or put the town under a tight siege.

November 1, 1835

SAN FELIPE — The group acting as the de facto government of Texas today disbanded after ruling the rebellious province for three weeks.

The General Council stepped down and turned the reins of government over to the long-awaited Consultation — a general convention of elected delegates from almost every municipality and region of Texas.

R.R. Royall, president of the General Council, issued a formal report to the Consultation, which is expected to convene within the next few days.

The Consultation had been scheduled to convene today, but many delegates have not yet arrived in this Brazos River center of Anglo power. The convention is expected to begin within 48 hours.

In his report, Royall listed the major acts of the council, which consisted of the members of the San Felipe Committee of Safety and delegates for committees of safety throughout the province.

The General Council actions Royall listed included:
● Forming a ranger corps to protect the frontier regions from Indian attack.
● Contracting for a large amount of supplies for the Texas Army.
● Appealing to the citizens of the United States for assistance.
● Issuing letters of marque to allow privateers to attack Mexican ships at sea.
● Establishing mail routes including major points in Texas and connections with the United States.
● Suspending of the proceedings of all land offices.
● Authorizing Thomas F. McKinney to borrow $100,000 from private sources in the United States.

November 2, 1835

ARMY HEADQUARTERS NEAR SAN ANTONIO — A council of war held here today by Texas Army senior officers voted not to attack the besieged Mexican Army in San Antonio.

The council was called by the commander in chief, Gen. Stephen F. Austin.

A force of more than 600 Texans occupies positions north and south of San Antonio. One contingent is camped at the Old Mill, less than a mile north of town. The other occupies Mission Concepcion, less than two miles south of the center of town.

The Texans are besieging an army of between 800 and 1,000 Mexican troops under the command of Gen. Martin Perfecto de Cos.

The officers voted not to assault the town because of a lack of heavy artillery. The Mexicans have fortified the plazas of the town of 2,500 in addition to holding strong positions at the Alamo, an abandoned mission with strong limestone walls that has been used as a fort.

The opinions of the officers were that without artillery to knock down fortified positions, a direct assault on San Antonio would cause an unacceptable number of Texas casualties.

The officers urged Austin to tighten the siege of San Antonio and wait for expected reinforcements and heavy artillery.

November 3, 1835

SAN FELIPE — A general convention of Texas met here today with a quorum of 55 delegates representing most of the municipalities in the rebellious province.

The convention, referred to as the Consultation, was called by Stephen F. Austin, the organizer of the largest colony in the province. Austin called the Consultation to form a Texas government during the present conflict with the Mexican Army.

The delegates consist of three members from each municipality. Several members are reported to be en route. The only area of settled Texas not represented is the Irish-Texas areas along the Nueces, although delegates from San Patricio have been elected. Observers think the Irish representatives may be involved in military action which is expected in the Fort Lipantitlan area near San Patricio.

The Consultation takes over as de facto government from the General Council, which ruled Texas from Oct. 15 until relinquishing power Nov. 1.

The Consultation elected Dr. Branch T. Archer of Brazoria president.

Archer is a political ally of Austin and is expected to follow the policy guidelines urged by the leading colonizer and acknowledged political leader of Texas Anglos.

Austin wants the Consultation to adhere strictly to the legalities of the Mexican Constitution of 1824.

Austin sent a statement to the Consultation, which Archer submitted to the delegates. The statement urged the delegates to declare themselves in a state of war because the Mexican government of President Antonio Lopez de Santa Anna had abolished the guarantees of the Constitution of 1824.

"Austin wants the rest of the world and particularly the United States to realize that the Anglos in Texas are not seeking independence or annexation by the United States," one political observer pointed out.

November 4, 1835

GONZALES — Texas soldiers rioted in this Guadalupe River settlement today, breaking into houses and assaulting at least one resident.

The soldiers are from the Ayish Bayou settlement in the Redlands on the Texas-Louisiana border. They were on their way to join the main Texas Army besieging San Antonio when the incident occurred.

Eyewitnesses reported the troops were delayed by an accident which capsized the ferry operating between the east and west banks of the Guadalupe River near this town of 500.

About 30 men were in the contingent. After working about 10 hours to repair the ferry, they came into town. A number of the troops apparently became upset at the lack of supplies allocated for them and began to break into private residences, looking for food and clothes.

Most of the men of the town are serving in the army. A number of women whose husbands were away from town had to flee the rioters. They took refuge in the homes of some of the few remaining men, most of whom are invalids or elderly.

One man, Lawrence Smither, attempted to protect a woman's property and was dragged from the house and beaten by several of the rioters.

Smithers was furious after the assault and wrote a stinging report to the commander of the Texas Army, Gen. Stephen F. Austin.

"Savage Indians would not be guilty of such conduct," Smithers reported.

"They twice entered the house by bursting every door and window and coming in crowds and dragged me into the street and beat my head. They would have killed me had not one of their party intervened," Smithers reported to Austin.

Included in the items Smithers listed as stolen by the rioters were $100 in cash, one buffalo coat, two fur coats and several blankets.

Eyewitnesses said they believed most of the men had been drinking heavily before the rioting which involved about half of the men. They were eventually calmed by some of the other members of the detachment and marched back to the ferry.

November 5, 1835

FORT LIPANTITLAN — A troop of 30 Mexican militiamen today surrendered Fort Lipantitlan to a force of 40 Texans without firing a shot.

The garrison consisted mainly of militia — local Mexican-Texan ranchers and Catholic-Irish residents of San Patricio.

When a Texan force under the command of Capt. Ira Westover unexpectedly appeared, the garrison stacked arms and marched out with hands raised.

The commander of the garrison and 80 Mexican Army regulars were in the field searching for Texas troops at the time.

Fort Lipantitlan is on the west bank of the Nueces River about 12 miles south of San Patricio. It was the last Mexican outpost in Texas besides the besieged town of San Antonio and its capture isolates the troops there.

Westover said he expects a counterattack by Mexican regulars within 24 hours. Texans stripped the fort of all usable military equipment, including two cannons, and moved out to meet the expected counterattack.

Several members of the surrendered garrison joined the colonists. Some of the Irish told of being pressed into service by the Mexicans.

November 6, 1835

FORT LIPANTITLAN — Forty Texans today repulsed an attack by 80 Mexican troops bent on recapturing Fort Lipantitlan, killing or wounding at least 15 men.

The Texans, under the command of Capt. Ira Westover, had taken up positions on the west side of the Nueces River and repulsed the Mexican attack with rifle fire and several shots from two cannons captured at Fort Lipantitlan.

The Texans had only one casualty, William Bracken of the LaVaca settlement. The Texan force consisted of militia from the coastal plains.

The attack developed when the Mexicans advanced upon the Texas force, which was in the process of retiring across the Nueces River. When scouts brought information that the Mexicans were advancing quickly, Westover deployed his men.

Only about 15 of the Texans were in a position to fire during the encounter, which was held in a driving rainstorm that made rifle reloading difficult.

The Mexicans charged the Texans and were greeted with accurate fire which cut them down before they were able to move within range of their muskets.

They retreated toward the west after the encounter and were not pursued.

After the battle, the Texans continued their march toward San Patricio. Because of muddy conditions, the Texans abandoned both of the six-pounder cannons they had captured the day before at Fort Lipantitlan. The cannons were thrown into the Nueces River.

November 7, 1835

SAN PATRICIO — A Mexican Army officer was buried today with full military honors in this Nueces River town of Irish-Texans.

Lt. Marcelino Garcia died of wounds received in a battle yesterday near Fort Lipantitlan.

Garcia had become friends with a number of the Irish-Texas settlers in the Nueces River area. When he was discovered among the wounded Mexicans after the battle, he was taken to San Patricio for medical treatment.

Garcia was taken to the cabin of James McGloin, one of the leading citizens of the town. The wounds were treated, but Garcia had lost too much blood, according to McGloin.

"With his last breath, Lt. Garcia deplored the unhappy relations existing between Texas and the mother country in consequence of (President Antonio Santos de) Santa Anna's ambitious purposes," McGloin reported.

McGloin added that Garcia was, at heart, a sympathizer with the Texans but, being an officer of the regular Mexican Army, had no option but to follow his orders and fight his friends.

November 8, 1835

ARMY HEADQUARTERS NEAR SAN ANTONIO — Light skirmishing was reported today on the outskirts of San Antonio between Texan and Mexican patrols.

No casualties were reported in the encounters, which mostly consisted of patrols exchanging long-range shots.

Mexican activities since the Battle of Concepcion 10 days ago have been limited to skirmish action, patrols and occasional attempts to gather corn and cattle from nearby ranches.

The Texans have countered by increasing their own patrols and attempting to isolate the town and cut off food supplies.

Several Mexican troops have been killed or wounded in the skirmishing. Texans have reported no casualties since the Battle of Concepcion, in which about 60 Mexicans and one Texan were killed.

While the Texas Army has been relatively inactive on the military front, it has moved to put its political house in order.

In a democratically-run army, which uses ballots to resolve issues or select officers, a vote early this month did not allow officers who were also delegates to the general convention to leave for San Felipe.

Many of the delegate-officers complained and a compromise was reached. Line officers could attend, but staff officers were required to stay with the Army.

Observers pointed out that, while the compromise kept a number of competent officers with the Army, it also deprived the crucial convention of the political abilities of such staff officers as Stephen F. Austin, William Travis and William Wharton.

November 9, 1835

ARMY HEADQUARTERS NEAR SAN ANTONIO — The judge advocate of the Texas Army today resigned his position following repeated disagreements with senior officers.

William H. Wharton, the long-time War Party leader, tendered his resignation to the commander in chief, Gen. Stephen F. Austin.

In his letter of resignation, Wharton stated:

"It is useless and unusual to give reasons for tendering my resignation. I will, however, say that from a failure to enforce general orders and from an entire disregard of the grave decisions of councils of war, I am compelled to believe that no good will be achieved by this army except by the merest accident under heaven."

Wharton was named to the judge advocate position one month ago by Austin. Sources said at the time that Austin was trying to balance the senior officer staff between the Peace Party and War Party and that Wharton obtained his position because of politics.

Sources close to Austin said that Wharton's resignation comes as no surprise. Several other key officers have tendered resignations, but most have withdrawn them when Austin personally intervened and asked them to stay on.

Among the officers who have resigned and then withdrawn their resignations are Lt. Col. William Travis and Col. Jim Bowie. Both men are currently commanding key portions of the army.

Austin is not expected to ask Wharton to stay on. Wharton has been lobbying for the army to become more politically involved and push for a declaration of independence from the Consultation now meeting in San Felipe.

Austin is opposed to such a move and has let it be known he disagrees with the idea that the army should involve itself in politics.

"The business of the Texas Army is to drive every Mexican soldier out of Texas, not to attempt to do the work of the elected representatives of the people," one aide to Austin explained.

November 10, 1835

ARMY HEADQUARTERS NEAR SAN ANTONIO — A Texas officer today offered to sell 36 slaves to raise money for the war effort.

Capt. James Fannin of Velasco sent a letter to the president of the Consultation authorizing the government to sell all of his property in Texas, consisting mainly of the slaves, to meet the expenses of purchasing artillery for the army.

Fannin has played a key role in the siege of San Antonio. He commanded a company during the Battle of Concepcion and has led several patrols seeking to block food and supplies from entering the town.

Fannin is one of a growing number of trained officers in the Texas Army. He attended West Point for two years and served in the Georgia militia.

Sources close to army headquarters said it is widely known that Fannin has been active as a slave trader in addition to growing cotton on his farm near Velasco. They point out that such action would account for the relatively large number of slaves he has.

Fannin has been a leading advocate of strengthening the artillery of the army.

He has said that it would be impossible to attack San Antonio without heavy artillery.

In his letter to the president of the Consultation, Fannin urged the purchase of two pieces each of long 12-pounders, 18-pounders, 24-pounders and 32-pounders and from two to four mortars of 12 to 24 inches each.

He also informed the president that the current commander of a U.S. fort in Alabama — an artillery officer — was willing to join the Texas Army if a suitable commission was offered to him.

Slave trading experts said Fannin's slaves could bring from $400 to $600 each at current market prices.

November 11, 1835

TAYLOR HOMESTEAD NEAR THREE FORKS OF LITTLE RIVER — A Texas frontier family repulsed an attack by Kickapoo Indians here today, inflicting several casualties.

A Ranger patrol arrived on the scene several hours after the Indians had retreated. They immediately set out in pursuit of the Kickapoos.

The Taylor family homestead is located three miles above the Little River Falls, about 70 miles north of Bastrop. It is one of the most exposed positions on the Robertson Colony frontier.

The family consists of Joseph Taylor, his wife, two grown daughters and two teen-aged sons.

According to Taylor, the first warnings of an attack came with the barking of a watchdog quickly silenced by an arrow.

One Indian spoke English and demanded to know how many men were in the house. Taylor replied that there were a lot of armed men, but the Indian was able to look into the house through a crack and yelled out, "You lie, one man."

Taylor beat the Indian away with a board, but then the attack began in earnest. A total of 11 Indians began firing at the house with muskets and arrows.

The Indians then offered to stop the attack if the Taylors provided them with tobacco, to which Mrs. Taylor replied, "No admittance and no presents for red devils."

The attack grew more fierce. One Indian grabbed an ax and headed for the door, but was shot dead by one of the boys.

Another Indian attempted to drag the dead body away and was also shot dead by the youth.

The Indians next tried to burn the family out. They got on top of the cabin and set fire to the roof.

Taylor considered the situation hopeless and suggested the family surrender.

"They will kill me, but they may take you and the kids prisoner and you will have a chance to escape," Taylor recalled saying.

His wife refused the offer. Instead, she called on the family to fight to the end. Then, grabbing hot coals in a shovel, she threw them in the face of an Indian looking through the burning roof.

The home consisted of a double log cabin with covered but unfloored passage between — a door to each cabin opening to the passage.

She then climbed onto the roof and doused the flames with a barrel of milk and one of homemade vinegar.

The house was gutted, but remained intact enough to provide a refuge for the family. After another Indian had been wounded by Taylor and seeing that the house was not going to be engulfed in flames, the Indians retired.

After daylight, the family hid in the river bottom until the Ranger patrol arrived. None of the family members was wounded.

November 12, 1835

NASHVILLE ON THE BRAZOS — A frontier family who survived an Indian attack on its home today arrived at this outpost on the Brazos River.

The Joseph Taylor family was escorted into town by a patrol of Rangers commanded by Capt. George Chapman. The Rangers had discovered the family hiding in a river bottom near Three Forks of Little River, about 20 miles west of Nashville on the Brazos.

The family had fled from its burned-out cabin after beating off an attack by 11 Kickapoo Indians. Two of the Indians were killed.

The Rangers dispatched a patrol to search for the Kickapoos. They cut off the heads of two dead braves and mounted them on poles as a warning to other Indians.

Taylor described the action and the events leading up to the fight.

"A party of Tonkawa Indians were camped near the house. A party of Kickapoos were known to be in the vicinity.

"The Tonkawas told me they were going to steal the horses of the Kickapoos. I insisted they should not, because their proximity to my home might implicate me.

"They agreed to move away, but failed to do so till they had stolen the horses and maneuvered so as to cause the Kickapoos to blame me," Taylor explained.

Rangers said that incidents involving Indians are increasing in the northern frontier areas. They have appealed to the government for more men to patrol the area, but with the military crisis around San Antonio escalating, the Rangers fear they will have to protect the entire area with the 25 men they now have, plus a few militiamen.

Rangers are urging exposed frontier families to band and fortify their homes. Patrols have been increased and efforts are being made to recruit friendly Indians to help scout the region.

November 13, 1835

GOLIAD — Martial law today was declared for the town and surrounding area of Goliad by the Texas Army commander for the region.

Capt. Philip Dimmit, commander of more than 80 soldiers in the Goliad area, issued the proclamation declaring martial law.

The proclamation states:

"The following order has been called for by occurrences too recent to require recital and of a character too flagrant to admit of explanation. The necessity which compels it is met with regret, but with unhesitating firmness.

"All persons manifesting an opposition dangerous to the cause espoused by the people of Texas — all who oppose or threaten to oppose the observance of order, discipline and subordination or who endeavour to excite discontent within the fortress (La Bahia) or within the town — will be regarded as public enemies, arrested as such and dealt with accordingly."

The proclamation adds that all persons currently in Goliad who are not permanent residents and all arriving persons are required to report immediately to Texas Army authorities. All travel is restricted to those persons given passports by the Army.

Sources close to Dimmit reported that he took the action to stop what he considered to be the threat of a subversion movement headed by some Texas-Mexicans and Irish Catholics. The sources added that the majority of Texas-Mexicans in the predominantly Texas-Mexican town of 1,000 and the overwhelming majority of Irish colonists backed the rebellion.

"Dimmit is just trying to nip a problem in the bud. We know there are Mexican government agents in this area trying to whip up racial or religious fears among the population," the source explained.

November 14, 1835

SAN FELIPE — The general convention of Texas today adjourned after naming Henry Smith provisional governor and Sam Houston commander of the Army.

The Consultation of 55 delegates from most of the municipalities of Texas met from Nov. 3 until today. It passed a series of laws and regulations which have been termed the Organic Law.

Smith, a former Velasco leader of the War Party, was a surprise choice for provisional president according to observers. He will share authority with a General Council, composed of one representative from each municipality. While Smith is considered an advocate of separation of Texas from Mexico, the majority of the council is thought to favor defense of the Mexican Constitution of 1824.

The council majority favors keeping Texas in a loose confederation with Mexico, feeling that growing Anglo strength in Texas will ensure the autonomy of the province, according to political observers.

Houston, a former governor of Tennessee and close associate of U.S. President Andrew Jackson, has had considerable military experience. He was an officer for three years in the regular American Army and was decorated for bravery in the Creek Indian War.

He was an overwhelming choice for the post of Army commander. The council, however, stipulated that Houston would command a regular army to be recruited for two years. It expressly forbade him from exercising any authority over the 600-man volunteer army now besieging San Antonio. As volunteers formed before the Consultation, legal experts said that army could not be under the control of any officer appointed after it was formed. The army besieging San Antonio will keep its right to elect its own commander in chief.

Houston was given the authority to recruit, equip and put into the field a force of 2,500 regular troops. The soldiers would enlist for two years and be paid in grants of public land.

Among the most significant accomplishments of the Consultation, according to political observers, was a declaration passed Nov. 7 stating that "The people of Texas, availing themselves of their natural rights, solemnly declare that they have taken up arms in defense of their rights and liberties which were threatened by the encroachments of military despots and in defense of the Republican principles of the federal constitution of Mexico of 1824.

This motion was passed 33-15 over the objections of a minority of delegates who favored an immediate declaration of independence from Mexico.

In other significant action, the Consultation appointed three of the most prominent men in Texas to go to the United States as commissioners seeking aid in the war.

Appointed were Gen. Stephen F. Austin, who was the commander of the Texas

Army outside San Antonio, Branch T. Archer, the president of the Consultation and William T. Wharton, a prominent War Party leader.

November 15, 1835

TACUBAYA, Mexico — President Antonio Lopez de Santa Anna today began meetings in this suburb of Mexico City.

He met with members of his cabinet and the general staff of the army concerning the Texas crisis.

Santa Anna arrived in Tacubaya last night. He was anxious to begin discussions about the worsening situation in the province and sent word ahead for his aides, cabinet ministers and high-ranking Army officers to meet him here.

The president is expected to continue on to Mexico City after initial plans for dealing with the Texas situation are drawn up and preliminary orders issued.

Taking part in the discussions are Maj. Gen. Miguel Barragan, president pro tem of the nation, Jose Maria Tornel, minister of war and marine, Maj. Gen. Vicente Filisola, and dozens of aides and advisors.

Santa Anna was delayed in reaching Mexico City from Veracruz by storms which made roads impassable for days. Aides said he had hoped to reach the capital 10 days ago.

One reason for the hurried meeting in Tacubaya, according to aides, was Santa Anna's desire to get troops moving before winter makes large-scale deployments impractical.

November 16, 1835

GOLIAD — The commander of this key coastal plains post today issued an appeal from reinforcements to save San Patricio for a retaliatory raid by Mexican troops.

Capt. Philip Dimmit sent an urgent request for troops to the inhabitants east of the Guadalupe River and to the committees of safety of the towns of Matagorda, Columbia, Brazoria, Velasco and Quintana.

In his appeal, Dimmit wrote:

"You are again called upon by the return and reinforcement of the enemy on your frontier to rally and chastise him.

"An express just arrived at this fort (La Bahia) direct from San Patricio announces a return of the enemy in considerable force to Fort Lipantitlan.

"The movement places the friendly and well-disposed garrison of that town in momentary peril of life and liberty."

Dimmit went on to report that he fears for the safety of San Patricians who cooperated with an expeditionary force that captured Fort Lipantitlan Nov. 5.

"They (the town's inhabitants) may at this moment be flying to the woods for concealment or writhing in the agony of indiscriminate massacre. It is our duty to protect these people," Dimmit wrote.

Military sources said Dimmit has fewer than 100 men to defend the fortress of La Bahia and several posts in the area. Dimmit has made it clear that he will gather what troops he can spare and march to San Patricio's aid, but that a timely arrival of reinforcements might make the difference in the campaign.

Troops under Dimmit's command captured Fort Lipantitlan, but in a move that has been criticized, the troops dismantled the battery of the fort, but did not destroy the installation.

About 60 Mexican troops survived the encounter with the Texans and are believed to be the nucleus of the force which reportedly has reoccupied the fort. They are believed to have been reinforced by a few dozen militia still loyal to Mexico and some soldiers from the Matamoras garrison.

San Patricio is the closest colonial settlement to Mexico. It consists mainly of Irish Catholics, who have experienced divided loyalties during the insurrection between the mainly Anglo anti-government movement and Mexican appeals to their religion.

Sources report that the majority of the Irish settlers have sided with the Anglos and, for that reason, Dimmit is fearful for their safety.

San Patricio is located 40 miles south of Goliad on the east bank of the Nueces River. It is about 12 miles from Fort Lipantitlan.

November 17, 1835

ARMY HEADQUARTERS NEAR SAN ANTONIO — Word was received here today that a small force of Texans has captured a major Mexican horse herd in a bold attack 70 miles west of San Antonio.

Capt. William B. Travis commanded a patrol of 12 men who trailed the herd for four days before launching a surprise attack two days ago.

Army sources explained that Texans have stepped up patrol activity south and west of the besieged town of San Antonio since learning that the Mexican commander, Gen. Martin Perfecto de Cos, has decided to remove a portion of his horses to Laredo for safe keeping.

With the siege tightening, the sources explained, Cos was finding it difficult to keep his horses fed.

In his report to Texas Army commander Gen. Stephen F. Austin, Travis reported that his force seized 300 tame Spanish horses, including 10 mules. They also seized five prisoners, six muskets and two swords.

Travis explained that his patrol picked up the herd's trail on the Laredo road about 20 miles from San Antonio. The Texans trailed the herd for 50 miles, coming upon it at night on the west bank of San Miguel Creek.

"I did not think it prudent to attack at night. We thought there were about 20 men in the escort and we would lose the advantage of our superior marksmanship in a night action," Travis wrote.

After camping without fire, water or shelter for the night, Travis mounted his patrol and charged directly into the Mexican camp at first light.

"We took them completely by surprise. They surrendered without firing a shot. Two of them escaped," Travis reported.

Travis explained that his patrol would take the horse herd to Gonzales, where it would be available to provide remounts for the Army.

November 18, 1835

NASHVILLE ON THE BRAZOS — The Ranger company based in this far northern frontier town was increased today with the arrival of 15 men.

The reinforcements bring the number of Rangers based here to 40. In addition, 25 Rangers are stationed at smaller outposts on the Robertson Colony frontier.

The reinforcements are part of a general buildup of fighting forces aimed at preventing Indian attacks.

The provisional government in San Felipe has increased the number of Rangers to about 125. In addition, there are more than 200 militiamen on the frontier who are cooperating with the Rangers.

The increase in Ranger activity comes at a time when reports are circulating of unrest among several Indian tribes, including the Comanches, Kiowas, Kickapoos and Wacos.

Military authorities here believe Mexican government agents have been agitating the Indians to attack the exposed settlements while the bulk of the Texas fighting forces are concentrated in the San Antonio-Goliad area.

Rangers have recruited a number of friendly Indians, mainly Tonkawas, to help scout the area.

"The Tonks have been a big help. They know the area and are good warriors. We couldn't provide the protection we do without their help," one Ranger commented.

November 19, 1835

GOLIAD — Capt. Philip Dimmit today was removed from command of the Texas troops in the Goliad area by the commander in chief of the army.

Gen. Stephen F. Austin issued the order to remove Dimmit two day ago at his headquarters near San Antonio. The order was effective upon receipt.

Austin ordered Dimmit to turn over command of the garrison at the fortress of La Bahia to Capt. George M. Collinsworth. There are more than 80 Texas soldiers in the Goliad command.

In Austin's letter, the commanding general rebuked Dimmit for failing to treat Agustin Viesca, the exiled governor of Coahuila-Texas, with proper respect.

Austin wrote he was taking the action because of complaints by Viesca, the acting alcalde to Goliad and other sources.

"These complaints show in substance that great harshness had been used toward the inhabitants of Goliad. This conduct is the reverse of what I expected and have ordered and is well calculated to injure the cause we are engaged in," Austin wrote.

Austin went on to explain that he had been counting on the intervention of Viesca's military aide, Col. Juan Gonzales, to induce the cavalry units stationed with the Mexican Army in San Antonio to desert and join the cause of the colonists.

"Colonel Gonzales did not come here, as I am informed, owing to the reception Governor Viesca and himself met with at Goliad," Austin wrote.

Informed sources said complaints about Dimmit had been increasing since he placed the town under martial law and gave orders requiring passports be issued by the army before any movement was allowed in or out of town.

November 20, 1835

GOLIAD — The former commander of Texas forces in this South Texas town today told aides he was fired for political reasons.

Capt. Philip Dimmit, whose troops registered victories at the battles of La Bahia and Fort Lipantitlan, was dismissed effective yesterday as Goliad commander by order of Gen. Stephen F. Austin.

Austin wrote he was taking the action because of complaints by Coahuila-Texas Gov. Viesca, the acting alcalde to Goliad, and other sources.

"These complaints show in substance that great harshness had been used toward the inhabitants of Goliad. This conduct is the reverse of what I expected and have ordered and is well calculated to injure the cause we are engaged in," Austin wrote.

Dimmit told aides he believed Austin fired him because he was jealous of his victories and the lack of dissension in his command when compared to the main Texas forces besieging San Antonio.

Dimmit pointed out that charges that he was treating the inhabitants of the area harshly were ridiculous because most of his troops are militia drawn from the area.

As far as charges that he showed anti-Mexican sentiment, Dimmit pointed out that he was married to Luisa Laso, the daughter of Carlos Laso, one of the most prominent Texas-Mexicans in the coastal plains area.

Dimmit said that he had treated Viesca with correct military courtesy. Viesca fled into Texas after Santa Anna dismissed the state legislature of Coahuila-Texas and arrested supporters of the federalist system.

"I sent Col. James Power, John Linn and James Kerr, the three most prominent citizens of this part of Texas with an escort to meet, welcome and conduct Viesca into Goliad. All three of these gentlemen speak Spanish fluently and were, moreover, personally acquainted with Gov. Viesca," Dimmit explained.

Dimmit pointed out that Viesca was welcomed with a military salute and hospitably entertained until he left for San Felipe.

"We did everything but recognize Viesca as governor, which we could not and would not do on the eve of the formation of a government by our own people. This, and this only, was the grievance of Viesca."

Aides to Dimmit said Austin's policy has become so vacillating that it is likely that he would have recognized Viesca's jurisdiction over Texas if he had had the chance.

Such a move would have been denounced by the vast majority of the Army and brought on a crisis, the aides maintained.

November 21, 1835

GOLIAD — The Texas soldiers stationed in this coastal plains stronghold today unanimously rejected a Gen. Stephen F. Austin order firing the commander of this post.

By a vote of 67-0 the soldiers stationed at the fortress of La Bahia and the town of Goliad rejected Austin's order replacing Capt. Philip Dimmit as commander and replacing him with Capt. George M. Collinsworth.

All the troops, with the exception of Dimmit, took part in the emotion-filled meeting, which was held inside the imposing walls of the powerful fortress of La Bahia.

About 20 soldiers attached to the Goliad campaign were not present for the vote. Some are guarding the key port of Copano Bay and others are on patrols west of the Nueces River.

The soldiers passed a resolution specifying five points, including:

"That we (the soldiers) enter the service of our country as citizen volunteer-soldiers, that as such we claim and can never surrender but with life, the right to elect and to elect freely our immediate commander."

The resolution goes on to explain that Philip Dimmit was elected and is recognized as their captain and that while the soldiers have respect for Collinsworth, they refuse to recognize his authority.

The soldiers also dispute the validity of any charges against Dimmit.

Army sources said that Dimmit enjoys great popularity among his troops because of his aggressive action. He has two important victories to his credit and has taken vigorous action to curtail subversive activity.

The sources point out that Austin is expected to withdraw from the Army within a few days and that Collinsworth is on assignment several days' journey from Goliad. It is expected that Collinsworth will not press the issue and that Dimmit will continue as commander of the Goliad detachment.

November 22, 1835

MACON, Ga. — A group of more than 60 men from the Macon area today volunteered for the Texas Army in an emotion-charged meeting.

A committee to aid Texas was formed during the public meeting, which attracted nearly 1,000 people.

A collection to aid "freedom fighters" in Texas netted more than $6,000, according to organizers, who added that at least that much more was secured in pledges.

Speakers, including Robert Beale, Robert Collin, Lewis Eckerly and Thad Holt appealed to the crowd to "come to the aid of kith and kin as they fight military tyranny."

Col. William Ward, a veteran officer of the Georgia militia, was elected commander of the volunteers, who adopted the name the Georgia Battalion. Ward said after the meeting that he hoped to recruit at least 60 more men before the battalion sails for Texas.

The town meeting is one of at least a dozen such gatherings that have been held recently in all parts of the United States, but principally in the South.

Several hundred volunteers and thousands of dollars' worth of military supplies have already been sent to Texas as the result of such meetings.

Federal authorities have warned organizers that they face criminal charges if they openly interfere with the internal affairs of another country. Informed sources said federal authorities have limited their actions to sending observers to some of the meetings. Mexican diplomats have also been observing the meetings and formally protesting the gatherings to the U.S. State Department.

November 23, 1835

ARMY HEADQUARTERS NEAR SAN ANTONIO — One of the most popular and victorious officers in the Texas Army today was granted an honorable discharge before leaving camp.

Capt. James W. Fannin of Brazoria was granted the discharge by commander Gen. Stephen F. Austin.

In a terse announcement from headquarters, Austin stated:

"Capt. J.W. Fannin having represented to me that of the absolute necessity of returning home, I have granted to him an honorable discharge and have to say that he has uniformly discharged his duty as a soldier and as an officer."

Fannin commanded the most exposed company in the Battle of Concepcion. He has led several patrols to cut off supplies from Mexican troops in San Antonio. He has commanded the barricades closest to the town and has been under enemy fire almost daily.

Sources close to Fannin said that the personal business the Brazoria planter and slave trader alluded to might be connected with an offer he is reported to have received from Gen. Sam Houston.

Houston, who has been named commander of all Texas troops except those besieging San Antonio, is reported to have offered Fannin a high position on his staff.

Fannin has considerable military experience. He attended West Point for more than two years and served as an officer in the Georgia militia.

November 24, 1835

ARMY HEADQUARTERS NEAR SAN ANTONIO — The Texas Army besieging San Antonio today elected Col. Edward Burleson its commander in chief.

Burleson replaces Gen. Stephen F. Austin, who has been recalled to San Felipe by the General Council to prepare for a mission to the United States. Austin and two other commissioners will go to the United States to seek aid for the war against the Mexican Army.

Austin has commanded the Army since Oct. 11. He took command nine days after the victory of militia troops over Mexican cavalry at the Battle of Gonzales.

The troops, then called the Army of Texas, marched to San Antonio, defeated the Mexicans at the Battle of Concepcion and have carried out a sometimes effective siege of the town of 2,500.

The Texans have 800 Mexican soldiers bottled up in the town. The size of the Texas forces has varied from 400 to 1,000 men, with many soldiers coming and going at will.

The vote for Burleson, a 50-year-old Indian-fighting veteran from Bastrop, was unanimous.

In one of his last acts as commander in chief, Austin asked for pledges from troops to maintain the siege. A total of 405 troops out of the 500 assembled agreed to maintain the siege until reinforcements and supplies arrive.

Burleson appointed F. W. Johnson adjutant and inspector general, William T. Austin, aide-de-camp. He appointed himself, Lt. Col. Philip Sublett and Lt. John York to appraise the value of private equipment being used by the volunteer army.

Military sources said that Burleson is expected to maintain Austin's strategy of siege until reinforcements and heavy artillery build up his strength prior to storming the fortifications in San Antonio.

November 25, 1835

SAN FELIPE — An ordinance creating the Texas Navy was signed here today by Gov. Henry Smith.

The ordinance was drawn up by the Naval Affairs Committee of the General Council, the supreme governing body for the rebellious colonists of the faction-torn Mexican province of Texas.

Sources close to the committee said the action was taken because of an increased Mexican naval presence on the Gulf Coast, including the operations of two revenue schooners.

The bill calls for a strict policy concerning the action of privateers, disposition of prizes and division of prize money.

It calls for the creation of a publicly owned and operated navy consisting of four schooners, two of 12 guns each and two of six guns each, "for the security of our coasts and the protection of our commerce."

Several incidents have occurred in recent weeks along the Texas coast between Mexican naval vessels and Texan and American merchant ships.

Naval committee sources said the creation of a small but hard-hitting Texas

Navy will ensure the rapid arrival of supplies and reinforcements should hostilities continue to intensify between Texans and the Mexican Army.

November 26, 1835

ON THE LAREDO ROAD WEST OF SAN ANTONIO — A Mexican pack train was intercepted today by Texas forces five miles west of San Antonio and captured after a furious fight which involved hundreds of troops on both sides.

Mexican losses are estimated at 70 killed and wounded. Four Texans were slightly wounded and one was reported missing.

According to a report filed by newly elected Texas commander Gen. Edward Burleson, Chief Scout Deaf Smith brought news that 150 Mexican cavalry troops were escorting a mule train into San Antonio on a path near the Laredo Road.

Burleson immediately ordered Col. James Bowie and Col. William Jack with about 100 infantry and 50 cavalry to intercept the train.

After skirmishing began, the Mexicans were reinforced by 200 infantry and one piece of artillery from the San Antonio garrison. Burleson responded by personally leading the Texas reserve of 50 cavalry to reinforce the Texans.

At one point, Texas cavalry was fired on from ambush at a distance of 50 yards, but escaped with only minor casualties. The Texans then charged the Mexican infantry, which was hidden in a drainage ditch. Meanwhile, Texas infantry turned the Mexican flank and began pouring fire on the Mexican infantry from both flanks, while the Texas cavalry charged head-on.

The result was a rout, Mexicans fleeing in disorder before they were reformed by officers from the reserve sent from San Antonio.

Mexican artillery fire proved ineffective and the Texans began a long-range rifle fire which quickly persuaded the Mexican commander to abandon the open field.

The Mexicans pulled back into the fortified town of San Antonio, with the Texans close on their heels.

More than 20 Mexican bodies were found on the field and several wounded Mexicans were captured and allowed to be taken into San Antonio for medical treatment.

The entire pack train of 30 mules was captured. Disappointed Texans discovered it contained only hay meant to feed the starving horses of the Mexican cavalry in San Antonio.

The Texan camp had been alive with rumors for days that a large pack train carrying silver to pay the troops in San Antonio and the merchants for supplies was on its way to town. Patrols had been increased and agreements reached to split the loot among the troops.

Texas military sources pointed out, however, that the hay was probably more important to the Mexican Army than silver. The Mexicans have endured a six-week siege and have nearly exhausted the supply of fodder for their horses.

November 27, 1835

NACOGDOCHES — The governing body of Nacogdoches today urged the General Council of Texas to revoke a controversial order to close all land offices.

The Committee of Vigilance and Safety of the Municipality of Nacogdoches passed a resolution urging Texas lawmakers to allow the resumption of the granting of land titles.

The order to close all land offices was issued by the Permanent Council Oct. 18 and was reaffirmed by the Consultation Nov. 4.

There has been a great deal of discontent with land office operations since the scandal last summer in which more than one million acres of Texas public land was sold by the legislature of Coahuilla-Texas.

Public outcry forced a suspension of the granting of land titles involved in that transaction. Further questions about land transactions led to the Permanent Council's decision to suspend all land transactions until a more adequately regulated land office could be put into operation.

The suspension of land offices was met with opposition in most parts of far East Texas, especially in the Nacogdoches area. The Nacogdoches committee stated in its appeal to the authorities in San Felipe:

"This committee has endeavored to ascertain the wishes of the whole community of the eastern part of Texas on the subject just mentioned, and would suggest the propriety of your authorizing the commissions to proceed to finish all land business surveyed previous to Nov. 1 and to retain their papers in their hands as anticipated by the law authorizing them to issue titles, it is the wish of the inhabitants of this part universally."

November 28, 1835

SAN ANTONIO — The Mexican Army has placed increased restrictions on movements and begun to ration food supplies in this besieged town of 2,500 residents.

The moves were ordered by the garrison commander, Gen. Martin Perfecto de Cos, following a stunning defeat his forces suffered two days ago.

A mule train was sent out with a large escort to gather grass for the horses of the garrison. Texans intercepted the train. Both sides sent reinforcements and, in the ensuing battle, 70 Mexicans and five Texans were killed or wounded.

The defeat was the second major fight the Mexicans have had with the Texans since the colonists put this center of Hispanic power in Texas under siege six weeks ago.

Four weeks ago, a force of 400 Mexicans was routed with heavy casualties by the accurate rifle fire of fewer than 100 Texas infantry.

Military sources close to Cos said the general is unwilling to risk anymore encounters in the open with the sharpshooting Texans until reinforcements arrive.

Despite losing nearly 200 men in the major battles and minor clashes since the siege began, Cos is reported to have about 800 men fit for duty. In addition it is reported that he has dispatched his most trusted officer, Col. Domingo de Ugartechea, with 100 dragoons to Laredo to escort back a force of 500 conscripted convict infantry.

While awaiting reinforcements, Cos has tightened movement in the town, strengthened barracades at Main and Military plazas and made improvements at his major fortified position at the improvised fortress known as the Alamo.

If he is forced out of town, Cos has told his staff he will make his last stand at the Alamo.

November 29, 1835

SAN FELIPE — A group of leading citizens and legislators from coastal municipalities today petitioned the Provisional Government to fortify the Texas seacoast.

The petition, signed by 12 men, urged the adoption of a 20 percent customs fee on all imports to pay for the defenses.

The petition states:

"The undersigned petitioners would respectfully represent to you that the sea coast of Texas is in a totally defenseless and unprotected state and the commerce of the country as well as the lives and property of the people upon the sea coast is at the mercy of the enemy.

"To remedy this evil we would suggest to you the expediency of building forts at the east end of Galveston Island, at the mouth of the Brazos and at the entrance of Matagorda Bay.

"Also to provide a naval force able to capture the enemy's cruisers or drive them off the coast."

The petition urges the government to establish ports of entry and custom houses. It suggests a duty of 20 percent be collected upon all imported articles except arms, ammunition, bagging, bale rope and the furniture and effects of immigrant families not intended for sale.

Political observers said the government would give the petition serious consideration. The legislators recently passed a bill creating a Texas Navy and authorizing construction of several powerful warships.

The legislators are searching for revenue to pay for the navy, and one possibility, according to observers, is the imposition of customs duties.

November 30, 1835

SAN FELIPE — A company of Rangers today was ordered to head off a war party of Indians near Mill Creek, about 12 miles north of this center of Anglo power in Texas.

Sam Houston, commander in chief of the Texas Army, issued orders today to Maj. Robert Williamson of the Ranging Corps.

Houston ordered Williamson to raise a company of between 30 and 70 men and to proceed to the Mill Creek area.

Houston said he had received reports that a party of hostile Indians was lurking in the area with intentions to murder settlers and steal horses.

Williamson was ordered to pursue the Indians, but not to expose his command to any possibility of defeat.

"Should you overtake the Indians, you will chastise them in such sort as will prevent them from future incursions into our frontier settlements and give security to our inhabitants," Houston commanded.

Williamson is one of several officers added to the Ranging Corps, or Rangers as they are called. The force has grown from 60 men authorized six weeks ago to more than a 100 because Indian attacks have increased in frontier areas.

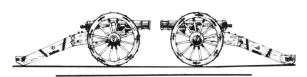

December 1, 1835

LAREDO — Political authorities in this Rio Grande town today received instructions to gather supplies for use by a large division of the Mexican Army marching into Texas.

Gen. Joaquin Ramirez y Sesma sent instructions to the political chief of Laredo for the gathering of supplies for 1,500 troops under his command. The division is expected to reach Laredo Dec. 11 from San Luis Potosi.

Sesma is leading the advance element of a 10,000-man invasion force under the overall command of Gen. Antonio Lopez de Santa Anna.

Santa Anna has vowed to crush all opposition to his rule in the rebellious province of Texas.

Sesma's troops include many of the elite units of the regular army, including veteran lancers and dragoons.

Many of Sesma's troops took part in tough fighting in northern states against opponents of centralist rule last summer.

Other elements of the invasion force are assembling in various locations along the Rio Grande and in northern cities from Saltillo to San Luis Potosi.

December 2, 1835

SAN FELIPE — A group of Beaumont citizens today urged the provisional government to pass a law banning all free blacks from immigrating to Texas.

In a letter addressed to Henry Millard, the Beaumont representative on the legislative council, the citizens stated they had discovered a plan by abolitionists in the United States to procure large tracts of land in Texas to set up a colony of free blacks.

"If such a scheme is allowed to be carried on, it will greatly impede the much desired emigration from the southern and western states to Texas," the citizens wrote.

The letter warns that the creation of a large black community would have an undesirable effect on slaves in Texas, agitating them to flee the plantations of their owners or use violence against whites.

Political observers in this Anglo Texas capital doubt that the council will take action on the measure. There are a number of free blacks living in Texas, including many who have moved to the province to escape racial persecution.

Several blacks are serving with the armed forces of Texas and others are performing valuable service in the making and repairing of arms.

"At a time when Texas needs every able-bodied man to fight the Mexican Army, I doubt we will give in to the hysteria of the slave owners who are constantly raising fears of a slave rebellion," said one observer close to the council.

December 3, 1835

BRAZORIA — News was received here today of the defeat of an expedition by federalist forces at the Mexican port of Tampico.

Gen. Jose Antonio Mexia reported the defeat in a letter to the exiled governor of the state of Texas-Coahuila, Augustin Viesca. Survivors of the expedition mingled with excited crowds at the docks and told their version of the disastrous expedition.

According to survivors, Mexia recruited about 200 men, including a number of

Americans, Texans and Mexicans in New Orleans and outfitted a ship with military supplies in October.

His plan was to sail to Tampico, link up with federalist supporters who opposed the centralist policies of President Antonio Lopez de Santa Anna and seize Tampico. The force would then move on to the key port of Matamoros, where Mexia reported federalist feelings were running high.

The ship ran into the sand bar near Tampico harbor and most of the ammunition was spoiled by sea water. When the expeditionary force finally waded ashore, it was attacked by more than 300 Mexican troops loyal to Santa Anna.

Not having the ammunition to fight a protracted battle, the federalists closed on the centralists and routed them with a bayonet charge.

Mexia's forces succeeded in seizing the fort and custom house of Tampico, but without ammunition and with almost none of the promised support from sympathizers, their position became precarious.

With more centralist troops arriving in the area and threatening to block their retreat, Mexia ordered his force to retire to the ship.

In the confusion of the retreat, more than 30 men, including a number of Americans, were taken prisoner. At least 60 of Mexia's troops were killed or wounded.

Centralist losses are estimated at between 50 and 75 killed or wounded.

December 4, 1835

ARMY HEADQUARTERS NEAR SAN ANTONIO — In a dramatic scene here today, orders were given to abandon the Texas Army siege of San Antonio. The orders were then reversed minutes later in favor of a plan to storm the town of 2,500.

Col. Edward Burleson called a meeting of officers yesterday. They voted in favor of breaking off the seven-week-old siege because of dwindling provisions, worsening weather and lack of warm clothing.

The officers voted in favor of a plan for the army to retire to winter quarters in Gonzales and Goliad and to resume the siege in early spring.

The number of Texas troops conducting the siege has dwindled from a high of about 1,000 men to fewer than 500. Most of the troops now in the army surrounding San Antonio are volunteers from the United States who have come to Texas for the purpose of fighting the Mexican Army. The majority of soldiers residing in Texas have left the army to return home to their families for the winter.

The troops were paraded in front of the camp and read the orders to abandon the siege by Burleson. The volunteers shouted their objections to breaking off the siege and confusion ensued.

At the same time the debate was going on with the entire army on the parade ground, a Mexican Army lieutenant who fled from the San Antonio garrison was escorted to the scene.

Burleson was forced to interview the deserter in front of the whole army. He informed Burleson that the morale of the 900 Mexican troops in San Antonio was very low and that he could lead the Texans into town undetected at night.

Choosing this moment to act, a 47-year-old adventurer named Ben Milam called out, "Who will follow old Ben Milam into San Antonio?"

Almost all of the volunteers and many of the remaining Texas militia yelled out their approval of an attack.

Burleson reluctantly agreed to allow Milam to organize an attack on the provincial capital, which is lined with fortified stone buildings and protected by the heavily gunned fortress of the Alamo.

Plans for the assault are in the process of being drawn up with the help of the Mexican officer and several Anglo residents of San Antonio who managed to slip out of town.

A tight lid of secrecy has been clamped on the camp, but observers said the assault will probably take place within 24 hours.

December 5, 1835

SAN ANTONIO — The long-awaited Texan assault on this center of Mexican provincial power began at 3 a.m. today with a three-pronged attack that caught the defenders by surprise.

An artillery detachment under Capt. James Neill bombarded the old presidio, the Alamo, with a single six-pounder to create a diversion, while two divisions totaling 300 men slipped into town.

The overall attack was commanded by Col. Ben Milam, who led one of the divisions. The other division consisted mainly of New Orleans Greys and was commanded by Col. Frank Johnson. A reserve force of 200 men under the commander in chief, Col. Edward Burleson, guarded the Texan camp.

The Texans were aided by a Mexican officer who had deserted yesterday and helped the attackers draw up plans for the assault.

The town of 2,500 inhabitants is defended by a garrison of more than 1,000 men under the command of Gen. Martin Perfecto de Cos.

Cos has split his forces into two divisions. One is holding the heavily fortified Alamo, while the other is concentrated around two fortified plazas in town. A number of stone buildings have been loopholed and prepared as defensive bastions by the Mexicans.

Details on the early stages of the fighting are sketchy, but reports indicated the feint against the Alamo drew many troops away from the town and allowed the Texans to seize several strategically located houses.

December 6, 1835

SAN ANTONIO — An icy norther blew into this town of 2,500 inhabitants today while furious fighting continued between the attacking Texans and the Mexican Army.

A number of casualties have been reported on both sides as Texans advanced slowly from house to house toward the barricaded center of town.

Several civilians have been killed or wounded in the exchange of cannon and musket fire, including a Texas-Mexican woman who had offered to draw water for pinned-down attackers.

One of the attackers, Herman Ehrenberg of the New Orleans Greys, described the death of the woman.

"We were under intense fire in the house we had seized. There was no well in the building; if we wanted a drink we had to go to the river, which was about 50 yards away. Pails in hand, we would hurry to the river and run back to shelter under a hail of bullets.

"The Mexicans soon became aware of our predicament and took positions close to the spot where we ran to the water's edge. It became so dangerous that we had to pay a man $3 or $4 each time he filled up a pail of water. After a time, even larger sums failed to induce anyone to undertake the dangerous assignment.

"There was in our quarters a Mexican woman we had found there who stayed with us to cook our food and bake our bread. As soon as she saw our predicament, she offered to go alone to the river to get water for us all."

Ehrenberg reported that the officers and men at first would not allow the woman to take the risk, but that she insisted, saying, "You do not realize the fondness of the Mexicans for the fair sex. I will be in no danger."

The woman filled up two buckets and was preparing to return to the house when Mexican troops opened fire on her. Four bullets struck her and she died instantly.

While the Mexicans were reloading, several Texans dragged the woman's body inside while other Texans refilled water buckets.

December 7, 1835

SAN ANTONIO — The officer who led a Texas division into this hotly contested center of Mexican power today was shot dead while running to a conference with another officer.

Col. Ben Milam, whose flaming rhetoric roused more than 300 Texans to attempt an assault on the 1,000-man garrison, died in the courtyard of the house of Martin Veramendi.

Milam was the commander of the assault group and led one of two attacking divisions. He was attempting to reach the commander of the second division, Col. Frank Johnson, when a Mexican sharpshooter shot him through the head. He died instantly.

In keeping with the democratic traditions of the loosely-organized Texas Army, an election was held in the midst of heavy fighting to select another commander. Johnson was named to take Milam's place as assault commander.

The overall commander of the army remains Col. Edward Burleson, who is in charge of the reserve force guarding the Texan camp.

Burleson has been feeding reinforcements to the steadily advancing Texans, who have seized about half of the town. Texans are using their superior marskmanship and hand-to-hand fighting abilities to clear the town in a house to house battle.

Milam is the second Texan known to have died in the assault. At least 15 have been wounded. Mexican casualties are much heavier. They are estimated at more than 150 killed or wounded.

In keeping with Masonic traditions, Milam was buried by fellow Masons at almost the exact spot where he fell. The burial was carried out shortly after Texans seized the house from which the Mexican sharpshooter had shot and killed Milam.

December 8, 1835

SAN ANTONIO — Despite the arrival of a large number of reinforcements, the Mexican military position in this provincial capital continues to deteriorate under unrelenting pressure from attacking Texans.

Military Plaza, one of the two key fortified plazas in town, fell to Texans this afternoon. Several artillery pieces in the plaza were captured by the steadily-advancing attackers, who outflanked the barricades designed to stop them.

Late in the day, Col. Domingo de Ugartechea arrived with 600 reinforcements at the Alamo, the heavily fortified presidio on the east side of the San Antonio

River. At least 100 of the reinforcements were convict soldiers brought into town in iron hobbles.

The commander of the Mexican garrison, Gen. Martin Perfecto de Cos, has reportedly decided to forgo holding the town, instead concentrating his forces at the Alamo.

However, late tonight, fighting continued around Main Plaza, the last strongly held position of the Mexicans in the town. The Texans were methodically outflanking that position and using deadly accurate rifle fire to shoot down every gunner who attempted to man the numerous artillery pieces in the plaza.

Military observers with the Mexican commander at the Alamo said that his forces were not prepared for the fury of the Texan assault. Texans have used battering rams to knock holes in the walls of houses so that they are not exposed to fire from the street. The Mexicans had been counting heavily on their battery of 30 cannons, but the Texans' strategy has reduced the effectiveness of the field pieces.

Mexican morale appeared to be cracking under the devastating fire from the much-superior Texas riflemen. The town is littered with more than 200 Mexican dead, while Texas casualties are reported to be four dead and fewer than 20 wounded.

December 9, 1835

SAN ANTONIO — Mexican troops defending this provincial capital from assaulting Texans today pulled back to the fortified presidio of the Alamo, leaving the town in the hands of the attackers.

Resistance appeared to be slackening after the Mexican commander, Gen. Martin Perfecto de Cos, ordered the abandonment of Main Plaza, the last fortified position in town.

Texans have captured at least a dozen cannons from the retreating Mexicans and have opened a steady bombardment of the Alamo. Mexican gunners manning artillery pieces in the Alamo have been subjected to accurate rifle fire when they have attempted to man their exposed field positions.

Mexican military sources said Cos was shocked to discover that nearly 200 of his best troops, the dragoons, deserted during the early morning hours and have fled toward Laredo.

In an effort to bolster morale, Cos ordered a red flag of no quarter flown from the Alamo. The effect of the move was said to be negative, however, since his troops are fearful that the Texans may take him at his word and execute them if they are forced to surrender.

Mexican casualties have been heavy. It is estimated that more than 200 have been killed and nearly as many wounded. Texas casualties are reported to be four dead and 20 wounded.

December 10, 1835

SAN ANTONIO — The furious, five-day Texan assault on this center of political and military power in the colony ended today with the surrender of more than 1,100 Mexican soldiers.

The Mexican commander, Gen. Martin Perfecto de Cos, ordered a white flag flown above his main fortification at the Alamo after it became apparent Texans had seized control of the town of 2,500.

Texan military sources reported that under terms of the surrender, Cos and all of his officers signed an agreement never to bear arms again against the colonists. He agreed to march his force across the Rio Grande. His troops were allowed to keep one cannon and 150 muskets with 10 rounds of ammunition each to protect themselves from Indian attack in the barren stretches between San Antonio and Laredo.

The capture of the Alamo yielded huge amounts of arms and ammunition for the Texas Army. Hundreds of pounds of powder, 30 cannons and about 2,000 muskets were captured, according to Texas military sources.

"Hopefully, this will end the war," commanding Gen. Edward Burleson said shortly after accepting the surrender.

After a siege of seven weeks, bitter house-to-house fighting began Dec. 5 when 400 Texans attacked the town in two columns commanded by Col. Ben Milam and Col. Frank Johnson. Cos had divided his forces between the Alamo, east of the San Antonio River and two heavily fortified plazas in the center of the town, which is west of the river.

The Texans used their superior marksmanship and the range advantage of their Kentucky long rifles (300 yards compared to 70 yards for the British-made Mexican muskets) to drive the Mexicans back. They used battering rams to break through adjoining walls of the mainly adobe and limestone structures to avoid exposing themselves to musket and cannon fire in the streets.

The Mexican troops barricaded key intersections and swept the streets with cannon fire, but the Texans kept up a methodical house-to-house advance, flanking the artillery positions one by one and capturing a number of cannons.

Despite the arrival of Col. Domingo de Ugartechea on Dec. 8 with 600 reinforcements, the Mexican position continued to deteriorate. After nearly 200 cavalry troops deserted yesterday, Mexican military sources said Cos felt that he must put an end to the fighting, which was causing civilian casualties as well as mounting losses to the demoralized garrison.

Texan sources list casualties at four dead and 25 wounded. Among the dead was Milam, the commander of one of the assault groups. At least 200 Mexican troops were estimated to have been killed in the fighting. Another 150 Mexicans are estimated to have been wounded.

December 11, 1835

SAN FELIPE — The General Council of the provisional government today issued an appeal to the Mexican people to understand the reasons Texans have taken up arms against the government.

"The people of Texas have taken up arms in defense of the rights and liberties menaced by the attacks of military despotism and to sustain the republican principle of the Constitution of 1824. The Mexican nation ought to be fully informed on this subject in order to correct the falsehoods circulated by the Centralists who have attempted to give the character of the revolution here a different look than it really is and painting it in the blackest colors," the circular states.

The council hopes the publication will circulate throughout Mexico and the Mexican communities of Texas.

"Texas was left without any government owing to the imprisonment and dispersion of the executive and legislative authorities of the state by the military Centralists and everything was rapidly falling into anarchy and ruin.

"It certainly was not the fault of the Texans that this state of things existed. They were living in peace when the revolutionary flame reached their homes. "Their situation may be compared to that of a peaceful village that is suddenly assailed by a furious hurricane . . . . The truth is that a storm which originated elsewhere threatened to involve them in its ravages. They wish to save themselves as they have a right to do, by the laws of nature," the publication states.

The council reaffirmed its decision to stand by the Mexican Constitution of 1824 and not to seek independence of the Mexican nation.

The publication closes with an appeal to all patriotic Mexicans to take up arms and make common cause with the Texans.

December 12, 1835

GOLIAD — A young cadet taken prisoner when the fortress of La Bahia was seized by a surprise Texas assault has switched sides and has thrown his support to the colonists, according to the Texan commander at Goliad.

Cadet Juan Garzar was one of 25 prisoners taken Oct. 9 when a force of 47 Texans under Capt. James Collinsworth stormed the fort. One Mexican was killed and three wounded in the assault. The Texans suffered no casualties.

In the seven weeks since his capture, Garzar has been allowed the freedom of the town and reportedly has talked to many prominent Mexican-Texans supporting the rebellion.

Following his denunciation of the dictatorial policies of President Antonio Lopez de Santa Anna, the Goliad commander, Capt. Philip Dimmit, issued a safe conduct pass and sent the cadet to the main Anglo command center at San Felipe.

In his dispatch to the president of the general convention at San Felipe, Dimmit commented:

"I have the honor to dispatch herewith for the disposal of the convention Cadet Juan Garzar.

"I confide his safe conduct hence to the care and fidelity of Capt. Pedro J. Miracle, formerly attached to the division of the Mexican army commanded by Gen. Barragan — but discharged from the service in consequence of his uncompromising detestation of Centralism and firm adhesion to the Republican system of 1824."

Dimmit went on to explain that Miracle was carrying important dispatches.

Miracle made his decision to join ranks with the colonists at least three months ago, according to observers. He told his friends he had always supported federalism and was opposed to rule by a military dictator.

Miracle is thought to have had great influence on Garzar, an 18-year-old from a wealthy family residing in Mexico City.

December 13, 1835

TAMPICO, Mexico — An American volunteer under sentence to be executed today for his part in the abortive federalist attempt to seize Tampico claimed that he and other volunteers had been tricked into joining the expedition.

G.F. Leeds, one of 27 Americans captured during the November attack, was allowed to write the following letter to his family:

"Dear brother, sisters and other relations and friends,

Before this comes to your hand, I shall be in eternity. In 24 hours, I and about 30 others who have been sentenced to be shot were treacherously deceived by Gen. Jose Antonio Mexia (leader of the federalist attack on Tampico), or rather by his agent, William Christy.

"We shipped in New Orleans for Texas on board the Mary Jane, through the agency of Christy. After being at sea, as we thought, long enough to have arrived in Texas, the passengers became anxious to know why we had not made our port of destination. The answer was that the schooner had lost 40 miles the first day she went out; nor did we know we were going to Tampico until the day we were wrecked on the bar.

"We all know it is appointed unto man once to die — and after death to come to judgment. I place myself under the protection of Jesus Christ, who has died for all. He has said come unto me, all ye that are heavy laden, for I will give you rest.

"Break the news of my untimely end to my family in as delicate a manner as possible. I wish you and all my relations and friends to forgive any injury which I may have done them or you. Clear my name from any crime. Pray for your affectionate brother."

Mexican military sources said the letter was made public in order to convince other Americans of the foolishness of attempting to come to the aid of rebellious Texans. They point out it is a capital offense for foreigners to bear arms against the government on Mexican soil.

United States diplomats have attempted to intervene on behalf of the prisoners, but have been told the death sentences must be carried out.

December 14, 1835

TAMPICO, Mexico — A last attempt by United States diplomats today to save the lives of 27 men sentenced to die for their part in an abortive attempt to seize the port Tampico failed and the men were executed.

Sources close to the scene said U.S. authorities attempted to purchase the freedom of the men, but that all attempts to stop their execution failed.

George R. Robertson, a U.S. diplomat attached to the Mexico City embassy, issued the following report to American authorities:

"I have now to inform you that the prisoners taken on the morning of Nov. 16 were all shot about an hour ago. I herewith enclose a correct list of their names.

"I was allowed to see them yesterday, and they all agreed that they were deserters from (Gen. Juan Antonio) Mexia and that they had been deceived, as they had enlisted for Texas, and never for a moment supposed that they were coming to Tampico.

"The poor creatures, it is said, met their fate with calm resignation."

The list of persons shot by order of the military commander at 8 a.m. Dec. 14, 1835:

Arthur H. Clement of Pennsylvania, age 40, no parents; Thomas Whitaker of Pennsylvania, age 30, father in Pennsylvania; William C. Barclay of New York, age 20, parent in New York; Jacob Morison of New York, age 21, parents in Kentucky; Edward Mount of New York, age 23, mother in New York; Charles Cross of Pennsylvania, age 23, mother in Pennsylvania; Isaac F. Leeds of New Jersey, age 30, no parents.

Also, Mordecai Gist of Maryland, age 22, parent in Oswego County, N.Y.; David Long of Ohio, age 25, mother in Ohio; William H. Mackay of Virginia, age 20, mother in Virginia; Jonas R. Stuart of Vermont, age 23, mother in Vermont; Daniel Holt of Canada, age 18, parents in Canada; Thomas H. Rogers of Ireland, age 23, parents in Ireland; James Farrall of Ireland, age 23, father in Green County, N.Y.; John Martin Ieves of England, age 35, no parents; Auguste Saussier of

France, age 22, parent in France.

Also, (no first name) Demoussent of France, age 25, parent in France; Fred Dubois of Germany, age 24, parent in Germany; Fred William Maiier of Germany, aged 22, parents in Saxony; Henry Wagner of Germany, age 24, no parents; George Iselle of Germany, age 27, parents in Germany; William H. Morris of New Providence, age 23, no parents; L.M. Bellefont of Hanover, age 26, no parents.

December 15, 1835

RANCH SALINAS — Gen. Martin Perfecto de Cos, writing from this ranch 100 miles north of Laredo, issued the first formal report to his commander in chief explaining the reasons for the Mexican Army's recent defeat in San Antonio.

After moving his demoralized and defeated command 50 miles south of San Antonio, Cos ordered a halt to rest his troops while he composed the following letter to his brother-in-law, Gen. Antonio Lopez de Santa Anna.

"After 56 days of siege, without the slightest hope of supplies of forces, ammunition and food, I have withdrawn from Bejar (the municipality of San Antonio) by means of an honorable agreement which I was forced to make in order to save the honor of the army which has been entrusted to me.

"The arrival of Col. (Domingo de) Ugartechea with replacements at the time my few soliders were fighting for the sixth day, inch by inch, over the plaza did not help, as we could not utilize them.

"This was due to the fact they lacked training and were tired from a long march to the city. They only aggravated matters by increasing the consumption of provisions of which there was an absolute lack.

"In such critical circumstances, there were no other measures than to advance and occupy the Alamo, which, due to its small size and military position, was easier to hold. I took with me the artillery, packs and the rest of the utensils I was able to transport.

"This was in spite of the fact that two companies of the Presidiales de Rio Grande with their officers plus those at Agua Verde and some pikemen with their captain had deserted me. This occurrence had demoralized the other soldiers so much that almost all of them followed the example. Only 120 of the Permanent Battalion of Morales and some Presidial Dragoons remained faithful. The rest of those who had not deserted were wounded or dead.

"I was in a very difficult situation. My retreat was cut off. The troops were dead tired and without a single horse to bring provisions to maintain their positions. Under those circumstances I decided to draw up some terms, copies of which will be forwarded to you.

"The captains, officers and men who have accompanied me have conducted themselves with courage and steadiness as usual. I have the satisfaction of having saved most of the garrison when it was thought that worse would result."

Cos went on to explain that most of the military equipment and all the cannons except for one four-pounder were turned over to the Texans.

Mexican military sources with Cos were reluctant to discuss the matter, but indicated that the general was putting the best twist possible on a disastrous defeat.

The battle cost the Mexicans more than 400 casualties, including more than 200 dead. Texas casualties were about 25, including four dead. In addition, a number of Mexican troops declined to retreat with Cos and preferred to take their chances making their own way back to Mexico or staying in Texas. More than 1,100 soldiers surrendered to about 400 Texans.

"I wouldn't want to be in Cos' shoes when he first meets up with Santa Anna and has to explain this," one officer said.

December 16, 1835

SAN ANTONIO — The Arc of Texas, a 90-year-old strategic defense line, has been occupied by Texas forces and strategists believe the rebellious colonists are in a strong military position should Mexico attempt an invasion.

Military authorities said that the conquest of San Antonio six days ago by Texas troops led by Col. Edward Burleson completes the occupation of a defense line constructed in 1749 by the Spanish Army.

According to the military experts, the Spanish were fearful of an invasion of Mexico by France and constructed a defense line that included the fortresses and missions in San Antonio, La Bahia fortress in Goliad and fortifications in the Copano Bay area near Aransas Pass on the Gulf Coast.

The strategists pointed out that the defense line works both ways — protecting Texas from a thrust from the south while holding a line against forces moving from east to west.

Goliad fell to a Texas attack force Dec. 9 and Copano Bay was occupied several days later without resistance.

"Arc of Texas has been the key to holding this land for 100 years. The Copano area is the only protected bay suitable for sailing ships to land men and materials. Goliad guards the southern route inland and protects the road to San Antonio. Holding San Antonio is the key to holding the center of Texas," one military expert explained.

The Arc of Texas defense line was drawn up by the Spanish military commander Alonzo Alvarez de Pineda in 1749. It roughly parallels the end of heavily vegetative terrain. Beyond the line is mostly semi-desert area.

Texas military authorities pointed out that any invading army from Mexico would have to march over rough terrain and then could be pinned against the powerful fortresses of San Antonio and La Bahia.

December 17, 1835

SAN ANTONIO — The commander of the Federal Volunteer Army of Texas today issued a strong complaint against the commander of troops stationed at Goliad.

Col. Frank W. Johnson distributed copies of a strong protest he made to the provisional governor of Texas concerning the actions of Capt. Philip Dimmit.

Johnson pointed out that strong protests against Dimmit's conduct have previously been issued by the former commander of the Army of the People, Gen. Stephen F. Austin and Col. Edward Burleson, who succeeded Austin as army commander.

Johnson reported that Dimmit has been criticized by the two previous commanders and himself for "repeated attacks on individual property and for a total disregard of the civil authorities and civil rights of the citizens of Goliad and the area west of the Guadalupe River."

Dimmit has been under attack since declaring Goliad under martial law six weeks ago.

Dimmit said he took the action to stop infiltration of enemy agents and to halt the spread of rumors injurious to the cause of Texas freedom.

A previous attempt to remove Dimmit from command resulted in a unanimous vote by the garrison of Goliad to support Dimmit and to refuse to serve under any other commander.

Following the vote Nov. 21, the matter of removing Dimmit was dropped. No further action to replace him has been taken by senior Army officers.

December 18, 1835

SAN LUIS POTOSI, Mexico — The Mexican Army of Operations today was given its general orders by Gen. Antonio Lopez de Santa Anna.

The First Division, under the command of Gen. Joaquin Ramirez y Sesma will be comprised of the battalions from Matamoros, Jimenez and elements from San Luis Potosi, a regiment from Dolores and eight pieces of artillery.

The Second Division will consist of three brigades. The first, under command of Gen. Antonio Gaona, will be composed of the Aldama, Toluca and Queretary battalions, light auxiliaries from Guanajuato and six pieces of artillery. The second, under command of Gen. Eugenio Tolsa, will consist of a battalion from Guerrero, the first battalion from Mexico City and battalions from Guadalajara and Tres Villas plus six pieces of artillery. The elite Morales battalion is scheduled to join the brigade in several weeks.

The permanent regiment from Tampico, the active battalion from Guanajuato and auxiliaries from El Bajio will form a cavalry brigade under Gen. Juan Jose Andrade. The Sapper Battalion will be attached to headquarters.

Gen. Vicente Filisola was appointed second in command. Juan Arago was appointed major general and Brig. Gen. Adrian Woll was appointed quartermaster.

Lt. Col. Pedro Ampudia was appointed commanding general of the artillery and Lt. Col. Luis Tola was named chief of the corps of engineers.

The general order of the day stipulated that Santa Anna "very emphatically recommends that the generals and corps commanders zealously watch so that the armaments be in good condition, that infantrymen be provided knapsacks, two changes of wearing apparel, capes, spare shoes, canteens and plates."

Mexican military sources estimated that the Army of Operation will consist of at least 10,000 men when fully formed. The sources pointed out the army will consist of the best troops available in Mexico.

December 19, 1835

SAN LUIS POTOSI, Mexico — News of the fall of San Antonio has prompted Gen. Antonio Lopez de Santa Anna to make significant changes in his plans for deployment of troops for the invasion of Texas.

Reacting today to news that Gen. Martin Perfecto de Cos and more than 1,100 men had surrendered in San Antonio nine days ago, Santa Anna today sent urgent messages to his top commanders now deploying troops for the invasion.

Gen. Jose Urrea was ordered to break off his march toward Laredo and proceed with his division to Guerrero. He was ordered to link up with the first division of Gen. Vicente Filisola at Guerrero, a town near the Rio Grande 70 miles up-river from Laredo.

Guerrero was formerly known as Presidio de Rio Grande and for 200 years has been the traditional jumping off point for Hispanic expeditions into Texas.

Gen. Ramirez y Sesma, and 1,500 troops, including several elite cavalry units, arrived in Laredo a few days ago.

Laredo is about 150 miles from San Antonio.

Cos' defeated army is on the march to Laredo after its shattering defeat by 400 Texans in San Antonio during a five-day assault that ended Dec. 10.

Mexican military sources indicated that Santa Anna was concerned that the intermingling of too many troops with Cos' defeated soldiers might injure morale at a time when he said the most important thing is building up the army's fighting spirit.

December 20, 1835

GOLIAD — The first declaration of Texas independence was made here today during a dramatic meeting of La Bahia's fortress garrison.

A total of 92 men serving under Capt. Philip Dimmit took part in the meeting and voted unanimously on the resolution.

Of the 92, 31 are from Irish communities in San Patricio and Refugio, while the remainder are mostly Anglos from the coastal plains with a sprinkling of volunteers from the United States.

A six-man committee, consisting of Thomas H. Bell, Benjamin J. White Sr., William G. Hill, William S. Brown, J. Dodd Kirkpatrick and John Dunn, was delegated to present the declaration to the Provisional Government in San Felipe.

The resolution states:

"That the former province and department of Texas is, and has the right to be a free sovereign and independent state.

"That we hereto set our names, pledge to each other our lives, our fortunes and our sacred honor to sustain this declaration — relying with entire confidence upon the co-operation of our fellow-citizens and the approving smiles of the God of the living to aid and conduct us victoriously through the struggle, to the enjoyment of peace, union and good government; and invoking His maledictions if we should either equivocate or, in any manner whatever, prove ourselves unworthy of the high destiny at which we aim."

The subject of a declaration of independence from Mexico is one of the hottest debates among Anglos in Texas.

A move to declare independence from Mexico was voted down 33-15 on Nov. 3 by delegates to the Consultation. At that time, reasons for not declaring independence included the need to establish an alliance with Mexican federalists opposing the centralist policies of President Antonio Lopez de Santa Anna.

It was also thought it imprudent for 40,000 colonists to, in effect, declare war on 8 million Mexicans. Outside help, principally from the United States, was thought to be jeopardized by a hasty declaration of independence. The support of Texas-Mexicans was also thought endangered by such a move.

Instead, the Consultation voted to reaffirm its adherence to the Mexican Constitution of 1824, which Santa Anna has declared null and void.

Political observers here said that in the time since that vote was taken, opinion has been steadily drifting toward an outright declaration of indepedence.

Disappointment over the lack of activity among Mexican federalists and the growing desire of the Anglo colonists to be rid of confused Mexican politics are said to be the reasons for a shift in public opinion.

December 21, 1835

WASHINGTON-ON-THE-BRAZOS — Lt. Col. James Neill today was ordered by the commander of the regular Texas Army to take command of the garrison at San Antonio.

Gen. Sam Houston ordered Neill to take command of the key town of 2,500, which had been the center of Mexican power in Texas before it was seized Dec. 10.

Houston issued Neill specific instructions to inventory the military equipment at the post and to have chief engineer Lt. Green Jameson make a list of items needed to put the fortifications of the town and the Alamo in order.

Houston also included in Neill's packet of instructions blank recruiting forms and orders to enlist as many men as possible in the regular army.

Military sources here reported that Neill is a 45-year-old resident of Robertson's Colony. He is a native of North Carolina and moved to Texas in 1831.

Neill entered the Texas Army on Sept. 28, 1835, and was given a commission as captain of artillery. He is reported to have distinguished himself during the siege of Bexar and to have commanded an artillery company during the storming of San Antonio in December.

During that battle, the legislative council appointed him lieutenant colonel of artillery.

Military sources said Neill was appointed because he is one of the army's leading experts in artillery. There are almost 30 cannons in San Antonio, nearly all captured from the defeated Mexican garrison and Houston is eager to get the field pieces in working order.

"It's the biggest concentration of firepower between New Orleans and Matamoros," one source said, pointing out that Neill was the logical choice to command such a battery.

December 22, 1835

GOLIAD — The first flag of Texas independence was unfurled today in ceremonies conducted in the imposing La Bahia fortress.

The flag was made to honor the first declaration of independence of Texas. The declaration was unanimously approved two days ago by 92 members of Capt. Philip Dimmit's militia command.

The banner was made of white cotton domestic cloth, 2 yards long, 1 yard wide. In the center, painted with red ink, is a severed arm and hand holding aloft a drawn sword.

Designers of the flag said it symbolized the feeling, "I would rather cut off my arm than bow to the orders of a dictator."

Nicholas Fagan of Rufugio cut a sycamore pole from the trees along the San Antonio River bottom and placed it in the center of the fortress quadrangle.

As the troops paraded and the flag was unfurled in the breeze, it was pierced with a bullet from a musket fired from the streets of Goliad outside the fort.

Soldiers rushed into the streets, but could not find the person who fired the shot.

Dimmit said afterwards that it proved that enemy agents and sympathizers were active within sight of the fortress.

Goliad and the surrounding area have a population of more than 2,000, mainly

Mexican-Texans. Many are not in sympathy with the Anglo-led rebellion, according to officers in Dimmit's command.

December 23, 1835

QUINTANA — A controversial Mexican federalist leader today withdrew his services from Texas, saying he was being ignored by authorities of the provisional government.

Gen. Antonio Mexia, who led a disastrous raid on Tampico last month, sent an official report to Gov. Henry Smith, informing him that he was withdrawing from active cooperation with Texas forces.

Mexia said he would return to New Orleans and attempt to organize exiled Mexican federalists in an attempt to continue the struggle against the centralist rule of President Antonio Lopez de Santa Anna.

Mexia led about 200 men, mostly Americans, in an abortive raid on the northern Mexican port Tampico. Troops loyal to Santa Anna crushed Mexia's forces. Mexia and about half his force escaped by sea.

Twenty-seven Americans and Europeans who claimed they had been tricked into accompanying Mexia on the expedition were captured. Despite appeals for leniency by U.S. diplomats, they were executed earlier this month.

Mexia's letter to Smith expressed bitterness at the inaction of Texas authorities in cooperating with him in further plans.

"Since my arrival in Texas Dec. 3, I have communicated all of my movements. During all this time I have not received a single official communication.

"This circumstance plus the victory at Bexar convinces me that my services are neither of any utility in Texas nor are they desired," Mexia wrote.

The federalist leader said he would leave in the hands of Texas military authorities all the arms, artillery and ammunition he had accumulated at Copano Bay for another invasion attempt.

December 24, 1835

SAN LUIS POTOSI, Mexico — Gen. Antonio Lopez de Santa Anna today moved to shore up the deteriorating Mexican Army supply situation by appointing Col. Ricardo Dromundo purveyor of the Army of Operations in Texas.

The Army of Operations in Texas is the name given to a force of soldiers Santa Anna is massing in northern Mexico to invade the rebellious, Anglo-dominated province. The force consists of 8,000 to 10,000 men.

Santa Anna ordered Dromundo to go immediately to Guerrero (formerly the Presidio Rio Grande) to purchase food and stores for the army.

Dromundo, an experienced staff officer specializing in supply problems, was told that the second in command of the army, Gen. Vincente Filisola, would have most of the funds necessary for supplies by the time he reached Guerrero.

Santa Anna specified that Dromundo must have ready 1,000 boxes of flour, 2,000 of corn, beans, rice, lard and salt and two months' supply of rations for 6,000 men.

In addition to the funds in Filisola's possession, Santa Anna provided Dromundo with 30,000 pesos.

Because of the defeat of the Mexican troops in San Antonio and their forced expulsion from Texas, Santa Anna has been forced to juggle his plans for deployment of the Army of Operations.

Guerrero has been picked as the main jumping-off point for the invasion, although sizable detachments will move out from Laredo and Matamoros. Guerrero is located on the Rio Grande about 70 miles northwest of Laredo.

December 25, 1835

GALVESTON — Three commissioners armed with extraordinary powers today sailed from this Gulf Coast port to New Orleans to seek aid for Texas colonists in their struggle with Mexico.

Stephen F. Austin, Branch T. Archer and William Wharton, all prominent political figures in Texas, boarded a commercial sailing ship due to arrive in New Orleans within 72 hours.

The provisional government of Texas has given the commissioners broad authority to raise money for the revolutionary movement. The men can negotiate loans at the best interest rates possible, pledge public lands as collateral and make whatever other arrangements are needed to secure funds.

The commissioners also have been instructed to seek contributions of money and war materials and to aid in the enlistment of volunteers for the Texas Army.

New Orleans has been the main staging area for groups supporting the Texas cause. Hundreds of men and thousands of dollars' worth of war materials have already been sent from the city to ports in Texas.

U.S. authorities have attempted to stem the flow of volunteers and equipment for Texas. The commissioners are expected to be cautious in their appeals for support, taking care to follow the letter of U.S. neutrality laws, according to sources close to the government.

December 26, 1835

WASHINGTON-ON-THE-BRAZOS — The commander of the Texas Army today issued instructions to recruiters specifying the organization and pay of volunteers from the United States.

Gen. Sam Houston dispatched the following communique to all recruiting officers:

"Should you find it practical to introduce volunteers from the United States into Texas by March 1, they will be accepted by the government.

"A platoon will consist of 28 men rank and file, two sergeants and two corporals. A company will consist of two platoons, or 56 men rank and file, one captain, one first and one second lieutenant, four sergeants, four corporals and two musicians.

"Five companies will constitute one battalion and two battalions one regiment, commanded by one colonel, one lieutenant colonel and one major.

"The monthly pay of the privates will be $8, corporals $10, sergeants $11. The pay of the officers and non-commissioned staff will be the same which is established in the regular army of the United States. The volunteers will elect their own officers.

"Bounty land given is 640 acres besides the rights of citizenship to those who volunteer their service for two years or the duration of the war and 320 acres for one year. If, for a shorter period than one year, no bounty of land will be given.

"All accepted volunteers will be given pay rations and clothes."

December 27, 1835

NASSAU, Bahamas — A British warship today seized a U.S. merchant ship loaded with volunteers for the Texas Army and brought the vessel under guard into Nassau port.

British authorities said the brig Serpent came upon the American ship, Matawamkeag, off the Bahamian coast. Seventeen Americans from the Matawamkeag were arrested while in the act of raiding a plantation on the British crown colony island, according to government officials.

After taking the prisoners, the Serpent sent a boarding party on the Matawamkeag and forced it to sail to Nassau.

A total of 210 men, all volunteers for the Texas Army who signed up in New York City, were taken into custody and marched off to the colony's prison.

British authorities who questioned the Americans said that they identified themselves as a volunteer battalion made up of New Yorkers who had sailed 10 days ago for Texas.

The commander of the battalion, E.H. Stanley, decided — apparently on his own authority — to stage a raid on the Bahamas while en route to Texas.

Most of the men were in opposition to the plan, but Stanley used his authority to force the raid, according to some of the prisoners questioned.

British authorities said all 210 men could be charged with piracy. Theoretically, that means that they could all face death by hanging, but sources here doubt that such drastic measures will be taken.

"It's a delicate situation. We will not put up with such lawlessness, but we can't hang 210 Americans unless we are prepared for another war with the United States," one British official explained, adding that the men will probably be detained for several months, forced to pay a large fine and then probably released.

December 28, 1835

SAN LUIS POTOSI, Mexico — Gen. Antonio Lopez de Santa Anna today issued a series of sharp orders to his second in command as momentum grew for an invasion of Texas by the Mexican Army.

Gen. Vicente Filisola, second in command of the Army of Operations, was instructed by Santa Anna to establish the army's line of operations from Guerrero through Monclova to Leona Vicario. Filisola was warned to remain on the defensive until preparations are completed for advancing into Texas.

Santa Anna issued orders for Gen. Martin Perfecto de Cos to march with all the men he can muster to Monclova, where he is to replenish his troops, replacing supplies and equipment left behind at the surrender in San Antonio to Texans Dec. 10.

Cos has previously been instructed by Santa Anna to ignore his pledge not to bear arms against Texans, which was part of the terms of his surrender in San Antonio.

Filisola was told not to concern himself with the defense of Matamoros, since Gen. Francisco Vidal Fernandez had already marched there with a large division of men.

Santa Anna expressed concern that too many troops were massing in Laredo and that the town could not supply such a large force.

He stressed to his second in command that troops should be dispersed from Guerrero to Monclova and preparations speeded up for the invasion of Texas.

Santa Anna also gave Filisola permission to spend 30,000 pesos being sent to him by special courier in any way he sees fit to supply his forces.

The commander in chief informed Filisola that he would arrive at Leona Vicario Jan. 5 and that he would make that location the army's general headquarters.

He ordered cavalry forces to remain at Laredo in order to scout the area for movements by Texas forces.

The loss of San Antonio is the latest in a series of defeats that has shaken the Mexican high command. Santa Anna is said to be determined to regain the initiative, but has stressed to his officers that no more combat will be risked against Texas troops until he can bring overwhelming force to bear against them.

December 29, 1835

HORNSBY'S STATION ON THE COLORADO RIVER — A company of 60 Rangers today began assembling here under the command of Capt. John Tumlinson.

Provisional government authorities ordered Tumlinson to assemble the new company of Rangers to add to the protection of the frontier area north of Bastrop.

Authorities have become increasingly concerned over the danger of families in newly-settled areas along the Colorado River because of incursions by Comanche Indians.

The area has traditionally been occupied by Tonkawas, a tribe usually allied with Texans, but pressure from Comanches, Kiowas, Wichitas and Wacos has gradually driven the friendly Tonkawas south, opening the area to attacks by raiding parties.

After assembling at Hornsby's Station, the Rangers under Tumlinson have been ordered to proceed up the Colorado to Brushy Creek and to construct a strong blockhouse capable of withstanding any attack by hostile Indians.

Rangers said the area is certain to be a hot spot because the Comanches, the most feared tribe in Texas, have begun to use the Brushy Creek area as a camping ground on raids against other Indian tribes and, more recently, against Anglo settlers.

Meanwhile, Texas authorities are continuing efforts to secure peace treaties with all the Comanches. Many of the approximately 12 Comanche tribes operating in Texas have pledged either neutrality or support for Anglos in the war with Mexico, but the chiefs have pointed out that they have almost no control over small raiding parties made up of young men eager to prove themselves in battle.

December 30, 1835

SAN ANTONIO — A force of 530 Texas soldiers today departed this former provincial capital on an expedition to capture the key Mexican port of Matamoros.

Col. Frank Johnson commanded the troops under the authority of the General Council of the provisional government.

The Matamoros expedition has been rejected by Gov. Henry Smith and by the commander of the regular Texas Army, Gen. Sam Houston, but Johnson decided to begin the expedition with volunteers on the authority of the council.

In an official report to the council, Johnson reported that the troops, almost all volunteers from the United States, took up a line of march to the fortress of La Bahia in Goliad.

"I have left in garrison at San Antonio 100 men under the command of Lt. Col. James Neill. This force I consider to be barely sufficient to hold the post and it will require at least 50 additional troops to place it in a strong defensive position. I have ordered all the guns from the town into the Alamo and the fortifications in the town to be destroyed," Johnson reported.

Johnson commented that he had no hesitation in saying that the controversial expedition is practical and that "not one moment should be lost as the enemy is concentrating its forces at many points in the interior with a view to suppress the liberals of the interior and also for the purpose of attacking us in Texas."

Johnson has been one of the most ardent supporters of an attack on Matamoros, arguing that seizing the key port would deprive the Mexicans of a staging point for an invasion of Texas, while making common cause with liberals in Mexico who are resisting the rule of President Santa Anna.

Arguing against the expedition have been such men as Smith and Houston. An invasion of Mexico, they argue, will bring the entire Mexican nation of 8 million down on the 40,000 Anglo colonists of Texas.

"The last thing we want is to make this a racial war," complained one opponent of the expedition.

December 31, 1835

NEW ORLEANS — The steamboat Yellow Stone today left the port of New Orleans carrying war supplies for Texas and 47 volunteers from Alabama.

The volunteers, formed into a company called the Mobile Grays, are under the command of Capt. David N. Burke.

Unconfirmed reports indicated the Grays are armed with 50 of the latest rifled muskets from the U.S. Army armory in Mobile. U.S. Army authorities have emphatically denied such rumors, but sources close to the company said support for the expedition has been tremendous among the people and military authorities in Alabama.

The Yellow Stone is a vessel of deep draft with a keel 130 feet long and equipped with one engine, two stacks and one rudder.

It was built in 1831 in Louisville, Ky., for a cost of $7,000. Another $1,000 was spent to construct a blacksmith shop on board.

The Yellow Stone has reportedly been purchased by a group of Texas financiers and is expected to be employed in transporting troops and supplies on the navigable Texas rivers, particularly the Brazos and Trinity.

The Mobile Grays are expected to be landed at the port of Copano Bay near Aransas Pass and to join the Texas forces now assembling in Goliad for an expected attack upon the Mexican port of Matamoros.

The addition of the Yellow Stone is expected to greatly enhance the Texas naval situation. The Texans have two smaller steamboats presently in service. The boats are particularly useful in towing larger sailing ships over the sandbars found along the Texas coastline.

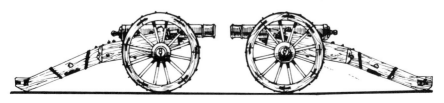

January 1, 1836

AT THE HEADWATERS OF BRUSHY CREEK — A young Anglo woman today staggered into a partially-built Ranger blockhouse saying she had escaped from Indians who had captured her and killed her family.

The woman, Rebecca Hibbons, said Indians captured her two days ago, after ambushing and killing her husband and brother-in-law while the family was traveling along the Colorado River, about 10 miles from the headwaters of Brushy Creek.

After the Indians killed the men, they took her and her two children captives, Mrs. Hibbons said.

Sobbing and nearly hysterical, she told the Rangers that when she couldn't get her 6-month-old infant to stop crying, an Indian took the baby by the legs and bashed its brains out against a tree.

Her other child, a 3-year-old boy, was still held captive by the Indians, the mother said.

The Rangers treated Mrs. Hibbons for cuts and abrasions and immediately mounted a rescue party, which moved out in the direction Mrs. Hibbons indicated the Indians were traveling.

January 2, 1836

AT THE HEADWATERS OF BRUSHY CREEK — A young Anglo mother today described her ordeal at the hands of Comanche Indians.

A Ranger patrol has been dispatched from this partially-built blockhouse in an attempt to save the 3-year-old son of Mrs. Rebecca Hibbons.

Rangers at the post were able to determine the Indians who captured Mrs. Hibbons were Comanches from her description of their weapons, clothing and war paint.

The young mother seemed to be in shock when she first appeared at the station yesterday, but recovered to describe what happened to her family.

According to Mrs. Hibbons, the Comanches ambushed and killed her husband and brother-in-law before they were able to defend themselves.

After bashing her 6-month-old daughter's head against a rock, the Indians bound Mrs. Hibbons tightly to a horse and tied her 3-year-old son to another horse.

Traveling leisurely, unconcerned about the discovery of the murder victims, the war party of a dozen Indians headed west, making camp early because of bitterly cold weather.

Apparently deciding the mother would not attempt to leave the camp without her child, the Indians untied her, then wrapped themselves in buffalo robes and went to sleep without posting guards.

Mrs. Hibbons decided her only chance to escape was to leave her child behind. She slipped out of the Indian camp after she was sure the braves were all asleep.

She traveled down the river, hiding her tracks in the icy waters. She knew there were settlements somewhere to the south.

She said she came upon a herd of cattle she recognized as milch cows, but she feared to expose herself because Indians might be tracking her. She hid in a clump of trees until the cows finished their evening meal and headed for the station.

She followed them and found the blockhouse.

Rangers treating her said she came through her ordeal remarkably well, suffering only cuts and scratches from the underbrush and rope burns from being tightly bound for more than 12 hours.

January 3, 1836

AT THE HEADWATERS OF BRUSHY CREEK — A Ranger patrol returned today to this post with a 3-year-old Anglo boy rescued from a war party of Comanche Indians.

The boy's mother, Mrs. Rebecca Hibbons, was joyous at seeing the only other surviving member of her family. Her youngest child, husband and brother-in-law were killed by the war party four days ago.

One of the Rangers, Noah Smithwick, had a bloody Indian scalp tied to his saddle.

Smithwick described what happened:

"We came upon them about 10 a.m. when they were just preparing to break camp. Taken completely by surprise, they broke for the shelter of a cedar brake, leaving everything except such weapons as they hastily snatched up.

"I was riding a fleet horse, which, becoming excited, carried me right in among the fleeing savage, one of whom jumped behind a tree and fired on me with a musket, fortunately missing his aim.

"Unable to control my horse, I jumped off him and gave chase on foot, knowing his gun was empty. I fired on him and saw him fall. The brave I shot lay flat on the ground and loaded his gun, which he fired at Capt. (John) Tumlinson, narrowly missing him and killing his horse. Conrad Rohrer ran up and, snatching the gun from the Indian's hands dealt him a blow on the head, crushing his skull."

Smithwick went on to describe how the rest of the war party made good their escape to the cedar brake.

The Rangers decided not to pursue them because of the danger of trying to fight them in the wooded area.

Smithwick said that the Rangers held a meeting and decided that his gunshot had proved fatal to the only Indian killed in the fight. They voted to award Smithwick the dead Indian's scalp.

"I decided to go along with the boys. Rohrer scalped the Indian and I allowed the loathsome trophy to be tied to my saddle, thinking that it might provide the poor woman (Mrs. Hibbons) some satisfaction to see the gory evidences that one of the wretches had paid the penalty of his crime."

January 4, 1836

HARRISBURG — A military hero and former leader of the radical War Party today urged the legislative council to sell government property to raise funds for the war effort.

Andrew Briscoe, whose arrest in July 1835 by Mexican customs officials in Anahuac set off one of the earliest confrontations between Texans and centralist troops, distributed copies of a letter he sent to the council.

Briscoe suggested in the letter, "It seems to have been forgotten by the council that there is a good deal of public or government property in Texas which will hardly be of any use to the government and which if sold would aid considerably in raising funds."

Among his specific suggestions was the selling of public buildings at the port of

Anahuac.

Briscoe admitted that the buildings in question probably wouldn't raise more than $1,200, but pointed out that they are going to ruin and could be put to commercial use to benefit the economy of Texas.

Briscoe commanded a company at the opening battle of the rebellion in Gonzales Oct. 2, 1835. Two months later, he was singled out for commendation for bravery during the storming of San Antonio.

January 5, 1836

BESIDE THE SAN ANTONIO RIVER NEAR GOLIAD — More than 200 Texas troops marching to Goliad were halted here today by a vast herd of wild horses.

The troops, almost all volunteers recently arrived from the United States, are under the command of Col. Frank Johnson and Col. James Grant. They are scheduled to rendezvous in Goliad with other troops committed to an attack upon the Mexican port of Matamoros.

The command consists of one company of the New Orleans Greys and the Mobile Grays, plus detachments from other fighting units. Most of the troops took part in the storming of San Antonio one month ago.

The troops were forced to halt on the left bank of the San Antonio River, less than two miles from the large fortress of La Bahia, located within the city limits of Goliad.

La Bahia has been held by Texas militia troops since it was seized from the Mexican garrison in a surprise attack Oct. 9.

Texas troops engaged in the Matamoros expedition are critically short of horses. Less than 10 percent of the men are mounted and there are barely enough spare horses to pull the baggage carts and four pieces of artillery.

Since halting on the river bank, the troops have been attempting to chase down and capture wild horses and tame them to be of use to the army.

Very few of the soldiers are Texas residents and almost all are unfamiliar with the techniques needed to catch and tame the mustangs. A few horses have been caught, but most managed to break free.

"It's good training for the boys," one officer remarked.

"They are going to have to learn how to handle mustangs. This is wide-open country, cavalry country, and these boys are infantrymen. The Mexicans have some of the best cavalry in the world. If we meet them in the desert, these boys are going to have to be able to handle horses better than this," the officer said.

January 6, 1836

SAN ANTONIO — The commander of this key town has reported that supplies are running dangerously low and that the garrison has been reduced far below minimum requirements.

Lt. Col. James Neill issued a stinging report received today by the governor and legislative council detailing the deficiencies he said exist in the Texas forces stationed in this former provincial capital.

Neill complained that Col. Frank Johnson and Col. James Grant stripped the garrison of men and supplies to equip their expedition to Matamoros.

"We have 104 men and two distinct fortresses to garrison and about 24 pieces of artillery. You, doubtless, have learned that we have no provisions or clothing since Johnson and Grant left. If there has ever been a dollar here, I have no knowledge of it. The clothing sent here by the aid and patriotic exertions of the council was taken from us by the arbitrary measures of Johnson and Grant," Neill wrote.

Neill complained that many of his men had only one blanket and one shirt for comfort during a severe winter storm that has plunged temperatures to below freezing.

Neill's main concern appeared to be the lack of manpower in his garrison.

"About 200 of the men who had volunteered to garrison this town for four months left my command contrary to orders and thereby violated the policy of of their enlistment.

"I want here, for this garrison, at all times 200 men, and I think 300 men until the repairs and improvements of fortifications are completed," Neill wrote.

Military sources in San Antonio said that unless the garrison is built back up to minimum strength, plans to defend both the town and the Alamo may have to be abandoned in case of a Mexican attack.

Current plans call for forces to be split between the town's fortified plaza areas and the rebuilt fortress of the Alamo.

January 7, 1836

WASHINGTON-ON-THE-BRAZOS — The commander in chief of the Texas Army today reacted angrily to a report from San Antonio that essential supplies had been stripped from the garrison.

Gen. Sam Houston, in a report to Gov. Henry Smith, demanded that the government take action to halt officers from fitting out an expedition against Matamoros.

Houston also demanded that the needs of the soldiers in the garrison at San Antonio, especially the sick and wounded, be attended to as quickly as possible.

"The government must adopt some course that will redeem our country from a state of deplorable anarchy. Manly and bold decision alone can save us from ruin. I only require orders and they shall be obeyed.

"If the government now yields to the unholy dictation of speculators and marauders upon human rights, it were better that we had yielded to the despotism of a single man," Houston stated.

The commanding general went on to state, "In the present instance, the people of Texas have not even been consulted. The brave men who have been wounded in the battles of Texas, and those who are sick from exposure in her cause, without blankets or supplies, are left neglected in her hospitals, while the needful stores and supplies are diverted from them, without authority and by self-created officers, who do not acknowledge the only government known to Texas and the world."

Houston promised to leave within 30 hours for Goliad to try to head off the planned expedition to seize the Mexican port of Matamoros.

The expedition is under the command of Col. Frank Johnson and Col. James Grant. The expedition was authorized by the legislative council, but was vetoed by Gov. Smith. A political stalemate resulted and Grant and Johnson moved to organize the expedition despite conflicting orders from political authorities.

Observers close to the scene said Houston and Smith are strongly opposed to the Matamoros expedition, considering it little more than a piratical attack.

Houston closed his letter to Smith with this plea:

"No language can express my anguish of soul. Oh, save our poor country! — send supplies to the wounded, the sick, the naked and the hungry, for God's sake!

What will the world think of the authorities of Texas. Prompt, decided and honest independence is all that can save them and redeem our country. I do not fear — I will do my duty."

January 8, 1836

LEONA VICARIO — Gen. Antonio Lopez de Santa Anna today authorized a retaliatory raid against Indians in the Laredo area.

Santa Anna issued orders to Gen. Vicente Filisola, the second in command of the Army of Operations, allowing him to carry out plans to suppress hostile Indians along the Rio Grande from Laredo to Mier.

Filisola had been under strict orders not to divide his forces for any reason and had not allowed area commanders to pursue Indians who have carried out a number of raids on ranches and military outposts along the Rio Grande.

Military sources close to the high command said that Santa Anna was forced to take action against Indians because of increased raids which have begun to affect military operations. He was moved to action, sources said, because of appeals of Mexican rancheros who have had wives and children carried into captivity.

Filisola reported that the Indians involved were mostly the feared Comanches. They have been at war with Mexicans for a number of years and have been known to occasionally attack Texans, but have taken a generally pro-Texan position during the current hostilities.

Mexican authorities have been, without much success, seeking to interest Comanche chiefs in a pact to make war on Anglo Texans.

Sources pointed out that the Comanches consider it more profitable to attack Mexican rancheros, who rarely retaliate, rather than Texans, who almost always send forces to track down raiding Indians.

January 9, 1836

NEW ORLEANS — Texas representatives today negotiated a loan for $250,000 in exchange for 400,000 acres of land in the embattled former province of Mexico.

A report, prepared for Gov. Henry Smith by commissioners Stephen F. Austin, William H. Wharton and Branch T. Archer, revealed details of the transaction.

The lenders have offered to land 500 men in Texas within six weeks. The force would be armed and equipped to serve during the war on the terms of the military laws of the provisional government, and after the war would receive pay for the cost of their arms and outfit, with interest in the meantime of 8 percent.

"This is the true way to obtain troops. To undertake to receive them here and pay their way to Texas is now impossible — we have not the means and it is an open violation of the laws of this country," the report stated.

The commissioners urged the governor and council to suspend granting large tracts of land for volunteers, pointing out that the volunteers would probably come to Texas for the standard 640 acres.

"Some of the best informed persons of this place confidently assert that this loan ensures the triumph of our cause and the independence of Texas," the commissioners reported, adding:

"The stock in this loan will soon be in the hands of hundreds of capitalists who will feel as much interest in Texas and exert themselves as much for it as those of us who have long lived there."

The commissioners defended their actions in selling prime farming land for 50 cents an acre because of the pressing need to raise funds for the war effort, even though comparable land in the United States currently sells for at least four times that price.

January 10, 1836

SAN FELIPE — Gov. Henry Smith today issued a blistering attack upon the members of the General Council, saying their continued support of a plan to invade Matamoros will bring ruin to Texas.

The governor suspended the council until a general convention meets March 1.

Smith blasted the council for issuing resolutions without quorums, for appointing officers to organize an attack upon Matamoros and for passing bills aiding "marauding parties of pirates."

"Let the honest and indignant part of your council drive the wolves out of the fold, for by low intrigue and management they have been imposed upon and duped into gross error and absurdities. Some of them have been thrown out of folds equally sacred and should be denied the society of civilized man.

"Your services are now no longer needed until the convention meets. I will continue to discharge my duties as commander in chief of the Army and Navy and see that the laws are executed.

"You are further notified that audience will not be given to any member or special committee other than in writing. I will immediately proceed to publish all the correspondence between the two departments by proclamation to the world and assign the reasons why I have pursued this course, and the causes which have impelled me to do it," Smith reported.

Political observers in San Felipe have been expecting a split between the governor and council, but the severity of Smith's actions caught most of them by surprise.

Observers said the crisis was brought on by a report from Lt. Col. James Neill in San Antonio that the garrison of that strategic post had been stripped of arms, clothing and men by officers organizing an expedition to seize Matamoros.

Smith heads a faction violently opposed to meddling in Mexican politics. The council seeks to seize Matamoros as a means of uniting with Mexican liberals who are opposing Santa Anna, as well as denying any invasion army a strategic base.

January 11, 1836

SAN FELIPE — The General Council of the provisional government today impeached Gov. Henry Smith and declared vacant the office of Texas' chief executive.

A committee of the council, headed by John McMullen, president pro tem of the council, drew up a list of grievances against Smith.

The action came as a direct result of Smith's move yesterday to disband the council.

The council appointed Lt. Gov. James Robinson acting governor until a general convention meets March 1.

While problems between the executive branch and the council have been escalating since the formation of the government, political observers in San Felipe said the breaking point in relations was a violent disagreement between Smith and the council over the proposed expedition to seize the Mexican port of Matamoros.

The majority of the council approved the plan, while the governor and his allies opposed it.

In a statement to the people of Texas, the council reacted to Smith's proclamation disbanding the body by stating:

"By what sort of delusion could he have been so blindly actuated as to put forth a document so degrading to himself, so mortifying to his countrymen and disgraceful to the office he holds? Could his success in imposing himself upon the people as their governor encourage him to attempt the assumption of all the power, authority and domination he now claims?

"Heaven forgive his delusion and may he learn from this act that a gallant people engaged in a perilous contest for right with a foreign foe cannot be thus gulled and cheated of their liberties."

Political observers said the council's actions in refusing to disband and in impeaching the governor have the effect of creating two competing governments in Texas.

"It's a battle of wills now, and Texas will be the big loser. We can't afford this kind of bickering in the middle of a war," one observer warned.

January 12, 1836

MEXICO CITY — Mexican officials today declared the ports of Galveston and Matagorda on the Texas Gulf Coast closed to all foreign commerce.

The order includes all vessels pursuing coastal trade or wishing to take on provisions.

The order takes effect 30 days after its publication in Mexico City for ships sailing from foreign ports in the Mexican Gulf and 90 days from the same date for ships coming from ports outside the Gulf of Mexico.

The order was issued by Jose Maria Ortiz Monasterio, the secretary of foreign relations.

The order states:

"The order will be in effect for the whole period in which these ports may be occupied by the rebels of Texas."

Mexican naval sources said that two fighting ships are currently cruising in the Gulf and will be instructed to enforce the order. In addition, several other warships under construction in England are expected to be delivered within the next several months, which will greatly enhance the ability of the Mexican Navy to enforce the blockade.

January 13, 1836

NEW ORLEANS — Opposing attorneys hurled ink bottles and insults at each other as a federal court suit over the seizure by Texans of a Mexican warship today degenerated into near chaos.

Felix Huston represented Texas interests while Pierre Soule represented the Mexican government. Both attorneys have reputations as duelists. The suit concerns the detention of the crew and officers of the Mexican warship Correo, which was seized in September by the San Felipe.

The San Felipe was operating under the direction of Texas officers and engaged in the Texas trade. Mexico claimed in its suit that it is a pirate ship.

The Texans brought the ship to New Orleans for disposition in an admiralty claims court. They told authorities the Correo's commander, Lt. Thomas Thompson, could not produce papers from the Mexican government proving his authority. The Texans also alleged that the Correo was attacking peaceful commerce and was acting like a pirate ship.

Texas interests seek to have the ship declared legally seized and the officers and crew charged with piracy. Mexico insists the ship is one of its navy vessels, and was engaged in revenue patrolling when unlawfully attacked by pirates.

The two lawyers had to be restrained repeatedly by associates as they hurled insults at each other. They were warned repeatedly by the presiding judge that such conduct would result in severe penalties. The judge was seen arming himself with a brace of pistols in the midst of one outburst.

January 14, 1836

SAN FELIPE — James W. Robinson today told the General Council that he was assuming the office of governor over the embattled province of Texas.

Robinson acted on the authority of the council, which recently declared the office vacant and began impeachment proceedings against Gov. Henry Smith.

Smith has refused to recognize the right of the council to dismiss him and has, in turn, adjourned the council.

The council ordered Robinson, Smith's lieutenant governor, to occupy the governor's position and to seize all official correspondence and executive branch funds.

Smith and the council have been in disagreement since taking power from the Consultation. That body met Nov. 3-14 and drew up various documents called the Organic Law.

Legal experts here say the Organic Law does not clearly specify the differences of authority between the executive and legislative branches of government.

"In other words, we don't know who can fire who," one Texas political observer explained, adding that the government situation was deteriorating daily.

One part of the government is answering only to Smith; the other is answering to the council and Robinson.

Both sides are heavily armed. According to observers, Smith has the loyalty of the regular army, including the recruiting officer in San Felipe, Lt. Col. William; the commander of the San Antonio garrison, Lt. Col. James Neill; and the commander in chief of the regular army, Gen. Sam Houston.

The council is backed mostly by newcomers to Texas, who seek to extend the war into Mexico.

January 15, 1836

NEW ORLEANS — The officers of the Mexican warship Correo today were released from custody following a near-riotous, three-day trial that featured Texas interests opposing those of Mexico.

The jury acquitted Lt. Romero Ocampo, the second in command on the Correo, of charges of piracy. The jury deadlocked on the guilt or innocence of the ship's commander, Lt. Thomas Thompson, an American serving in the Mexican Navy.

The district attorney, Henry Carleton, then filed a nolle prosequi (an intention not to continue prosecution) and the prisoner was released.

The principal lawyers in the sometimes strident and combative trial were each given six hours' time to serve in jail as a result of "repeated insults to this court and to accepted behavior."

The lawyers involved included Carleton, who prosecuted the case, Felix Huston, a fiery Texas lawyer who defended Texas interests, and Pierre Soule, who represented the Mexican government. All three were held for six hours by the U.S. marshal.

The court case is considered a victory for Texas interests, despite the release of the Mexican officers. The Correo has been held in New Orleans since September. Its crew has scattered and it will be weeks before the Mexicans can get the ship ready to put to sea.

"We took out one of their key ships for six months," one Texan explained.

A New Orleans paper described the case another way, headlining, "Court lets pirates go free, jails lawyers."

January 16, 1836

GOLIAD — Two groups of Texas soldiers squared off today in the fortress of La Bahia and pointed loaded rifles at each other during a dispute over a flag.

Lower-ranking officers persuaded the men to unload their weapons after men from both parties threatened to start shooting following a argument over which flag should fly above the Spanish-built fort in the middle of Goliad.

The argument began when Col. Frank Johnson, in command of several hundred volunteers from the United States, ordered the Texas independence flag removed from the fortress flagpole and replaced with a Mexican flag representing the Constitution of 1824.

Capt. Philip Dimmit, in charge of about 90 Texas militia troops, refused the order. When some of the volunteers moved toward the flagpole, several of Dimmit's soldiers loaded their rifles and said they would shoot the first man who touched their flag.

Scores of men from both detachments grabbed weapons and stood by their comrades.

Dimmit, one of the most successful and combative officers in the Texas Army, refused to recognize Johnson's authority to remove the flag designed by his troops to signify their desire for complete independence from Texas.

With tempers boiling, several junior officers of the volunteers implored Johnson not to push the issue, pointing out that the resident Texans were in a fighting mood and a shootout would be disastrous.

Johnson finally agreed to a compromise because Dimmit was expected to be reassigned within a few days and the militia will withdraw with him.

Johnson explained later that he and his men were strong advocates of defending the Mexican Constitution of 1824 and were opposed to a declaration of independence by Texas.

The banner in question is made of white cotton domestic cloth, 2 yards long, 1 yard wide. In the center, painted with red ink, is a severed arm and hand holding aloft a drawn sword.

Designers of the flag said it symbolizes the feeling, "I would rather cut off my arm than bow to the orders of a dictator."

The flag has been called the first banner of Texas independence and was designed to honor the Goliad Declaration of Independence, a document written Dec. 20 by the Texas militia troops at La Bahia calling for an independent Texas.

January 17, 1836

SAN FELIPE — The battle between the General Council and the president heated up today with the public disclosure of an inflammatory letter sent to a political ally by the chief executive.

Gov. Henry Smith, who has refused to recognize the authority of the council following numerous disagreements, allowed the following letter to William G. Hill to be publicized.

"The council became corrupt and determined on mischief. I found that they were determined to ruin the interest of the country.

"A veto from me was useless and, instead of a veto, I sent them to the devil in the shape of an address.

"Their conduct was criminal and I could no longer stand it. They had everything combined against me — men, means and a damned corrupt council."

With the council consistently overriding Smith's veto, he recently adopted the tactic of refusing to accept any formal communication with that body.

The council reacted by declaring vacant the office of the governor and by appointing Lt. Gov. James Robinson acting governor.

The majority of the bureaucracy and the officers of the regular army have continued to take orders from Smith, however, and political observers in San Felipe predict showdowns between the council and governor are likely to intensify.

January 18, 1836

NEW ORLEANS — A Texas commissioner today reported that more loans were being negotiated for the revolutionary government, but that they are dependendent on a declaration of independence from Mexico.

Stephen F. Austin, considered the most influential Texas politician and a leadei of the moderate faction, reported that he had come to the conclusion that Texas must separate from Mexico and make it clear to the world that it seeks independence.

"Texas has continued to rise rapidly in public estimation all over this country — we (Austin and two other commissioners) have negotiated a loan of $200,000 with 10 percent advanced immediately, and the balance after the convention ratifies it. We expect to conclude another loan for $50,000 cash in hand.

"The loans are made on the firm belief that Texas will declare absolute independence in March — otherwise they would not have been obtained — public opinion all over the United States calls for such a declaration," Austin reported.

Until late last year, Austin had been a leader of the faction which sought to make common cause with the federalists in Mexico and to defend the Mexican Constitution of 1824. He had repeatedly urged Texans not to talk of independence, seeking instead to stay within a Mexico ruled by a federal system.

In a report issued today to Texas authorities, Austin gave the reasons for his change of position:

"All the accounts from Mexico agree that the Federal Party has united with Santa Anna to invade Texas and exterminate the 'rebels' as they call us. The reasons for adhering to the Constitution of 1824 have therefore ceased.

"Texas did her duty. She adhered to the position in which the nation placed her until self-defense compelled her to abandon it and made it a duty to do so.

"I hope there will be no difference of opinion and that all will be unanimous for independence."

January 19, 1836

LEONA VICARIO, Mexico — Communication between Mexico and San Antonio today was ordered cut off by Gen. Antonio Lopez de Santa Anna.

Santa Anna issued orders to Gen. Ramirez y Sesma in Laredo to seal the border and "stop all communication with Bejar (San Antonio) without permitting the passage of food supplies, only allowing trustworthy and discerning spies to pass who may be able to tell with certainty the conditions found in that city and the plans of the rebels."

Mexican military sources said Santa Anna has become concerned that the continuation of limited commercial activity between northern provinces of Mexico and San Antonio was allowing too much information about troop movements to filter through to Texas Army officers.

The port of Matamoros and the land routes to San Patricio and Goliad have been sealed for several weeks, but limited commercial activity has continued, mainly between San Antonio and Laredo.

Mexican troop movements have accelerated in recent weeks as the 10,000-man Army of Operations has begun to deploy for an expected spring offensive against the Texans.

"We can't allow the rebels to know where our main thrust will be. Right now they have to guard everything from their coastal towns to La Bahia and San Antonio. It is much better for us to keep them guessing," one Mexican military officer explained.

January 20, 1836

SAN FELIPE — The marshal of Texas delivered an order to Gov. Henry Smith for the General Council, ordering the chief executive to relinquish all documents and records of his office within two hours.

Smith allowed Marshal John H. Money to deliver the order, but refused to hand over the documents and declared the actions of the council illegal.

The order to Smith read in part:

"In accordance with the resolution passed by the General Council of the Provisional Government of Texas . . . the late Gov. Henry Smith is required within two hours after notice to surrender possession of all the papers, records, public correspondence and public documents of any kind belonging to the Executive Department of Texas."

Money delivered the document and reported to the council later in the day, "In accordance with the order directed to me I executed the notice on Henry Smith, late governor of Texas, by leaving a copy with him at 3 p.m. but did not obtain the papers because he refused to give them up."

The council declared vacant the office of governor and impeached Smith several days ago. Smith responded by dismissing the council and declaring their actions illegal.

Political observers in San Felipe said the dispute has brought an end to effective government in Texas. They pointed out, however, that both sides are holding to their positions, hoping to be vindicated by the General Convention of Texas, scheduled for March 1.

"We are just going to have to manage without a government for six weeks. Santa Anna isn't expected to launch an invasion of Texas until the spring grasses come in, in April. We have time," one political observer said.

January 21, 1836

SAN FELIPE — Acting Gov. James Robinson today authorized the use of force to retrieve governmental records from Gov. Henry Smith.

Marshal John H. Money received an order from Robinson stating, "You will take possession from the late governor of Texas, Henry Smith, all public documents belonging to the Executive Department . . . .

"Should Smith or any other person resist you in the execution of this command, you are hereby further commanded to call to your aid the power of the country, all officers of the civil and military and all citizens of the country who are hereby required and ordered to obey your call."

Money reported to Robinson's secretary several hours later: "In accordance with the order to me directing me to demand public document: The late governor, Henry Smith, refused to give them up.

"In accordance with your order I proceeded to summon 12 persons to enforce the order. Nine of those persons refused to act."

Political sources in San Felipe said frantic efforts are being made behind the scenes to avert an armed clash.

A committee composed of several members of the General Council and aides of Smith are meeting and urging both parties to remain calm.

Smith received support from several groups, including the regular army, most members of the executive branch and one group headed by Moses Hawkins. The group stated:

"You have men not sentiment at San Felipe to sustain you in the discharge of your duty as first magistrate of the nation. Be consoled. Fight the good fight and we are with you to a man. Let the low, intriguing land and Mexican speculators know that the sons of Washington and St. Patrick will not submit to delusion, rascality and usurpation.

"We are bound to you in the proper discharge of your duties and will not submit to anarchy and misrule."

The General Council and Smith had a long-running series of disagreements that started the day they inherited Texas government from the Consultation.

Meeting Nov. 3-14, the Consultation specified that the provisional government of Texas would consist of a governor and a General Council. Legal experts here said the Consultation's failure to specify what areas of authority each department had had resulted in the present confusion.

Ten days ago, the council ruled the post of governor vacant and elevated Lt. Gov. James Robinson to the top job. Smith retaliated by dismissing the council and declaring their actions illegal.

A standoff has resulted. Smith, a staunch supporter of the independence movement, seems to have more support from the average Texan while the council is relying more on support from friends and from advocates of an invasion of Mexico.

January 22, 1836

WASHINGTON, D.C. — Because of the escalating situation in Texas, the commanding general of all U.S. troops west of the Mississippi River has been ordered to postpone a scheduled inspection of Florida military installations.

In orders released today from military headquarters, Adjt. Gen. Robert Jones ordered Gen. E.P. Gaines to postpone his planned trip to Florida. Gaines is also responsible for U.S. military forces along the Gulf Coast west of Washington, D.C.

Jones instructed Gaines to remain in close contact with the government.

Some troop movements have been reported in the area. The 6th Regiment of the U.S. regular army is reported to be moving in the direction of the Sabine River, the boundary of the Mexican province of Texas and Louisiana.

The U.S. Army maintains a major post, Fort Jessup, near the Sabine River. It is reportedly garrisoned by more than 200 troops. The 6th Regiment is about 600 men strong.

In addition to these troops, Gaines has several hundred regulars scattered in posts along the border and coastal areas. He also has the authority to call out the militias of Louisiana, Mississippi and Alabama in the case of an emergency.

"We could put 2,000 fighting men on the Sabine within 10 days' notice," one military source estimated.

January 23, 1836

LEONA VICARIO, Mexico — The commanding general of the Mexican Army today issued warnings to soldiers who have seized supplies from civilians.

Gen. Antonio Lopez de Santa Anna, the commanding general of the Army of Operations and political head of Mexico, issued rebukes to top officers following a series of complaints received at headquarters from civilian merchants and political leaders.

The Army of Operations is massing 10,000 troops, complete with arms, equipment and foodstuffs, for a late-winter campaign against Texas rebels.

The effort is taxing the Mexican economy's ability to support a rapid buildup so far from the established centers of commerce in the country.

Mexican military sources explained that funds were often sent to wrong locations or were slow being delivered and hard-pressed commanders sometimes confiscated what they needed and issued promissory notes to merchants.

Santa Anna has been courting popularity in the northern Mexican states since his seizure of absolute power in Mexico City. He has crushed northern federalists, but aided the creation of centralist-leaning state governments. He is said to be particularly concerned that the army be seen in the most favorable light by the population of the northern states.

In orders to his second in command, Gen. Vicente Filisola in Guerrero, Santa Anna stated:

"All the troops that form the Army of Operations having their respective incomes, there is no reason why they should owe in the stopping-places along their route for any goods which are supplied them, but rather they must pay for them with exactness according to their just prices.

"With this in mind, please inform all the authorities in the department under your command thus so that through your zeal there might not be the least abuse of this kind.

"There is no reason why citizens should be deprived of the pay which they should deserve for the provisions which they give up, nor will I be able to allow that such a thing be permitted."

January 24, 1836

SAN ANTONIO — The commander of the Texas garrison in San Antonio today reported that he would blow up the fortifications at the Alamo and in the town and withdraw if he could find transport for the artillery.

There are more than 20 cannons in the Alamo, captured from the Mexican Army which surrendered last month. The artillery pieces are being reworked by Texas blacksmiths and ordnance experts and most are now in good working order.

Military sources here have estimated that there is more artillery firepower in the Alamo than at any other location between Mexico City and New Orleans.

Lt. Col. James Neill reported to Gov. Henry Smith and the General Council that he has obtained reliable information from Texas-Mexicans that Gen. Antonio Lopez de Santa Anna has arrived at Saltillo with 3,000 troops, that 1,600 more are in the town of Rio Grande (Guerrero) and that a total of 10,000 are massing for an early invasion of Texas.

Neill has concentrated his force of slightly more than 100 men in the Alamo and has begun an extensive renovation project on the old presidio.

The severe lack of horses or oxen in San Antonio has forced Neill to abandon the idea of retreating from San Antonio.

Sources close to Neill said they did not think the officer would abandon the Alamo even if he could move the artillery.

"Neill has desperately been trying to get the government to reinforce him here. He has good intelligence that an earlier attack upon Texas is about to be launched and that most of the troops are heading here. He just wants them to see the seriousness of the situation," one aide explained.

January 25, 1836

MEXICO CITY — The Mexican foreign office today responded to inquiries from U.S. officials concerning the execution of American citizens last month by military officers in Tampico.

Mexican authorities reported 13 American citizens were executed as a result of an abortive raid on Tampico in November by a federalist force led by Gen. Jose Antonio Mexia. U.S. diplomats said they have documented at least 22 Americans among 27 prisoners executed by a firing squad as a result of the attack.

The Mexican foreign minister, Jose Maria Ortiz Monasterio, addressed his reply to the American charge d'affaires, Anthony Butler.

Monasterio reported to Butler that the 13 persons who were citizens of the United States of America were punished for the crime of piracy.

"The unfortunate individuals received punishment for invasion of the national territory under the orders of the traitor Jose Antonio Mexia, during which action they were captured.

"It was declared at their trial that their aggression was an act of piracy as those adventurers belonged to no nation with whom the republic was at war and fought under no acknowledged flag.

"The authorities who tried them did nothing more than subject them to the rigor of the laws, observing all the proceedings prescribed by them with respect to those who venture to offend the sovereignty of the nation."

Sources close to the American embassy said the note infuriated Butler, who has been working on the case. Butler attempted to intervene on the Americans' behalf and halt their execution.

In a note attached to the Mexicans' official reply and forwarded to the U.S. State Department, Butler reported:

"They (the executed Americans) were not made prisoners in battle, but were arrested after Mexia had departed, abandoning them.

"All their companions did not suffer: the Mexicans still survive and will no doubt eventually be discharged. The foreigners alone suffered punishment.

"The flag was that of Mexico; as in every civil war here, both parties march under the same flag, and both insist that their object is to support the constitution and laws.

"There was no authority to judge them — no trial — Gen. Santa Anna ordered that they should be shot, and it was done."

January 26, 1836

SAN ANTONIO — Soldiers and citizens in this strategic town of 2,500 today pledged their support to Gov. Henry Smith.

Smith and his allies are engaged in a power struggle with the General Council of the Provisional Government. Neither group will acknowledge the constitutional authority of the other.

The garrison of San Antonio, including the Alamo, consists of about 120 men. Almost all of the soldiers plus scores of Anglo and Texas-Mexican citizens participated in a large rally chaired by the commander of the garrison, Lt. Col. James Neill.

A group of seven men was chosen to draft a preamble and resolutions for consideration at the rally.

Among those chosen to draft the document were James B. Bonham, James Bowie, Green B. Jameson, Dr. Amos Pollard, Jesse Badgett, Juan Seguin and Don Gasper Flores.

The resolution was adopted by voice vote. It included eight resolutions, including:

"We will support his excellency Gov. Smith in his unyielding and patriotic efforts to fulfill the duties and to preserve the dignity of his office, while promoting the best interests of the country and people against all usurpations and designs of selfish and interested individuals."

Other resolutions included a provision to refuse to honor any orders issued by the council and to invite a similar expression of sentiment from the army under Gen. Sam Houston and throughout the country.

The resolutions also accused the council of acting illegally in withholding a $500 loan pledged to maintain the San Antonio garrison which was never received.

The document dealt with the hotly-debated issue of the Matamoros campaign, stating that the members of the meeting do not recognize the "illegal appointments of agents and officers made by the president and members of the council in relation to the Matamoros Expedition."

The resolution requires the document to be printed in the Brazoria Gazette, the Nacogdoches Telegraph and the San Felipe Telegraph.

January 27, 1836

MEXICO CITY — The top U.S. diplomat in Mexico today charged that the government lied when it claimed 22 Americans were given trials prior to their execution last month in Tampico.

U.S. Charge d'affaires Anthony Butler reacted to the official Mexican reply to his inquiries on why a number of Americans were shot by a firing squad.

Butler sent an official report on the matter to U.S. Secretary of State John Forsyth stating that the note was a month late and contained falsehoods regarding trials for the accused men.

"According to every account received here, these unfortunate men were victims of the offended vanity and uncontrollable passions of Gen. Santa Anna, merely because the people of Texas have dared to oppose his will.

"The horrible crime is the work of Santa Anna alone. He was at San Luis Potosi when the news reached him of the capture of these unfortunate men, and he immediately ordered all foreigners taken to be shot. An order to that effect was immediately issued and executed. This is a sample of Mexican liberty, as well as Mexican justice," Butler wrote.

Butler pointed out that the men had embarked in New Orleans under the assumption they were being taken to Texas as settlers. Only when they were nearing the Mexican coastline were they told they were to be part of a federalist attack commanded by Gen. Jose Antonio Mexia.

Butler explained that the men refused to fight and that was the reason Mexia abandoned them when he sailed off for Brazoria with the defeated remnants of his force.

Butler urged American authorities to retaliate against the Mexican government for the execution of U.S. citizens.

"If this barbarous and inhuman act be submitted to — should the Mexican government be permitted to escape without making the most ample satisfaction, not only the property and lives of our countrymen in Mexico will hereafter be held at the mercy of every petty officer who pleases to exert his power. We will become the scorn of nations."

Sources close to the U.S. embassy said Butler had taken a personal interest in the fates of the captured Americans at Tampico. It is understood by these sources that Butler has been told that all foreigners found with weapons on Mexican soil will be shot as an example.

"The Mexicans are terrified at the thought of thousands of armed Americans fighting with the Texas rebels.

"They want to scare the Americans into not fighting for Texas by showing them they will not be treated as prisoners of war, but as pirates. It's a rough game they're playing," one political source explained.

January 28, 1836

SAN FELIPE — The commander in chief of the regular Texas Army was furloughed today at his own request by the governor.

Gov. Henry Smith granted Gen. Sam Houston a furlough from today until March 1.

In a dispatch to Houston, Smith wrote:

"You are hereby furloughed until March for the purpose of adjusting your private business, preparatory to your necessary absence, hereafter, from home, in the country's service.

"Your absence is permitted in part by the illegal acts of the council in superseding you, by the unauthorized appointment of agents to organize and control the army, contrary to the organic law and the ordinances of their own body.

"In the meantime, you will conform to your instructions and treat with the Indians."

Sources close to Houston said the general had decided he could do no further good for the armed forces of Texas until a general convention scheduled for March 1 makes clear his line of authority.

Houston and Smith have been active in attempting to stop a proposed attack upon Matamoros. The attack is being organized by officers who have been appointed by the General Council instead of Gov. Smith.

The regular army, headed by Houston, continues to support Smith. Sources close to Houston said he was successful in a recent visit in the Goliad-Refugio area in convincing most of the troops not to take part in the Matamoros attack.

Houston has told aides he will go to the Nacogdoches area immediately to carry out orders he received last month to seek a peace treaty with the Cherokee Indians.

Texas authorities are eager to conclude such a treaty to prevent the possibility of the Cherokees aligning themselves with the Mexican Army and opening a second front in the event the Mexicans attempt to invade western Texas.

January 29, 1836

BURNHAM'S CROSSING ON THE COLORADO — One of the top officers in the regular army today said that, unless enough money is raised to support a military establishment, the country will be ruined and unable to resist aggression.

Lt. Col. William B. Travis, en route from San Felipe to assume command of the San Antonio garrison, reported to Gov. Henry Smith, "The people are cold and indifferent.

"They are worn down and exhausted with the war, and, they have lost all confidence in their own government and officers . . . . money must be raised or Texas is gone to ruin.

"Without it, war cannot be again carried on in Texas. The patriotism of a few has done much; but that is becoming worn down. I have strained every nerve, I have used my personal credit, and have neither slept day nor night since I received orders to march, and, with all this, I have barely been able to get horses and equipment for the few men I have."

Sources close to Travis said he was bitter because he had been ordered to raise 100 men, but he was able to muster only 26 regular troops and four volunteers.

"We were recruiting right in the San Felipe district. That's where there are more Anglo settlers than anywhere in Texas. If we can't get help from there, what chance do we have in a war against 8 million Mexicans?" one Travis aide commented.

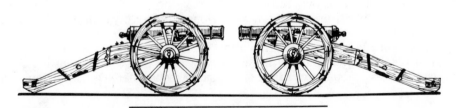

January 30, 1836

BURNHAM'S CROSSING ON THE COLORADO — The officer sent to take over command of the San Antonio garrison today asked to be reassigned.

Lt. Col. William B. Travis reported to Gov. Henry Smith that he had been able to raise only 30 men instead of the 100 men he had been instructed to gather.

Military sources explained that Smith, under fire from the General Council for opposition to the Matamoros expedition, sent the only San Antonio reinforcements available when he dispatched Travis.

There are about 100 men currently stationed in San Antonio. They are quartered at the Alamo.

Travis was the recruiting officer in San Felipe for the regular Texas Army. The regular army continues to take orders from Smith, who has been ousted as governor by the council. Smith has declared the actions of the council to be illegal.

In a report to Smith, Travis stated:

"I have been here with the troops under Capt. John Forsythe, but shall await your orders at Gonzales or some other point on the road. I shall, however, keep the 30 men of Forsythe's company in motion towards Bexar, so that they may arrive there as soon as possible.

"Not being able to raise 100 volunteers as you ordered and there being so few regular troops together, I must beg that your excellency will recall the order for me to go to Bexar in command of so few men.

"I am willing, nay anxious, to go to the defense of Bexar, but, sir, I am unwilling to risk my reputation (which is ever dear to a soldier) by going off into the enemy's country with such little means, so few men and with them so badly equipped. In fact, there is no necessity for my services to command these few men. The company officer will be amply sufficient."

Military sources said they doubted that Smith would act on Travis' request.

"Smith wants to get another good officer he can count on in Bexar and as many troops as he can. All he has is Travis and 30 men; that is all he can do," the source explained.

January 31, 1836

GALVESTON — The Texas Navy grew to four ships today as the latest addition arrived off Galveston Island, giving the rebellious colonists effective control of the sea lanes to New Orleans.

The navy was authorized Nov. 25, 1835, by an act of the General Council. Texas agents have been working in New Orleans since that time, purchasing ships, enlisting seamen and procuring armaments.

The navy consists of the flagship, the 125-ton Invincible, the 125-ton Independence, the 160-ton Brutus and the 60-ton Liberty.

The Independence mounts 11 guns. The Brutus has an armament of a long 18-pounder and six smaller guns. The Liberty has six six-pounders. And the Invincible is armed with a nine-pounder swivel gun and six carronades (easily maneuvered cannons).

The Invincible has a deep draught and fine lines. It is considered the fastest ship of the fleet.

The Texas Navy is opposed by a growing number of Mexican men-of-war, generally larger, slower, with more guns and manned mostly by European sailors.

"We can out-sail them, we can out-hit them and, if necessary, we can out-run them," one Texas Navy officer said in describing the new fleet.

Also maneuvering in Gulf Coast waters are elements of the British West Indies fleet and the U.S. Gulf Coast squadron.

February 1, 1836

NACOGDOCHES — Blood was nearly shed today in an angry confrontation between a group of volunteer soldiers from Kentucky, who sought to vote in the election of delegates to the March 1 General Convention, and election judges who ruled the soldiers non-resident.

Members of the War Party and those favoring independence urged that the 50 Newport, Ky., soldiers be allowed to vote. Mexican-Texans and Peace Party advocates sought to bar the soldiers from voting.

Tempers flared and Lt. Jacob Woods, the Kentucky company's commander, drew up his troops with loaded rifles and vowed if the men were not permitted to vote, he would order them to fire on the Stone House, where the election was being held.

To avoid bloodshed, the election judges agreed to allow a committee of citizens to rule on the voting eligibility of the recently-arrived volunteers.

After the group of citizens decided to rule against the soldiers, Wood again drew up his men in a firing line.

The citizen council reconsidered and voted to allow the soldiers to cast ballots.

Voting is going on today throughout Texas to select delegates to the convention. Most political observers think the convention will declare Texas an independent nation.

Four delegates are being chosen to represent the municipalities of Nacogdoches, Washington, Brazoria, San Augustine and Bexar.

San Felipe, Bastrop and Liberty will each have three delegates. The remaining 13 districts are to be represented by two delegates each.

February 2, 1836

SAN ANTONIO — A top commander in the Texas Army vowed to die defending San Antonio rather than retreat from this center of power in Texas.

Col. James Bowie today dispatched a report to Gov. Henry Smith. Bowie has been in San Antonio for the last two weeks analyzing the military situation for the commander in chief, Gen. Sam Houston.

According to military sources here, Houston ordered Bowie to blow up the fortifications at the improvised fortress of the Alamo and remove the numerous cannons there to Copano Bay and Goliad.

Houston, however, left discretion to Bowie, according to the sources. They said Bowie has now become convinced that holding the Alamo is critical for the defense of Texas.

Both Houston and Bowie, as well as all of the 130-man garrison at San Antonio support Smith in his political battle with the General Council. They report to him and not to the acting governor, James Robinson.

Bowie reported that he had conferred with Lt. Col. James Neill, who is the commander of the post.

"Col. Neill and myself have come to the solemn resolution that we will rather die in these ditches than give it up to the enemy.

"These citizens deserve our protection and the public safety demands our lives rather than to evacuate this post to the enemy," Bowie reported.

Bowie called on Smith to quickly send money, arms, provisions and reinforcements to the garrison.

He added that he had received information that Gen. Antonio Lopez de Santa Anna already had massed 2,000 men at Guerrero (Presidio Rio Grande) and that 5,000 more troops were on the march toward the river.

February 3, 1836

NACOGDOCHES — Four mostly-moderate delegates were elected to the March 1 General Convention in a contest marred by insults and threats of physical force.

Vote counting was completed today in the Stone House government building.

Elected delegates from the 17-man field were Thomas Jefferson Rusk with 392 votes, Oran M. Roberts with 263, Charles S. Taylor with 258 and Robert Potter with 235. Potter barely nosed out J.K. Allen, who tallied 232.

Potter's margin of victory came in the rural districts. Allen had held a seemingly comfortable lead after the city voting.

The elected candidates are generally considered moderates in the struggle between War Party advocates seeking a declaration of independence and Peace Party activists who seek to have Texas remain a part of a Mexico governed under the Constitution of 1824.

Defeated candidates are some of the biggest names in Texas politics, including Hayden Edwards and Sam Houston.

Houston, the commanding general of the regular Texas Army, finished 16th in the 17-man race.

Sources close to Houston said the general also had entered his name in the Refugio district, which is expected to be dominated by army voting. Houston is expected to win a seat on the council from Refugio.

Nacogdoches is Houston's home district. He made his home and carried on a law practice here before becoming involved in the rebellion.

February 4, 1836

COPANO BAY — The main division of the Texas Army's expedition against Matamoros today disembarked at this Aransas Pass port.

The division's commander, Col. James W. Fannin, immediately began moving troops and supplies to the nearest army base at Refugio, about 15 miles west of here.

Fannin landed a force of more than 200 men. He said he expects to link up with about 300 men from Refugio under Col. James Grant and Col. Frank Johnson.

Aides close to Fannin admitted there was some confusion in orders. Fannin has been named overall commander of the Matamoros expedition by the General Council. At various other times, however, the council has given the same job to Johnson and Grant.

The confusion is aggravated by the fact that Texas forces in San Antonio and almost all regular Texas Army officers take their orders from Gov. Henry Smith.

The governor and the council have disavowed the authority and actions of each other.

In a report to the council, Fannin stated that he had reliable information that an armed federalist movement against the centralist government was beginning to break out all over Mexico.

"The troops which occupied Laredo have retired to Saltillo and Monclova; those at Rio Grande town are expected to do likewise."

Fannin reported his spies informed him that dissatisfaction is growing in the Mexican Army and that 20 to 30 men desert each day.

"Matamoros is poorly supplied with troops. I have reason to believe if we move quickly, we can take the town without a shot," Fannin commented.

February 5, 1836

SAN ANTONIO — A meeting of the Texas Army garrison in San Antonio today elected two members to the March 1 General Convention and demanded that they be seated.

Samuel A. Maverick and Jesse B. Badgett, both residents of San Antonio and members of the garrison, were elected to represent the 150 soldiers stationed in this former provincial capital.

More than 2,500 people live in the town and at least as many live on ranches in the municipality of Bexar. Most of the population are Mexican-Texans.

The garrison occupies positions in the town, but has removed all of the cannons and most of its supplies to the Alamo fortress on the outskirts of town east of the San Antonio River.

In a letter addressed to the General Convention, Lt. Col. James Neill, the commander of the garrison, reported that the garrison had held an election for delegates to the convention.

"Our officers perceived that impediments were put in the way of our men voting in the municipal election, such as requiring an oath of actual citizenship in this municipality.

"Not wishing to cause any breach in the good understanding which has so happily existed between the citizens and our garrison . . . we decided to hold our own election," Neill reported.

Neill said that since four representatives were chosen from San Antonio, the garrison chose two, because that was the number agreed upon for a voting group the size of the army in town.

The letter is signed by every officer in the garrison, including Lt. Col.William B. Travis and Col. Jim Bowie.

February 6, 1836

NACOGDOCHES — A motion to solicit money from women in the United States to pay for a "Ladies Battalion" today was approved by Nacogdoches officials.

The town's Committee of Vigilance and Safety approved a motion made by Hayden Edwards that he be sent to the United States, "to solicit from the fair sex of our mother country donations for the purpose of raising a battalion of men to be known by the name of "Ladies Battalion."

Edwards said he planned to have every woman who contributes to the battalion sign her name on an elaborate parchment.

Edwards explained that the parchment would be suspended at each end of a banquet table. A banquet will be held every year to celebrate the Ladies Battalion.

Women contributors, members of the battalion and guests will be allowed to attend the banquet.

Texas officials have attempted to recruit American volunteers into the army by a variety of methods, ranging from patriotic appeals to grants consisting of hundreds of acres of land.

Political observers here said the plan to raise a Ladies Battalion may be the most unusual method yet attempted.

February 7, 1836

MATAMOROS — The commanding general of the Mexican troops here today declared Matamoros a military station, placing the port city under martial law.

Brig. Gen. Francisco Vital Fernandez issued an order from military headquarters in Matamoros that stated:

"As the Army of Operations against the rebels of Texas has commenced to march from Saltillo, and the campaign having been opened, I have ordered that from this date forward during the continuance of the campaign, the city of Matamoros be considered a military station."

Matamoros is one of Mexico's busiest ports. It has a population of about 15,000 and is considered the most strategic post on the Rio Grande.

Fernandez, who was recently named commander in Matamoros following the victory he won over invading federalist troops at Tampico in November, issued the following orders:

● No person, Mexican or foreigner, can leave the city without a passport issued by the military.

● The regulations are extended to the Brazos Santiago and at the mouth of the river in order to include all persons arriving by sea or river.

● Every person who receives any individual into his house as a lodger must report that fact to military authorities.

● Any person who spreads rumors or reports about movements or actions of the rebels will be considered an enemy of the people.

February 8, 1836

MEXICO CITY — Sources close to the U.S. embassy today said the top American diplomat in Mexico described the country's ruler as a total military dictator.

Anthony Butler, a personal representative of President Andrew Jackson and charge d'affaires at the embassy, reported to U.S. Secretary of State John Forsyth that Gen. Antonio Lopez de Santa Anna keeps a tight grip on the national government even when on military campaigns.

Butler said Santa Anna uses his "agent,"   Foreign Minister Jose Maria Tornel, to control the government in his absence.

Santa Anna is president of the Centralist Party controlled nation. Legally, he must give up his title of presidency when he is acting as commander in chief of the armed forces. He has turned the presidency over to Miguel Barragan while he is preparing the Army of Operations for an invasion of the rebellious Texas province.

"Santa Anna, even at a distance of 700 miles, rules and directs every movement here (in Mexico City) and no decision on any important question is given until Santa Anna has been consulted,"   Butler reported.

Government officials in Washington, D.C., are growing concerned over the extent of military preparations being made by Santa Anna to crush the Anglo colonists in Texas, according to sources here.

Butler reportedly was pessimistic in his evaluation of the situation, pointing out that untrained militia and farmers could not be expected to stand up to the large, well-equipped and professional army Santa Anna will use against them.

February 9, 1836

SAN ANTONIO — A former U.S. congressman and legendary frontier figure today joined the Texas Army garrison of this strategically important former provincial capital.

David Crockett, a 50-year-old former congressman from Tennessee who lost a bitter re-election bid last year, rode into San Antonio at the head of a dozen mounted riflemen.

Crockett refused an officer's commission offered to him by the garrison commander, Lt. Col. James Neill.

"I would be honored if you appoint me a high private. I want to fight for Texas as an ordinary soldier," Crockett said.

Crockett told Neill he would act as a squad leader for the 12 men who arrived with him. Most of them are from Tennessee.

Crockett is one of America's most renowned frontiersmen. His arrival with a contingent of expert riflemen excited the 140-man garrison stationed in town and at the fortified mission, the Alamo.

A number of persons asked Crockett to give a speech, noting his fame as a frontier humorist.

Crockett stood on a box in Main Plaza and addressed hundreds of soldiers and citizens.

He told several tall tales which have made him famous and took a couple of jabs at his bitter political enemy, U.S. President Andrew Jackson.

Crockett then told of the necessity of good men resisting tyranny. He ended his speech with a saying for which he has become noted:

"I leave this rule for others when I am dead, be always sure you are right, then go ahead."

February 10, 1836

MEXICO CITY — The Mexican government today extended the blockade of Texas coastal towns.

One week ago, the government ordered the closing of the ports of Galveston and Matagorda while they remain in the hands of rebel forces.

Today's decreee includes the towns of Matamoros, LaVaca, San Luis, Galveston, Brazoria, Harrisburg, Goliad, Anahuac, Copano and any other point occupied by the insurrectionists in Texas.

The order was issued by Foreign Minister Jose Maria Tornel.

The order will take effect 30 days after its publication in Mexico City for vessels proceeding from foreign ports on the Gulf of Mexico and 90 days for those beyond the Gulf.

Naval sources in Mexico City said the extension of the blockade will proabably be ignored by most maritime nations.

"A blockade is only recognized if a country has the naval power to enforce it. Right now, it is the Texas Navy that controls the Texas coast," the source explained.

During the last two years, Mexico has launched a vigorous campaign to upgrade its navy. Several major warships have been constructed for the Mexican Navy in England and are expected to be delivered within the next few months.

February 11, 1836

SAN ANTONIO — The command of the Texas garrison in this strategic former provincial capital changed hands today, with a former leader of the War Party assuming leadership of the 150-man garrison.

Lt. Col. William B. Travis took charge of the troops. He was placed in command by Lt. Col. James Neill, the outgoing post commander.

Neill explained that there was sickness in his family that forced him to return home to his farm near Nashville on the Brazos.

One of Travis' first acts as commander was to send an urgent dispatch to Gov. Henry Smith, requesting more money, supplies and troops.

"You have no doubt already received information that tremendous preparations on the Rio Grande and in the interior for the invasion of Texas. (Gen. Antonio Lopez de) Santa Anna by last accounts was in Saltillo with a force of 2,500 men and guns. (Gen. Ramirez y) Sesma was on the Rio Grande with 2,000 men," Travis wrote.

The new garrison commander went on to explain that Santa Anna had issued a proclamation vowing vengeance against the people of Texas.

"He threatens to exterminate every white man within its limits," Travis wrote.

The commander pointed out that San Antonio was the frontier post nearest the Rio Grande and will, in all probability, be attacked first.

"We are ill prepared, as we have not more than 150 men and they are in a very disorganized state — Yet, we are determined to sustain it as long as there is a man left; because we consider death preferable to disgrace," Travis explained.

In addition to money and supplies, Travis suggested sending the regular army company stationed at Copano Bay and one of the volunteer companies at Goliad, pointing out that those troops could be in San Antonio in four days.

February 12, 1836

NACOGDOCHES — A former governor of Mississippi today presented the commander in chief of the Texas Army with a gun used in the fight for Polish independence.

John A. Quitman, president of Mississippi's Senate and former governor of the state, sent the Polish yager to Gen. Sam Houston. Quitman's agents made the presentation today in Nacogdoches.

A yager is a short smooth-bore musket, favored by cavalry troops. It has a short range, but can be handled from a horse.

The yager was reportedly used during the long and unsuccessful attempt of the Poles to throw off Russian rule.

Quitman resigned as governor of Mississippi last month. He is raising and equipping a force of Mississippians to fight in Texas, according to his agents.

Houston responded to the gift by pledging to make sure the weapon was used in a cause as righteous as that of the fight for a free Poland.

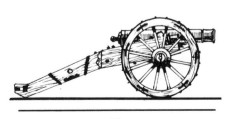

February 13, 1836

SAN ANTONIO — A dispute over the command of the Texas garrison at this strategic town threatens to undermine the military efficiency of the post, according to a high-ranking officer.

Maj. James J. Baugh, adjutant of the post, reported to Gov. Henry Smith that confusion exists over the position of commander.

Lt. Col. James Neill commanded the 150-man garrison until two days ago, when he was forced to go on a 20-day leave because of sickness in his family.

Neill, an officer in the regular army, turned command over to another regular Texas army officer, Lt. Col. William B. Travis.

The garrison is made up of about 50 regular army troops and 100 volunteers. The volunteers retain the right to elect their own officers.

According to Baugh, Travis announced to the garrison that he was assuming command, but that if the volunteers objected, they could elect their own officer.

Sources close to Travis said he expected the volunteers to approve of him as commander and was stunned when they rejected him and chose Col. Jim Bowie.

Baugh explained that Travis would not relinquish command to Bowie, but that Bowie insisted he be overall commander since he had more support than Travis.

Baugh commented that Bowie began to assume command, giving orders to release all prisoners and parading troops at the Alamo. Some of the troops and Bowie were drunk, according to the adjutant.

Baugh said Travis refused to be a part of such unprofessional action and removed the 50 regulars still answering to his command to a camp on the Medina River, several miles from town.

February 14, 1836

SAN ANTONIO — The dispute over the command of the Texas garrison at this strategic town was settled today with an agreement by the two top officers.

Lt. Col. William B. Travis and Col. Jim Bowie agreed to share command of the 150-man garrison.

Maj. James J. Baugh, adjutant of the post, had reported to Gov. Henry Smith that confusion existed over command position.

Lt. Col. James Neill had commanded the 150-man garrison. When he went on personal leave three days ago he handed command over to Travis, the ranking regular army officer.

Travis allowed the 100 volunteer troops to elect their own commander. He reportedly expected the election to be a formality, but Bowie won the vote count.

Travis withdrew the 50 regular army troops from the Alamo, where the garrison is stationed, to a campsite on the Medina River, several miles from town.

Aides of both officers were able to work out a compromise. The garrison command will now be jointly held by both men.

One source close to the scene explained, "There are disturbing reports of Mexican troop movements on the Rio Grande. Both Bowie and Travis knew that this is no time for a divided command. Things could get pretty hot around here before much longer."

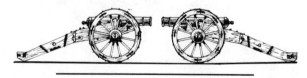

February 15, 1836

SAN FELIPE — A General Council advisory committee today urged that troops now stationed at Goliad be ordered not to retreat because of rumors of an impending Mexican invasion of Texas.

The Advisory Committee of the Executive, appointed by the General Council to advise Acting Gov. James Robinson, issued a report critical of suggestions that the far western defenses be abandoned because of reports of impending attack by large numbers of Mexican troops.

"The committee is of the opinion that the advances from the interior are not of so certain and definite a character as to require a retrograde movement on the part of Col. (James) Fannin or any of the troops designed for the Matamoros expedition, especially when the forces at San Antonio have considerably increased and the militia are being called upon to move upon the western frontier," the report stated.

"We believe these forces will be amply sufficient to sustain the posts of San Antonio and Goliad independent of the forces first designed for the Matamoros expedition and to meet any forces of the enemy which may come from the upper crossing of the Rio Grande.

"The committee advises that Col. Fannin be required to maintain his position at Copano and, if possible, at San Patricio until the movement of the enemy shall be well ascertained." the report concluded.

Military sources said that a debate is being carried on at the highest levels as to the proper strategy for Texas to adopt. The committee and its allies are urging a continuation of the plan to capture the Mexican port of Matamoros and to sustain troops as far west as possible.

The regular army commander, Gen. Sam Houston, has urged that fortifications in both San Antonio and Goliad be blown up and a line formed on the east bank of the Colorado River.

Officers in the San Antonio garrison and Gov. Henry Smith are urging all resources be thrown into a defense of San Antonio and the fortress of the Alamo.

February 16, 1836

SAN ANTONIO — The chief engineer at the Alamo today issued a report recommending significant changes to the fortress.

Capt. Green B. Jameson reported to Gov. Henry Smith on the improvements he had already made to the fortifications and offered suggestions for improvements.

Jameson, a respected military engineer, has been ordered to make the Alamo as secure as possible. In his report, Jameson stated:

"After seeing the improbability and perhaps the impracticality of stationing a large garrison here, I now submit a suggestion to square the Alamo and erect a large redoubt at each corner supported by bastions.

"A ditch should be dug all around and filled with water. When squared in that way four cannons and fewer men would do more effective service than 20 pieces of artillery can do in the way they are now mounted.

"The Mexicans have shown want of skill in this fortress as they have done in all things — I have seen many fortifications in the United States and find that all of the interior ones are square and those of the forts circular.

"Taking into consideration the scarcity of tools we have done well in mounting and remounting cannons and other necessary work. If I were ordered to construct a new and effective fortress on an economical plan, I would suggest a diamond with two acute and two obtuse angles. With few men and guns and with a sufficient entrenchment all around, such a fortress and its redoubts and bastions would command all points."

Texas military sources said that concern is mounting that a surprise Mexican attack would leave the garrison undermanned. There are now 150 men stationed in San Antonio. Plans call for the troops to make no attempt to hold the town, but to retire to the Alamo if attacked in force.

February 17, 1836

MEXICO CITY — An American diplomat stationed in Matamoros filed an angry protest today with the top Mexican Army officer in the area.

Consul D.W. Smith said armed soldiers had searched his house and mistreated members of his family.

Smith charged in a note to Brig. Gen. Francisco Vital Fernandez that:

"This morning a party of armed soldiers, during my absence from home, broke into my yard and forcibly took from there an American horse and two mules.

"My house was immediately surrounded by a party of armed soldiers, who not only prohibited all communications to the outside, but forcibly searched every room in my dwelling and grossly insulted the females of my family in open violation of the rights and immunities which belong to my official character.

"I have, therefore, to request that you inquire into the cause of this outrage and punish the delinquents."

The note was delivered to Fernandez in his official capacity as commandant general and inspector of the Departments of Tamaulipas and Nuevo Leon.

February 18, 1836

MATAMOROS — The commanding general of the Mexican Army in Matamoros today responded to an angry note from the U.S. consul, denying charges that soldiers had committed an outrage upon the diplomat's family.

Consul D.W. Smith charged yesterday that Mexican troops broke into his house, insulted the females of his family and searched the premises, seizing two horses and one mule.

Gen. Francisco Vital Fernandez, the commandant general and inspector of the Departments of Tamaulipas and Nuevo Leon, denied the charge.

He replied to Smith's note with an official memo of his own in which he explained that he had received orders to watch for persons who were conveying information from Matamoros to rebels in Texas.

"Two of them, one of whom is your step-son, were surprised in the act of departure and took refuge in your house.

"The soldiers placed guards around the house but did not enter your home.

"The soldiers in no way violated the security of your house and person or the consideration due your position as consul, which I will always see maintained in obedience to the prescriptions of international law," Fernandez replied.

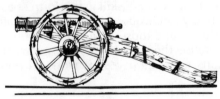

February 19, 1836

NASHVILLE, Tenn. — The leading colonizer in Texas today urged a united voice for complete independence in the embattled Mexican province.

Stephen F. Austin, who was the key figure in bringing about widespread Anglo immigration to Texas, said in the Tennessee capital that unity and independence, are essential if Texas is to be saved from rule by a tyrant.

Austin is credited with settling 1,500 families on his land grants.

Austin, William Wharton and Branch T. Archer are acting as commissioners for Texas in the United States. For six weeks they have been touring the country, urging Americans to provide the embattled colonists with money, war supplies and volunteers for the army.

The group has split up. Austin was planning on moving on to Washington, D.C. but severe weather has forced him to stay in Nashville.

While in Nashville, Austin reported to Gov. Henry Smith that the most important thing Texas needs to do in order to gain support in the United States is to declare complete independence from Mexico.

For years, Austin had been the leading member of the Peace Party, which sought to retain ties with Mexico under the federalist Constitution of 1824.

Since beginning his trip to the United States, however, Austin has told friends that it is apparent that no help can be expected from other Mexican states opposed to the centralist rule of President Santa Anna and that the only logical course is for Texas to declare itself independent.

Austin and the other commissioners have become concerned that the fight between Smith and the General Council is harming Texas' image abroad.

Both the president and the council have declared each other's actions illegal, creating, in effect, two separate governments.

"Union, union, union and concert of action and of purpose with a single eye to the independence and prosperity of Texas is absolutely essential," Austin commented to Smith.

February 20, 1836

MATAMOROS — The consulate in this Gulf Coast port today officially protested to the U.S. secretary of state the arrest of two Americans by Mexican officials.

In a report to Secretary of State John Forsyth, Chief Consular Officer J.W. Smith stated:

"On the morning of Feb. 17 William Hallett and my step-son, Zalmon Hall, were arrested in the street, near my house, by a party of armed soldiers, who brutally struck the latter in the face with a sword and forcibly took them to the principal barracks in this city, where they are confined as prisoners.

"They were arrested upon suspicion of being about to leave for Texas, which is altogether aside from the fact, so far as it applies to my son. A short time after this occurrence, sentinels were placed at the doors of my residence, under false pretenses, and all communication prohibited.

"Armed soldiers broke open my gate during my absence and forcibly took out of my yard a mare and two mules, being my private property and entered my house with drawn swords and searched every room in the building, contrary to law or justice."

Smith reported that he contacted the commander of the Mexican troops in Matamoros and demanded punishment for the soldiers involved in the incident, but, he reported, the demand was ignored.

Smith added that since the local commander, Gen. Fernandez, imposed restrictions on movements of civilians, "lawless depredations have been frequently committed with impunity by a licentious soldiery and that serious and well-grounded apprehensions are entertained by the resident American merchants for the safety of their persons and property."

February 21, 1836

CHEROKEE VILLAGE — The basic elements of a peace treaty between the Texas government and East Texas Indians have been negotiated and are in the final process of acceptance.

Eight Texas commissioners, headed by Gen. Sam Houston, have been carrying on delicate negotiations with Cherokee chiefs and representatives of other tribes in this village 40 miles west of Nacogdoches.

The Cherokees have been acting as spokesmen for a number of tribes, including the Shawnee, Delaware, Kickapoo, Quapaw, Choctaw, Biloxi, Ioni, Alabama, Coushatta, Caddo, Tahocullake and Mataquo.

The treaty is being taken by runners to several major villages not represented at the general meeting, which has been going on here for nearly two weeks.

The text of the treaty reads in part:

"The parties declare that there shall be a firm and lasting peace forever and that a friendly intercourse shall be pursued by the people belonging to both parties.

"It is agreed that the before named tribes or bands shall form one community and that they shall have and possess the lands within the following bounds. The lands lying west of the San Antonio Road and beginning on the west and the point where the said road crosses the Angelina River and running up the river until it reaches the mouth of the first large creek (below the great Shawnee village) emptying into the said river from the northeast and then running with the creek to its main source.

"From there due north to the Sabine River and with that river west, then starting where the San Antonio road crosses the Angelina River and with the said road to the point where it crosses the Neches River."

Other articles of the treaty guarantee that the Texas government will enforce the treaty and that the Indians will be responsible for their own government, so long as they are not contrary to the laws of Texas.

Included in the Indian chiefs negotiating the treaty are Colonel Bowles, Big Mush, Samuel Benge, Oosoota, Corn Tassle, The Egg, John Bowles and Tunnettee.

February 22, 1836

WASHINGTON, D.C. — The commanding general of all U.S. troops west of Virginia today was ordered to the Mexican border.

Maj. Gen. E. P. Gaines was instructed by the War Department to proceed immediately from Florida to the Sabine River area that separates the rebellious Mexican province of Texas from Louisiana.

"You will proceed to the western frontier of the State of Louisiana there to assume the personal command of all the troops which are or may be employed in any part of the region adjoining the Mexican boundary," Gaines was instructed by Adjutant Gen. Robert Jones.

Jones added:

"Lest the instructions herein referred to may not have reached you, the Secretary of War directs that a triplicate copy be now forwarded and that, on receiving the communication, you will not delay your departure for any reason."

Sources in the War Department said senior officers and President Andrew Jackson are growing increasingly concerned over the possibility of a bloody war breaking out between Anglo-American colonists in Texas and the Mexican Army under the personal command of Gen. Antonio Lopez de Santa Anna.

Jackson has told aides that it would be impossible to stand idly by and watch thousands of Americans slaughtered by a professional and ruthless army.

On the other hand, Jackson is determined not to go to war with Mexico over Texas unless provoked beyond limits.

Jackson is said to be hoping that Gaines, one of the most respected and veteran officers in the Army, will be the best man on the scene.

The Sixth Regiment, a crack infantry unit of 600 men, has recently been ordered to reinforce the troops along the Sabine.

Gaines has about 300 regular troops at Fort Jessup near the border and about the same number scattered in smaller posts. The general also has the authority to call out the militias of Louisiana and Mississippi.

February 23, 1836

SAN ANTONIO — A Mexican Army cavalry brigade nearly caught the 150-man garrison of this strategic town by surprise today, pushing to within two miles of the city before being spotted.

The cavalry brigade, including lancers in shiny breastplates and crimson uniforms, formed an extended line across the Laredo Road and advanced into the vacated town.

Many Mexican-Texans have left San Antonio for nearby ranches since rumors were heard 10 days ago that a large army under the command of Gen. Antonio Lopez de Santa Anna had crossed the Rio Grande and was moving rapidly toward this former provincial capital of 2,500 population.

The Texans had posted a sentry in the tallest structure in town, a church tower. He reported seeing the shining breastplates of hundreds of horsemen. Two scouts on horseback raced back into town a short time later verifying the sentry's report.

Confusion broke out in the two main squares as residents quickly rounded up possessions and fled, or returned to their homes to await events.

San Antonio is 95 percent Mexican-Texan and Santa Anna enjoys a good amount of support among the townspeople, according to Texas military intelligence officers.

The garrison, which was mainly located in dwellings around Main Plaza, carried out an orderly retirement to the Alamo, a fortified mission east of the San Antonio River on the outskirts of town.

The Mexicans ran up a red flag from the tower of San Fernando Cathedral, signifying no quarter. Co-commander Lt. Col. William B. Travis ordered the flag answered with a cannon shot.

Texas military sources estimated the number of Mexican troops in town by nightfall at between 1,000 and 1,500.

Travis and his co-commander, Col. Jim Bowie, dispatched urgent messages to commanders of Texas forces at Goliad and Gonzales requesting immediate reinforcements.

"We are determined never to retreat. We have but little provisions, but enough to last until you and your men get here," the dispatch to Col. James W. Fannin in Goliad explained.

February 24, 1836

SAN ANTONIO — The commander of the besieged garrison in the Alamo today sent an urgent appeal for help.

Lt. Col. William B. Travis, dispatched a messenger to Gonzales with the following appeal:

"To the people of Texas and all Americans in the world — fellow citizens and compatriots.

"I am besieged . . . I have sustained a continual bombardment and cannonade for 24 hours and have not lost a man. The enemy has demanded a surrender at discretion, otherwise, the garrison are to be put to the sword.

"I have answered the demand with a cannon shot, and our flag still waves proudly from the walls. I shall never surrender or retreat.

"Then, I call upon you in the name of liberty, of patriotism and everything dear to the American character, to come to our aid with all dispatch.

"The enemy is receiving reinforcements daily and will no doubt increase to three or four thousand in four or five days. If this call is neglected, I am determined to sustain myself as long as possible and die like a soldier who never forgets what is due his own honor and that of his country.

"Victory or death."

Travis added a postscript:

"The Lord is on our side. When the enemy appeared in sight we had not three bushels of corn. We have since found in deserted houses 80 or 90 bushels and got into the walls 20 or 30 head of beeves."

Texas military sources at the Alamo admitted that the arrival of large numbers of Mexican troops had nearly caught them by surprise.

"We were counting on having a couple of more weeks at least. Most of the garrison was in town when the alarm was sounded. We were nearly caught in an awkward situation," one source said.

The Texas garrison numbers slightly more than 150 men. More than 1,000 Mexican cavalrymen were in the first contingent to arrive in San Antonio and hundreds of infantry troops have augmented that force in the last 24 hours.

Texas officers are confident that the Mexicans will attempt no major assault until more heavy infantry and artillery arrive.

February 25, 1836

SAN ANTONIO — An attempt today by several hundred Mexican troops to erect a cannon battery within 100 yards of the Alamo gate was repulsed by the Texas garrison.

Estimates of Mexican casualties range from eight to more than 50, while no Texans were killed or wounded.

In a report on the action to Commanding Gen. Sam Houston, Lt. Col. William Barret Travis stated:

"Today at 10 a.m. some 300 Mexican troops crossed the (San Antonio) River below and came up under cover of the houses until they arrived within point-blank shot.

"We opened a heavy discharge of grape and canister on them, together with a well directed fire from small arms which forced them to halt and take shelter in the houses about 90 or 100 yards from our batteries. The action continued to rage about two hours, when the enemy retreated in confusion, dragging off some of their dead or wounded.

"During the action, the enemy kept up a constant bombardment and discharge of balls, grape and canister. We know from actual observation that many of the enemy were wounded, while we, on our part, have not lost a man. Two or three of our men have been slightly scratched by pieces of rock, but not disabled.

"I take great pleasure in stating that both officers and men conducted themselves with firmness and bravery.

"Captains William Carey, Almeron Dickinson and Samuel Blair of the artillery rendered essential service and Charles Despillier and Robert Brown gallantly sallied out and set fire to houses which afforded the enemy shelter, in the face of the enemy fire. Indeed, the whole of the men who were brought into action conducted themselves with such undaunted heroism that it would be injustice to discriminate.

"The honorable David Crockett was seen at all points, animating the men to do their duty. Our numbers are few and the enemy still continue to close in with entrenchments.

"I have every reason to fear an attack from his whole force very soon, but I shall hold out to the last extremity, hoping to secure reinforcements in a day or two.

"Do hasten to my aid as rapidly as possible, as from the superior number of the enemy, it will be impossible for us to keep them out much longer. If they overpower us, we fall a sacrifice at the shrine of our country, and we hope posterity and our country will do our memory justice. Give me help, oh my country. Victory or death."

February 26, 1836

SAN ANTONIO — Both sides continued to entrench and fought several brief engagements today during the fourth day of the siege of the Alamo.

Texans sallied forth early this morning and again tonight to burn down houses in La Villita, a part of San Antonio, which was providing Mexican troops with cover as they attempted to move in closer to the fortress.

The Texans were also after firewood, which is in short supply in the fortress. Several peasant huts were burned and others were ripped apart for firewood.

Mexican patrols fired on the Texans and brief exchanges of small arms fire took place. Several Mexicans were killed or wounded. No Texans suffered wounds.

An attempt at midday to cut off the garrison's water supply by damming an irrigation ditch was beaten off by accurate rifle fire. At least six Mexican troops were shot dead while attempting to construct a dam on the San Antonio River about 200 yards from the north wall.

The Mexicans kept up a determined bombardment, which caused damage to cannon mountings and portions of the limestone walls of the fortress. Alamo engineer Capt. Green B. Jameson is directing efforts to shore up weakened walls with timber and earth embankments. Ditches continue to be dug inside the fortress for secondary defense lines.

At Mexican headquarters, the arrival of three more battalions was greeted with relief. The Mexican troop strength is now above 3,000, although most of the elite infantry assault battalions have yet to arrive.

Texas troop strength of 160 is known to the Mexican commander, Gen. Antonio Lopez de Santa Anna, who has received excellent intelligence on the rebellious colonists' military position from Texas-Mexicans in San Antonio who have remained loyal to Mexico.

February 27, 1836

SAN PATRICIO — Mexican troops surprised and defeated a Texas Army unit early this morning in this Irish settlement.

Ten Texans were killed and 18 captured following a furious fire fight which began about 4 a.m. and lasted three hours.

Six Texans, including the commander of the force, Col. Frank Johnson, escaped and were assumed to be heading in the direction of the main Texas fortifications in Goliad, 50 miles east of the western outpost of colonization in the rebellious colony.

Mexican casualties were estimated at four dead and six wounded.

About 450 Mexican cavalry troops under the personal command of Gen. Jose Urrea arrived at San Patricio early in the morning after a 20-mile forced march through a freezing rain.

Urrea had received information that Johnson had split his small command of 60 men and was waiting out the bad weather in town.

Apparently because of the cold, rainy weather, the Texans had posted no guards.

The Mexican troops surrounded several houses in which the Texans were quartered and called out for them to surrender.

The Texans began firing. During the confusion of the first volleys, Johnson and five men who were billeted with him slipped out a back door and fled.

Their retreat was covered by the majority of the Texan troops, who held out in the largest house in the town square. They shot down several Mexicans who attempted to set fire to the house.

Eventually, the Mexicans succeeded in setting the house on fire and the surviving Texans surrendered.

Urrea ordered the prisoners taken to Matamoros.

Mexican military sources said Urrea would seek out the rest of the Texas forces operating in the Nueces River area and then proceed toward the next Texas position at Refugio before moving on the main Texas force at Goliad.

February 28, 1836

SAN ANTONIO — The sixth day of siege at the Alamo brought no relief for the 160-man garrison as cannon fire and crumbling entrenchments threatened the fortifications.

The Mexicans kept up a heavy bombardment, firing more than 100 rounds from howitzers and six- and nine-pounder cannons.

The Texans reported no casualties, but were kept busy propping up weakened portions of the limestone walls with earth and timber.

Several Mexicans were shot by sharpshooters as they worked on the trenches which are being dug steadily closer to the walls of the old fortress.

The Alamo fortress is composed of a series of rectangular buildings connected by a wall varying from nine to 12 feet in height. A 75-foot stretch on the south side between the chapel and the low barracks has no wall, but is protected by four four-pounders and an earth-and-timber stockade.

The Alamo encloses nearly three acres and is protected by 21 pieces of artillery. Defenders are stretched thin and the entire garrison has to remain on duty most of the time. Squads take turns sleeping inside the barracks for a few hours at a stretch.

One break they all look forward to is in the early evening, when two of the cattle are barbecued over a wood fire.

Soldiers cut thick slices of steak from the side of beef cooking over the fire. Cornbread and frijoles still are in good supply, but coffee ran out two days ago.

David Crockett has entertained soldiers at supper time with his fiddle playing. He has been joined in an unusual duo by John McGregor playing bagpipes while attired in full kilt.

The music of "Green Mountain Maiden" or "The Girl I Left Behind Me" was played in grim competition with the nighttime serenade of "Deguello" from one of the five Mexican Army bands taking part in the siege.

"Deguello" is the Moorish song of blood and death which means "throat-cutting." Traditionally, it is played to signify that no prisoners will be taken in the upcoming battle.

Texas military sources estimate Mexican troop strength at 3,000 and increasing daily. Texan gunners have had to suspend counter battery fire to conserve ammunition. They are limiting their fire to sharpshooters with Kentucky long rifles and three to five cannon rounds a day at selected targets.

February 29, 1836

SAN ANTONIO — The top-ranking Mexican-Texan in the Alamo was tonight sent out to hurry up reinforcements and supplies as the Mexican siege of this strategic fort intensified.

Capt. Juan Seguin and an aide slipped out of the fort after dark. Their mission was to ride to Gonzales to attempt a speed-up of the gathering of supplies and reinforcements.

Seguin was selected because commander Lt. Col. William Barret Travis thought the Mexican-Texan could slip through the tightening lines better than any other man at the fort.

Seguin was also thought better able to rally Mexican-Texan support in the ranchero area, where Travis is hoping to raise a company of Mexican-Texans and adequate supplies of grain and beef.

During the day, siege activities continued. Both sides are entrenching and throwing up earthworks. The Mexicans have succeeded in placing a battery 300 yards away from the south wall. Other batteries firing at the north wall and west wall are farther removed. Infantry slit trenches are being pushed closer to the rambling fort, which encloses nearly three acres.

Mexican troops have learned to be wary of Texas sharpshooters armed with 300-yard range Kentucky long rifles. The long-range rifles caught Mexican troops by surprise. They are accustomed to foes armed with conventional muskets barely effective at 100 yards.

Dozens of Mexican troops have been picked off while working on the trenches. A number of other Mexican soldiers have been killed or wounded by Texas raiding parties.

Texas military sources continue to report no casualties among their men, despite hundreds of rounds fired at the Alamo by Mexican howitzers and cannons.

March 1, 1836

SAN ANTONIO — Thirty-two reinforcements slipped through the Mexican lines tonight to bolster the besieged Alamo garrison.

The men, all from the town of Gonzales, were led through the lines on a moonless night by veteran scout John W. Smith.

Before they were able to gain access to the fortress, they were nearly lured into a trap by an imposter posing as a Texas soldier. When they approached the fort, one nervous guard fired a shot, wounding a man in the foot. All others made it safely inside.

The men explained that as they neared the fort a horseback rider appeared and asked in perfect English, "Do you gentlemen wish to enter the fort?"

Several men replied "yes." The rider said, "Follow me," and swung his horse around.

Smith became suspicious and said loudly, "Boys, I think it's time we should be shooting that fellow."

Hearing that, the stranger rode into the darkness and the company continued on to the Alamo.

Speculation was that the man was one of a few Englishmen in the Mexican Army, possibly Gen. Adrian Woll.

The Gonzales company is commanded by Capt. George Kimball and Capt. Albert Martin. One of the men carried the first Texas battle flag with him, the "Come and Take It" flag of the Oct. 2 battle of Gonzales.

The reinforcements raised the total fighting force in the Alamo to 189 men.

Texas military sources said the extra men were badly needed as riflemen. With 21 cannons to man and an enclosure of nearly three acres to guard, the available fighting force has been stretched thin.

"These men will give (Commander Lt. Col William) Travis a lot better chance of holding the outer walls and not having to fall back to his secondary positions inside the Alamo during an all-out assault," one Texas military source explained.

Even with the reinforcements, the garrison is outnumbered nearly 20 to 1 and more Mexican troops are arriving daily.

March 2, 1836

WASHINGTON-ON-THE-BRAZOS — The General Convention today declared Texas an independent nation, severing all ties with Mexico.

A committee chaired by George Childress prepared a declaration of independence, which was unanimously approved by the 58 delegates gathered in this small, bleak Brazos River community.

The convention was called into session yesterday, replacing the faction-torn government of Gov. Henry Smith and Acting Gov. James Robinson. The two had claimed executive authority. The General Council appointed Robinson governor in January after it declared the office of governor vacant. Smith refused to accept the council's authority and continued to function as governor as best he could.

The convention is expected to react to the worsening military situation by naming Sam Houston commander in chief of all Texas military forces.

Houston has insisted that he be given authority over all Texas military forces, including volunteers and the regular army and navy. Houston previously had commanded the regular army, but had no authority over volunteer forces.

Houston said the end result was confusion and lack of control of the military.

The former governor of Tennessee and close friend of U.S. President Andrew Jackson told delegates he would not serve unless granted wide-ranging powers to command all Texas military efforts.

He is expected to be confirmed as commander in chief within the next two days.

The declaration also states:

"The Mexican government has now a large mercenary army advancing to carry on against us a war of extermination. It has, through its emissaries, incited the merciless savage, with tomahawk and scalping knife, to massacre the inhabitants of our defenseless frontier.

"It has been, during the whole time of our connection with it, the contemptible sport and victim of successive military revolutions and has continually exhibited every characteristic of a weak, corrupt and tyrannical government.

"These and other grievances were patiently borne by the people of Texas until they reached that point in which forbearance ceases to be a virtue."

March 3, 1836

SAN ANTONIO — The commander of the besieged Alamo garrison sent out a final appeal for help tonight as the Mexican trenches came within musket range of the fortress.

Lt. Col. William Barret Travis dispatched veteran scout John W. Smith with a message to the president of the General Convention, now meeting in Washington-on-the-Brazos to proclaim an independent Texas.

Smith slipped through the Mexican lines once before with one of several appeals for help that Travis had dispatched. He is considered one of the best scouts in the Texas Army.

"This will be the last man we can send out," one Texas military source explained, adding that the Mexican entrenchments were getting so close and the siege tightening so that, by tomorrow, it would be suicide to try to slip through.

In his letter to the convention president, Travis stated:

"From the 25th to the present date the enemy has kept up a bombardment from two howitzers and a heavy cannonade from two long nine-pounders.

"During this period the enemy has been busy encircling us with entrenched encampments on all sides.

"I have fortified this place so that the walls are generally proof against cannon balls and I shall continue to entrench on the inside and strengthen the walls by throwing up dirt.

"At least 200 shells have fallen inside of our works without having injured a single man. We have not lost a man from any cause and we have killed many of the enemy.

"The spirits of the men are still high although they have had much to depress them. We have contended for 10 days against an enemy variously estimated from 1,500 to 6,000 with 1,000 more arriving today."

Travis went on to report that there was no indication that Col. James Fannin would send any aid from his force at Goliad.

Travis appealed for 500 pounds of cannon powder, 800 rounds of cannon balls, 10 kegs of rifle powder and a supply of lead as well as every able bodied man available.

"If these things are promptly sent and large reinforcements are hastened to this frontier, this neighborhood will be the great and decisive ground. The power of

---

Santa Anna is to be met here or in the colonies; we had better meet them here than to suffer a war of devastation to rage in our settlements," Travis reported. He added:

"A blood red banner waves from the church of Bejar and in the camp above us, in token that the war is one of vengeance against rebels; they have declared us as such; demanded that we should surrender at discretion, or that this garrison should be put to the sword.

"Their threats have no influence on me or my men, but to make all fight with desperation and that high-souled courage which characterizes the patriot, who is willing to die in defense of his country's liberty and his own honor."

Travis signed it, "God and Texas. Victory or Death."

Smith slipped over the east wall shortly before midnight with the message. He disappeared silently into the moonless night.

March 4, 1836

SAN ANTONIO — A decision to assault the Alamo was apparently reached at a high level strategy session today at Mexican Army general headquarters.

Mexican military sources said commanding Gen. Antonio Lopez de Santa Anna indicated his strong desire to end the siege as soon as possible with a full-scale infantry assault.

Heated discussion was held by a half-dozen aides and division commanders. A formal decision was delayed until tomorrow, but sources expect Santa Anna to order the attack within 48 hours.

Lt. Col. Jose Enrique de la Pena, a member of the general staff, reported that the council of war began with Santa Anna stressing the need to free the Army of Operations for further action by eliminating the Alamo garrison as soon as possible.

"I cannot take the responsibility for letting the military resources of the nation stand idle," Santa Anna said, according to de la Pena.

"Speaking in favor of an assault were Generals Sesma, Cos and Castrillon, Colonels Almonte, Duque, Amat, Romero and Salas and the interim mayor of San Luis," de la Pena reported.

"The problem centered around the method of carrying it out. Castrillon, Almonte and Romero were of the opinion that a breach should be made and that eight or 10 hours would suffice to accomplish this," de la Pena explained.

Several officers urged that the attack be put off until 12-pounder cannons could arrive in three or four days. With heavier cannons, it is believed, the crumbling limestone walls of the Alamo can be knocked down, exposing the garrison to point-blank grape and canister fire.

Santa Anna and most of his aides were of the opinion that the six- and nine-pounder cannons currently pounding away at the Alamo walls will be sufficient to breach the fortification and that a full-scale infantry attack from four directions will overwhelm the thinly-stretched garrison within a matter of minutes.

Mexican officers admit that siege operations have been unexpectedly costly, with more than 100 men killed or wounded by sharpshooters during the 11 days that trenches have been dug close to the Alamo.

At least 50 more men have been lost in a series of feints and skirmishes with Texas patrols. Texas casualties are not known, but are believed to be light, despite a heavy bombardment of the fort by light field guns.

Santa Anna repeated his orders that no prisoners should be taken because the rebels are considered pirates.

Speaking of the planned assault, one Mexican military observer said:

"If we hit them right, with surprise and with overwhelming force, we can be inside the fort and this whole thing can be over with quickly and with very few casualties."

March 5, 1836

SAN ANTONIO — In a dramatic gesture today in the Alamo courtyard, 188 defenders pledged to fight to their death.

Lt. Col. William Barret Travis, commander of the garrison, paraded all available men except the guard. Several wounded or sick men were brought out on cots, including Col. Jim Bowie.

Travis made an emotional speech to the men in which he fought back tears on several occasions.

"I have deceived you with the promise of help, because I, myself, have been deceived," Travis told the garrison, which has undergone 12 days of siege and continual shelling.

Travis went on to say that every letter he had received from the Texas government had promised help as soon as it appeared that the Mexicans were advancing in force.

"Now, it is clear that help will never come, not in the time needed. Our fate is sealed. In a few days, perhaps a few hours, we must all be in eternity. That is our destiny and we cannot avoid it," Travis told the silent troops.

Travis went on to outline the possibilities. To surrender was unthinkable; to cut their way through the enemy lines was impossible.

"All that remains is to die in the fort and fight until the last moment, selling our lives as dearly as possible," Travis said.

But the commander went on to say that every man had a choice. Anyone who wanted to slip over the walls and try to make it through the enemy lines was free to do so.

Travis then unsheathed his sword and drew a long line in the dirt in front of the file of men. He asked those who would stay with him and fight to the death to step over.

Without a second's hesitation, Tapley Holland, the 24-year-old son of one of Stephen F. Austin's original colonists, jumped over, yelling, "Here's one life for Texas."

Others began to cross over. David Crockett led his Tennesseans to join Travis. Jim Bowie and several other bedridden men were carried over the line by their comrades.

Within a few minutes, only Louis Rose, a 50-year-old private and veteran of the French Army during the Napoleanic Wars, stood on the other side.

"You might as well join us, old fellow," Crockett said, adding that it would be suicide to try to slip through the lines.

Rose packed a bundle of clothes and provisions and slipped over the west wall, hoping to throw off the Mexicans by making his way through town. Most of the Mexican cavalry is deployed east of the Alamo, in order to cut off support or flight toward the Anglo colonies.

An uneasy calm prevailed inside the fort after Rose's departure. The constant shelling of the past 12 days ceased and men began dropping to the ground to sleep during the respite.

Texas military sources are uneasy. They feel the suspension of the shelling, which had succeeded in opening a breach in the north wall this morning, means that the final assault is near.

Texans expect to face 6,000 Mexicans in the assault and are relying heavily on the firepower of 21 cannons to overcome 30 to 1 odds.

March 6, 1836

SAN ANTONIO — The 13-day siege of the Alamo ended today in a furious, six-hour assault that left every defender dead and more than 1,500 Mexicans killed or wounded.

After 12 days of continual bombardment by 10 cannons and howitzers, Mexican guns fell silent about 10 p.m. last night.

About 4,000 Mexican assault troops, grouped roughly into five battalions of 800 men each, moved into position about 1 a.m. and lay on the ground for three hours awaiting orders to attack.

The Mexican plan called for battalions to attack each of four walls of the Alamo, which is an improvised fort with nine to 12 foot limestone walls that enclose nearly three acres.

No artillery bombardment preceded the attack. Mexican president and Supreme Commander Gen. Antonio Lopez de Santa Anna told aides he hoped to catch the exhausted Texans asleep with a quick rush of the walls.

The 188-man Texas garrison, under the command of Lt. Col. William Travis, apparently realized that the end of the artillery bombardment meant the all-out attack was at hand.

The Texans were prepared to meet the first assault, which began about 4 a.m.

The Mexicans quickly formed for the assault after a bugle and the start-up of the Deguello (meaning throat-cutting and no prisoners) tune from five massed bands. Each battalion was massed in thick columns, 40 men per rank and 20 lines deep. About one-third of the soldiers in the first two ranks were equipped with scaling ladders and picks.

Hundreds of cavalry troops encircled the fort in order to prevent desertion from the Mexican assault troops and to cut off any attempt by Texans to flee.

Only the first two ranks of assault troops could use their weapons and the columns ran straight into a firestorm of cannon and rifle fire.

Twenty-one cannons, loaded with chopped up horseshoes, nails and other home-made shrapnel, tore into the densely packed Mexican columns. Hundreds fell and the first charge broke off in confusion and agony, with no Mexicans getting within 10 yards of the walls.

A cheer went up from the defenders as Mexican junior officers worked to reform lines and prepare for a second charge.

The second charge was also beaten back with cannon discharges and accurate rifle fire. Texas sharpshooters on the walls had a half-dozen loaded rifles each. They seemed to hit almost every target they aimed for. Mexican officers said after the fight that most of their men killed outside the walls were shot through the head.

A number of Texans were shot off the walls during the second charge. Many Mexican troops had made it to the walls, where it was impossible for the Texans to fire at them without standing on the walls and exposing themselves to massed musket fire.

With the issue still in doubt, Santa Anna ordered the entire reserve, and every

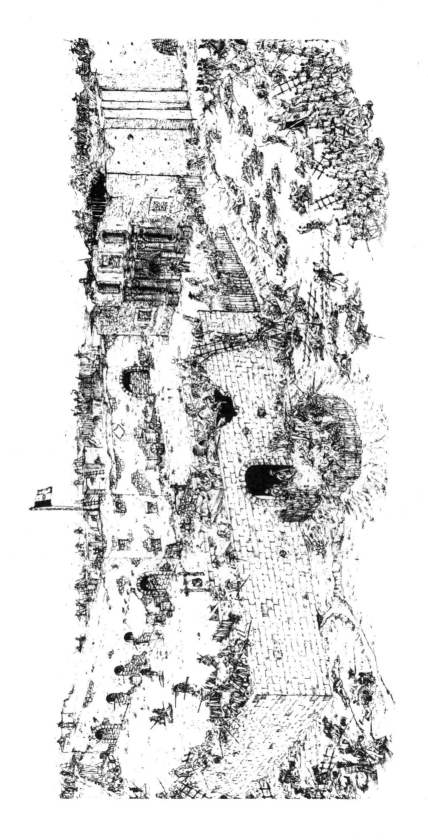

man who could carry a weapon in his 6,000-man army into the third assault. He directed almost every member of his personal staff to take part in the final attack.

The Alamo north wall was breached by cannon fire yesterday. It had been reinforced with earthworks and cannons. Mexican officers decided to concentrate on the weakened area for the third assault.

Shortly after 8 a.m., the Mexicans rushed the fort again from four directions, but the west and east assault forces moved toward the north wall and formed with the north assault group.

The Mexicans overwhelmed defenders on the northwest corner of the wall, dropped inside the compound and began shooting at north wall defenders from the rear.

The defenders began what was apparently a pre-arranged plan to fall back into a series of collapsing perimeters. The first was an earthwork and trench system about 10 yards behind the walls. With cannons and shotguns, the defenders raked the walls for the last time before the second perimeter was overrun.

The defenders formed a U-shaped hand-to-hand defense line in the plaza with the open end of the U facing the barricaded, sandbagged and loop-holed long barracks. They slowly gave ground, fighting bayonets with Bowie knives and clubbed rifles until the plaza was filled with Mexican troops.

Then the defenders dashed to the long barracks, exposing the massed Mexicans to the shrapnel fire from a cannon placed on top of the long barracks. The three gunners got off three rounds before they were shot down. One or two other cannons still in Texans' hands swung around to fire into the courtyard before the gunners were shot down.

The desperate fight began in the long barracks, which the garrison had carefully prepared as a last bastion with loaded shotguns, sandbags, loopholes and trenches inside the rooms.

The now-massed fire of the Texans brought down dozens of Mexicans with every volley, but were soon silenced by Mexicans manhandling captured cannons and firing point-blank into each room. Once the reinforced doors had been blasted open, each room was taken by bayonet with wounded and defiant Texans fighting until they were overwhelmed.

The last bastion to fall was the church. About 15 non-combatants, mostly Mexican-Texan women and children were housed in the chapel along with Susanna Dickinson and her 15-month-old daughter. Mrs. Dickinson was the wife of a Texas artillery captain. The chapel was the strongest building in the Alamo, with walls four feet thick and more than 22 feet high.

Stationed on top of the church was the main artillery post of three 12-pounders. Eleven artillerymen commanded by Capt. Almeron Dickinson and Capt. James Bonham manned the position. They were reinforced by several of the best sharpshooters in the command. A few Texans who had been defending the south wall and had been cut off from the long barracks were able to enter the chapel before the massive doors were barricaded.

Hundreds of Mexicans ripped the artillery post with musket fire and the captured Texan 18-pounder was used to blow down the door. A few men gathered to contest the entryway, but they were quickly overcome.

One Texas sharpshooter remained alive on the narrow ledge of the chapel's roof.

Santa Anna had waited for resistance to end before advancing. When it appeared that the garrison had ceased resistance, Santa Anna rode forward to within

500 yards of the fort when a single shot whizzed a few feet over his head. Santa Anna's aides hustled the commander back to the safety of San Fernando Cathedral in San Antonio. They said they were certain the shot came from the second story of the chapel.

Once the Mexicans had crushed organized resistance, they began to mutilate the bodies of the defenders. Several Mexican officers admitted they lost control of their troops.

For about 30 minutes after the last defender was killed, Mexican troops fired point blank into the bodies of the defenders and slashed and stabbed them with knives and bayonets.

Several wounded and stunned Texans who had lost the ability to resist were bayoneted.

In the hospital portion of the long barracks, Mexican troops killed 15 wounded Texans.

Mexican officers pointed out that Santa Anna had ordered no prisoners taken. Texas troops are considered pirates in the eyes of Mexican law and the penalty for piracy is death.

Other Mexican officers expressed shock at the brutality of the attack and the serious casualties that resulted from it.

Santa Anna issued a report to the government in Mexico City praising his army for the victory and claming 600 Texans were killed. He listed his own casualties at 70 dead and 300 missing.

Many Mexican officers admitted that casualties were much higher and that the Army of Operations had been dealt a severe blow.

The alcalde of San Antonio, Francisco Ruiz, was ordered by Santa Anna to dispose of the bodies of both Mexicans and Texans.

Ruiz reported that 1,544 Mexicans were killed in the assault and hundreds more wounded.

Ruiz ordered all carts in San Antonio to be used to carry Mexican dead and wounded. All available space in the city's graveyard was used in burying Mexican dead. Ruiz then ordered the Mexican dead to be thrown into the San Antonio River. The river was clogged with bodies.

Other Mexican accounts generally agree with Ruiz's carefully kept figures. The Toluca Battalion of 800 men was in the thick of the fighting and reported losing 670 soldiers. Other battalions suffered heavy casualties. Many officers and sergeants were killed or wounded by sharpshooters deliberately picking out targets wearing brass or stripes.

Ruiz was ordered by Santa Anna to burn all the bodies of the defenders. He had them stacked in layers with wood and kindling between each layer. The huge funeral pyre was located just outside the walls of the Alamo. It continued to burn with a sickening stench well into the night.

Santa Anna expressly forbade any religious service for the remains of the defenders.

Mrs. Dickinson and her daughter were escorted from the chapel to a personal audience with Santa Anna. Mrs. Dickinson was wounded in the calf by a stray shot as she walked across the plaza, but her wound was not considered serious. Santa Anna aides said he would probably question her and let her go to Gonzales.

"The whole idea is to spread terror among the Anglos, to get them to flee across the Sabine River and into the United States. Mrs. Dickinson is an eyewitness to what happens to rebels who resist the might of the Mexican Army," one aide explained.

Other aides worried about the almost total lack of medical facilities for the wounded.

A member of the general staff, Lt. Col. Jose Enrique de la Pena, said hours after the assault that hundreds of lives could have been saved if proper medical attention had been paid to the wounded.

March 7, 1836

SAN ANTONIO — Reports arrived today at Mexican military headquarters of the virtual annihilation of a Texas patrol near Agua Dulce.

Fourteen Texans, including the patrol's commander, Col. James Grant, were killed in a brief but fierce battle March 3 with forces under the command of Gen. Jose Urrea.

Urrea reported to supreme commander Gen. Antonio Lopez de Santa Anna that in addition to the 14 dead, six other Texans had been captured and taken to Matamoros. Another six Texans are reported to have escaped and fled in the direction of Goliad.

According to Mexican military sources, Grant had been operating with a force of about 40 men under Col. Frank Johnson.

The Grant-Johnson force had been roaming the desert below San Patricio seeking horses to help mount the planned invasion of Matamoros. The Grant patrol left Johnson's troops at San Patricio in order to secure more horses.

Urrea surprised Johnson Feb. 27 and killed most of the men in his command.

Urrea took about 300 lancers and set up an ambush near Agua Dulce, a creek about 25 miles southwest of San Patricio. Grant's patrol was trying to herd about 300 horses, many of them captured from Mexican-Texan ranches in the area, when Urrea's men attacked them from both sides of a draw.

At least six Mexicans were killed or wounded in an initial exchange of gunfire. Most of the Texas casualties resulted from horsemen being ridden down and stabbed by lancers.

Grant is reported to have escaped the initial assault, but refused to retreat and rode back into battle firing his pistols and drawing his sword. He is reported to have killed two Mexican cavalrymen before being overwhelmed and cut down.

Meanwhile, the smell of burnt flesh hung heavily over the town of San Antonio as the bodies of 188 Texan defenders of the Alamo were burned in a giant funeral pyre.

Hundreds of bodies of Mexican dead have been thrown into the San Antonio River after all available space in the city's cemetery had been used up in burials. The river is clogged with bodies.

Overwhelmed medical facilities in town are attempting to treat at least 400 seriously wounded Mexican troops.

More reinforcements continued to pour into San Antonio today. Most of the remaining elements of the First Infantry Brigade arrived today.

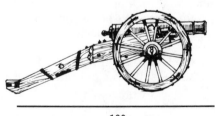

March 8, 1836

SISAL, Mexico — A Texas Navy warship tonight captured a Mexican schooner loaded with supplies destined for the army in the rebellious province.

The 60-ton Texas Navy schooner Liberty sent two boats with a boarding party to seize the Mexican commercial ship Pelicano.

The Mexican garrison commander had reinforced the crew of the Pelicano with 20 soldiers. A sharp battle broke out when the Texans attempted to seize the ship.

Seven Mexican soldiers were killed in the action. A number of others jumped overboard. Several of these men were attacked by sharks.

No Texans were reported killed or seriously wounded in the action.

The remainder of the Mexican crew retreated beneath the hatches and surrendered.

The Liberty sent a prize crew aboard the Pelicano and sailed for Galveston.

Texas naval sources said the cargo of the captured ship included 420 barrels of flour, 300 barrels of gunpowder and other supplies for the Mexican Army.

"I'm sure Gen. Sam Houston can put these supplies to good use," one naval officer remarked after inspecting the seized material.

March 9, 1836

BURNHAM'S CROSSING ON THE COLORADO — Gen. Sam Houston arrived today at this Colorado River crossing point and dispatched a series of orders concentrating Texas troops at Gonzales.

Houston, appointed five days ago as commander in chief of all Texas armed forces, ordered Col. James Fannin in Goliad to rendezvous with troops under Lt. Col. James Neill and Col. Edward Burleson in Gonzales.

Sources close to Houston said the commander is becoming increasingly concerned that Fannin, who is in charge of the largest and best-equipped Texas Army in the field, will be cut off before he evacuates the western frontier post at Goliad.

Houston has told aides he fears that the 188-man garrison defending the Alamo in San Antonio has already been overwhelmed. Before he left Washington-on-the-Brazos to take command of the army, he pledged to do all he could to save the besieged garrison.

Houston instructed Fannin to leave 120 men to help defend Victoria, 30 miles east of Goliad and to march to a rendezvous with other Texas forces using a route to be prescribed by Neill and Burleson.

Fannin is estimated to have about 500 men under his command.

Unconfirmed reports have reached Houston's mobile command headquarters that another 100 men under Col. James Grant and Col. Frank Johnson have been killed or captured in fighting at Agua Dulce and San Patricio west of Goliad.

"If Fannin doesn't start moving quick, he will be surrounded in hostile territory by (Gen. Jose) Urrea's cavalry. Urrea has the best cavalry units in the Mexican Army under his command. Fannin doesn't have a chance against them in open country," one source explained.

In other orders, Houston directed Neill to concentrate the troops available at Gonzales. Burleson was ordered to begin organizing a regiment out of the forces at Gonzales.

Fannin was ordered to blow up La Bahia and to march with only two light pieces of artillery and 50 extra muskets with forty rounds of ammunition apiece.

That would mean that Fannin would have to destroy seven pieces of artillery and at least 500 extra muskets. Most of the armament was captured from Mexican troops in battles in late 1835 in San Antonio and Goliad.

March 10, 1836

SAN ANTONIO — Gen. Antonio Lopez de Santa Anna today completed plans for the subjugation of the rest of Texas.

Four days ago, the Mexican Army overwhelmed and annihilated the 188-man Alamo garrison and captured most of the Texas Army artillery.

Santa Anna has told aides that the defeat of the Texans at the Alamo and the expected defeat of the Texas troops in Goliad should leave only mopping-up operations.

The commander in chief issued a series of orders that splits the 6,000 Army of Operations into four sections with orders to destroy all Anglo property and sweep all Anglos across the United States border at the Sabine River.

The first unit under General Juan Andrade was ordered to remain in San Antonio on the defensive and care for the hundreds of men wounded in the bloody assault on the Alamo.

The second unit under Col. Juan Morales was ordered to march from Bexar to Goliad to assist Gen. Jose Urrea's troops in eliminating the Texans still headquartered in La Bahia fortress.

Following the defeat of the Texans in Goliad, the combined force under Urrea's command was ordered to sweep east up the coast from Copano to Brazoria and to prevent Texans from forming large fighting groups.

The third unit, composed of 700 men under Gen. Antonio Gaona, was ordered to march from Bexar to Nacogdoches by way of Bastrop with the same instructions.

The fourth unit, under the command of Gen. Ramirez y Sesma was ordered to march from San Antonio to the Colorado River, cross to the east bank and march to the Anglo capital of San Felipe on the Brazos River. This unit will consist of about 1,500 men.

Meanwhile, reinforcements continue to pour into San Antonio and local Texas-Mexicans continue to join the Mexican Army. Mexican Army sources said several hundred local Texas-Mexicans have joined in the San Antonio area and hundreds more have joined Urrea's forces approaching Goliad.

The Cavalry Brigade under Andrade arrived in San Antonio today along with supply and headquarters companies.

Also arriving was the second in command of the Army of Operations, Gen. Vicente Filisola.

March 11, 1836

GONZALES — Gen. Sam Houston arrived at this Guadalupe River settlement today to take charge of the Texas Army amid reports that the Alamo has already fallen.

Houston took immediate action to squelch the rumors. He ordered the arrest of two Mexicans who had ridden into town March 9 spreading reports that the Alamo had been overrun.

Houston arrived with orders to prepare the Texas forces assembling at Gonzales to march to the relief of fewer than 200 men besieged at the Alamo by more than 6,000 Mexican troops.

Houston told aides he was surprised to find only 374 men ready for duty. He had hoped that more than 600 would have reached the assembly point.

Sources close to Houston said that he secretly believes that the Alamo may already have fallen, but that he feels he has to squelch the rumors to avoid a growing panic in the town and area.

Hundreds of civilians have jammed into Gonzales, a Guadalupe River community of about 500 people.

More than 30 militiamen from Gonzales reinforced the Alamo's garrison two weeks ago. No word has arrived from the commander of the garrison, Lt. Col. William B. Travis, since a message March 3.

In that message, Travis vowed that he and his men would fight to the death to defend their position.

Sources close to Houston said hundreds of Texas troops are expected to report to the army within the next several days. In addition, Col. James Fannin has been ordered to retreat from Goliad with 500 men and link up with the main army.

March 12, 1836

GONZALES — The commander in chief of the Texas Army today vowed never again to allow troops to be trapped in forts.

In a confidential dispatch to Capt. Philip Dimmit, Sam Houston wrote that he believes the rumors that say the Alamo has fallen and that the 188-man garrison has been killed.

Houston has officially denied the rumors and has jailed two Mexican-Texans who arrived March 9 and reported that the Alamo had fallen.

Gonzales is located on the west bank of the Guadalupe River about 75 miles from San Antonio.

He told aides at the time that he acted to prevent a panic in a town which has more than 40 of its residents in the Alamo garrison.

Houston ordered Dimmit to retreat from Victoria with his militia company, believed to be about 90 men strong.

In his communique, Houston wrote:

"I am induced to believe from all the facts communicated to us that the Alamo has fallen, and all our men are murdered.

"We must not depend on forts. The roads and ravines suit us best."

Aides to Houston pointed out that he sent Col. Jim Bowie to San Antonio in January with orders to remove the cannons and blow up the Alamo.

Houston has been a consistent opponent of fighting the Mexican Army on the far frontier and has urged a strategy of pulling back to the interior and using harassing tactics against the numerically superior Mexican Army.

March 13, 1836

GONZALES — This Guadalupe River community went into mourning today following the confirmed reports that the Alamo has fallen and its entire garrison has been killed.

More than thirty women living in Gonzales learned late last night they had become widows.

A total of 32 men from Gonzales had slipped into the besieged fortress March 1. At least a dozen members of the original 150-man garrison were from Gonzales, bringing the death toll of inhabitants of the town and surrounding area to nearly 45.

Gen. Sam Houston, who arrived yesterday to take command of Texas militia assembling at Gonzales, ordered all civilians and military personnel to immediately retreat to the east bank of the Colorado River.

Amid wails of anguish from grieving wives and mothers, troops began piling equipment and provisions into the few baggage carts available. Civilians, including many of the widows, were forced to fend for themselves. The fear of a sudden arrival by Mexican troops compelled many residents to flee with what they could carry. Some left dinners half-eaten as they bolted toward the Colorado.

News of the fall of the Alamo, which had held out for 13 days despite increasing pressure from more than 6,000 Mexican troops, was delivered by a party of scouts.

The scouts had come upon the only survivors of the Alamo battle, Mrs. Susanna Dickinson, her small child and two black slaves. Mrs. Dickinson is the 21-year-old widow of Lt. Almeron Dickinson, who was killed at the Alamo. The survivors had been released by Mexican commander Gen. Antonio Lopez de Santa Anna to report the Alamo defeat to Anglo colonists.

March 14, 1836

REFUGIO — A furious battle raged here all day and into the night between Texas and Mexican troops.

The Texans occupied the old mission at Refugio and beat off four charges by infantry and cavalry. Shortly after dark, the Texas troops slipped out of the mission in an attempt to make their way to either Goliad or Victoria.

Prior to the battle, colonists in the Refugio area sent a message to Col. James Fannin, the commander of the Texas Army at Goliad, requesting troops to guard them as they evacuated their homes.

Fannin dispatched the Kentucky Mustangs, a 29-man company, under the command of Capt. Amon King, who found the families in the mission surrounded by 150 Mexican-Texan ranchers and Indian allies. They fought their way through to the mission and dispatched a messenger to Fannin for reinforcements.

The Georgia Battalion, a 120-man unit under the command of Maj. William Ward, covered the 27 miles from Goliad to Refugio in seven hours.

After fighting their way inside the mission, the Georgia Battalion and the troops on hand beat off four separate charges from infantry and cavalry under the command of Gen. Jose Urrea, who had arrived at the battle site with 1,500 men.

About 15 Texans and more than 80 Mexicans and Indians were killed or wounded during the day-long action.

The colonists' families had been dispatched as soon as King's men had beaten back the initial threats from the rancheros and Indians. The remaining men split into two parties, with Ward taking his battalion in one direction and King moving out in another.

Both units were reported to be running short of ammunition.

March 15, 1836

MEXICO CITY — The ranking United States diplomat in Mexico today declined to discuss American troop movements near the Texas border.

Charge d'affaires Anthony Butler responded to a note yesterday by Mexican Foreign Minister Jose Maria Ortiz Monasterio that demanded to know why the U.S. Sixth Regiment was moving toward the frontier of the rebellious Mexican province of Texas.

Butler informed Monasterio that all the information in his possession concern-

ing the troop movements was handed to him by the Mexican foreign ministry.
"The diplomats of the United States are not consulted on troop movements within the borders of our nation," Butler responded.

Butler added that he could not conclude the communication "without remarking upon the novelty of the demand.

"It is well known that for more than 20 years the United States has maintained a chain of military posts throughout the northern and western frontier. Troops are regularly exchanged, augmented or diminished according to the needs of the moment.

"It is equally well known that Fort Jessup is the principal post of the United States on the western frontier and that the force stationed there is never less than a battalion and often more than that," Butler said.

The diplomat added that he could not understand why troop movements in the Fort Jessup area would be of such concern to the Mexican government. He also said he did not believe that troop movements within the borders of the United States was a legitimate concern of the Mexican government.

March 16, 1836

REFUGIO — Thirty Texas prisoners today were executed by Mexican troops in front of the mission they had defended.

The men were mostly members of the Kentucky Mustangs, a company under the command of Capt. Amon King. The company had fought at the Refugio Mission for two days, guarding colonists' families and combining with the Georgia Battalion to beat off several charges from vastly superior numbers of Mexican troops.

King's men slipped out of the mission and moved about three miles east of Refugio before being spotted by Indian allies of the Mexican Army.

King ordered his men into a clump of trees where they held off hundreds of attacking Mexican troops for 12 hours before running out of ammunition.

At least 20 Mexicans and five Texans were killed or wounded in the action.

King agreed to surrender his men if they would be treated as prisoners of war. Jose Urrea insisted that the men had surrendered at discretion, meaning without condition.

Supreme Commander Gen. Antonio Lopez de Santa Anna has ordered that all foreigners found bearing arms in Texas be executed.

Apparently in conformity with that order, an officer on Urrea's staff (the commander of the division had already left the scene) ordered the prisoners shot.

They were marched out into the square in front of the mission, tied two by two and shot at point-blank range. King was the last man to die.

March 17, 1836

WASHINGTON-ON-THE-BRAZOS — The General Convention today ratified a constitution for the newly declared Republic of Texas and elected an interim slate of officers to run the country until elections can be held.

David G. Burnet was selected by the convention to serve as president; Lorenzo de Zavala was named vice president.

Burnet, 48, is a native of New Jersey. He has been active in Texas affairs for the past six years.

Other officers include Samuel P. Carson, secretary of state; Bailey Hardeman, secretary of treasury; Thomas J. Rusk, secretary of war; David Thomas, attorney general; and Robert Potter, secretary of the navy.

The constitution is modeled after that of the United States. The main difference is the establishment of a unitary form of government rather than a federation of states.

All of the rights guaranteed to U.S. citizens are included in the constitution of Texas. Observers said the guarantees of individual freedom are somewhat stronger in the Texas Constitution than in its counterpart in the United States.

A sense of urgency hung over the proceedings as rumors of the advance of the Mexican Army filled townspeople and delegates with apprehensions.

March 18, 1836

GOLIAD — The Texas Army today began preparations for retreating from this key town on the western frontier.

Col. James W. Fannin, ordered the 300 men remaining at Fort Defiance (formerly La Bahia fortress) to pack ammunition and provisions for a retreat to Victoria, 24 miles southeast of here.

Fannin issued the orders after word arrived that two detachments he had sent to Refugio had apparently been cut off and surrounded by a large number of Mexican troops.

The 170 men in the commands of Maj. William Ward and Capt. Amon King were dispatched six days ago. Fannin had delayed a retreat until they returned, but was informed early today that King's 29 men had apparently been overwhelmed after a 24-hour fight with several hundred enemy troops. Scouts reported about 14 surviving Texas soldiers were executed at Refugio two days ago.

The fate of Ward's much larger force is unknown. He is in command of the 150-man Georgia Battalion. That force had been sent to relieve King, who had been surrounded in the Refugio mission.

Scouts reported that, after sharp fighting, Ward's force slipped away at night and is believed heading for Victoria.

Fannin ordered a speed-up in preparations to depart Fort Defiance after a scouting party returned to report that 1,500 troops were marching toward Goliad from San Antonio, where two weeks ago the main Mexican Army captured the Alamo and killed every member of the 188-man garrison.

Large billows of smoke could be seen rising from the courtyard of Fort Defiance. Hundreds of pounds of dried beef was being burned by Texans.

Sources explained that the army was short of trained oxen and carts and could carry only a limited amount of supply. The available transportation is being used to carry ammunition, nine pieces of artillery and 500 spare muskets.

Throughout the hectic day, Texas cavalry patrols clashed with the advance elements of Gen. Jose Urrea's main army, which is reported moving rapidly from Refugio to Goliad. Urrea is estimated to have more than 1,000 men under his command.

The cavalry encounters resulted in no serious casualties. Mexicans were entering the town of Goliad and then being chased out by Texas patrols. The patrols would then retreat when faced with superior numbers of Mexican dragoons outside of Goliad.

March 19, 1836

NEAR COLETO CREEK — A fierce battle was fought today on a prairie near here between Texas troops retreating from Goliad and a large force of Mexican infantry and cavalry.

About 300 Texas soldiers under the command of Col. James W. Fannin were overtaken as they attempted to retreat from Goliad to Victoria.

Mexican infantry and cavalry units under the command of Gen. Jose Urrea succeeded in surrounding the Texans on a prairie about 10 miles from Goliad.

Fighting broke out about 3 p.m. and continued until nightfall. The Texans utilized several pieces of artillery and Kentucky long rifles with deadly effect, killing or wounding more than 250 Mexicans.

The Texans were trapped about a mile from a wooded area that would have afforded them much more protection and access to water. Fannin ordered the command to halt the retreat when an ammunition wagon broke down. The troops were in the process of repairing the wagon when Mexican cavalry units placed themselves between the Texans and the woods.

The Texans drew up in a hollow square and beat off three charges by Mexican cavalry units supported by infantry and Indian auxiliaries.

Texas military sources reported nine men killed and nearly 60 wounded in the battle. Included in the wounded is Fannin, who sustained three wounds in his arm and leg.

The Texas military position is considered desperate. The Texans are surrounded in an open field, have no water and are faced by at least 1,500 enemy troops.

Texas military sources reported that Mexican artillery was being moved up under cover of darkness. The Texas artillery was practically silenced during the latter part of the battle today when every artilleryman was shot down. The field pieces cannot operate efficiently without water to cool them down.

The Texas troops spent the night digging trenches and piling their baggage into crude fortifications.

March 20, 1836

NEAR COLETO CREEK — More than 250 Texas soldiers today surrendered to a Mexican force which had them surrounded on a prairie two miles from Coleto Creek.

The command of Col. James W. Fannin laid down arms after lengthy negotiations with Mexican officers.

The Mexican force, consisting of artillery, crack cavalry units, and infantry fresh from the victory at the Alamo, was commanded by Gen. Jose Urrea. Fannin's was the fourth Texas unit to be eliminated by Urrea on his march from Matamoros. He previously met and defeated units at Agua Dulce, San Patricio and Refugio.

There was some confusion over the terms of capitulation. Texas military sources said Fannin surrendered only after being assured his men would be treated as prisoners of war and his wounded would receive medical attention.

European officers serving with the Mexican Army told several prisoners they would be in New Orleans in 10 days.

Most Texas troops thought the surrender included provisions for the prisoners to be paroled to New Orleans. The captured troops are mostly volunteers from the United States who have been in Texas only a few months.

However, Mexican military sources insisted that Urrea made no such guarantees to the Texas officers. They pointed out that Urrea was not authorized to deal with the rebels as a military force, but was ordered to consider them pirates.

An Oct. 30, 1835, decree from the Mexican Congress states:

"All foreigners who may land in any port of the republic or who enter it armed and for the purpose of attacking our territory will be treated and punished as pirates."

Under the Mexican code of justice, the punishment for piracy is death.

But most of the Texas prisoners seemed unaware of any controversy. They stacked arms and were marched backed to La Bahia fortress, which they had refurbished and renamed Fort Defiance.

The Texans were surrounded while attempting a 25-mile retreat from Goliad to Victoria. In a furious battle that lasted from 3 p.m. until nightfall, about 250 Mexicans and 60 Texans were killed or wounded.

The victory gave the Mexicans a large amount of captured war materials, including nine cannons, more than 1,000 muskets and rifles and 200 pistols.

March 21, 1836

ARMY HEADQUARTERS AT BEASON'S CROSSING — The commanding general of the Texas Army issued orders today to arrest all deserters from the army and all men of fighting age fleeing to the east.

Gen. Sam Houston said in an order to all committees of safety throughout the new republic to move quickly to arrest deserters who are adding to the panic in the country with unfounded rumors.

Houston has told aides his most serious mistake since taking command of the army in Gonzales 10 days ago was not to take action to keep about 20 men from deserting the army.

Houston said those 20 men fled east with horror stories about the Alamo and the intentions of the Mexican Army. Houston blames those rumors for the present panic of settlers who are fleeing for the safety of the U.S. border at the Sabine River.

Houston also ordered all able-bodied men to the front. He did make provision for one man to stay with each family, but all other men capable of bearing arms must report to the nearest militia company.

March 22, 1836

CAMP ON THE COLORADO — A Texas officer today called on the women of Texas to permit no able-bodied man to remain at home during the present crisis.

Capt. Mosely Baker issued a statement to the editors of the Texas Telegraph and Register newspaper in San Felipe, announcing that the Mexican Army is attempting to cross the Colorado River at Dewee's Crossing.

"The army consists of 800 men and will make a stand on the Colorado. Every man in Texas capable of bearing arms should join the army immediately," Baker commented.

Baker stressed that there is no reason for families to be moved. Roads leading to the Brazos and Trinity river crossings are jammed with refugees. Texas Army officers have said the confusion resulting from the panic of civilians is interferring with military activity.

"I call on the women of Texas to act well their parts and drive from their presence father, brothers and friends. Permit no man to stay at home, but bid them where duty and honor calls them," Baker commented.

March 23, 1836

VICTORIA — The survivors of the Georgia Battalion of the Texas Army today surrendered to Mexican troops under the command of Gen. Jose Urrea.

About 80 Texas survivors of the battle of Refugio eight days ago surrendered to about 1,000 Mexicans after an exchange of several shots.

The Texans, under the command of Maj. William Ward, were out of ammunition and had no means to offer resistance. They were captured while trying to hide near the banks of the Guadalupe River.

Ward said his men had followed the coastline after slipping out of the Refugio Mission the night of March 14. Ward said he expected to meet Col. James Fannin and the main Texas Army.

Ward told Mexican officers his men heard shooting on the afternoon of March 19, but could not reach the battlefield. Ward found out later about the battle of Coleto Creek in which Fannin and 250 men were captured.

The Georgia Battalion was formed in the fall of 1835. Many of the members of the unit come from prominent Georgia families. It landed at Copano Bay on Feb. 4 and was a key unit in Fannin's command. The battle at Refugio was the battalion's only fighting in Texas before its capture.

Mexican military sources said the Georgia Battalion prisoners would be taken to La Bahia, where all of the men taken prisoner with Fannin are held.

The sources were reluctant to talk about the fate of the men. It has been reported that Supreme Commander Gen. Antonio Lopez de Santa Anna has ordered all Texas prisoners shot.

March 24, 1836

SAN ANTONIO — Gen. Antonio Lopez de Santa Anna today ordered the execution of hundreds of Texas soldiers taken prisoner in fighting near Goliad.

Santa Anna dispatched the order to execute the prisoners to the southern front commander, Gen. Jose Urrea.

The supreme commander of the Mexican Army remarked to Urrea that he had been informed that Urrea had sent 234 prisoners to La Bahia fortress in Goliad.

Santa Anna went on to comment:

"The supreme government has ordered that all foreigners taken with arms in their hands, making war upon the nation, shall be treated as pirates. I have been surprised that the order has not been fully complied with.

"I therefore order that you should give immediate effect to the said ordinance in respect to all those foreigners who have yielded to the force of arms, having had the audacity to come and insult the republic, to devastate with fire and sword, shedding the precious blood of Mexican citizens.

"I trust that in reply to this you will inform me that public vengeance has been satisfied by the punishment of such detestable delinquents."

Mexican military sources said that the use of the term "pirates" meant that the prisoners must be executed.

Sources estimated that there were more than 400 prisoners at Goliad, including the 234 captured with Col. James Fannin at the recent battle of Coleto Creek.

March 25, 1836

HARRISBURG — Every inhabitant of Texas was placed under martial law today in a sweeping decree from Gov. David G. Burnet.

Burnet issued the decree from government headquarters in this temporary capital of the new Republic.

The decree places all the land claimed by the Republic and all of its citizens under martial, or military, law for a three-month period.

In the decree, Burnet wrote:

"The situation of Texas imperiously demands that her utmost possible energies be put in requisition and that every man take the field and repel the audacious invader, who has been too long permitted to desolate our country.

"Unity of action is necessary to our salvation, from an odious and detestable tyranny, or from an inglorious removal from the land we have so long laboured to cultivate and reclaim from barbarism."

In the decree, Burnet also issued the following orders:

● Texas will be divided into military districts.

● Each military district shall be governed by a committee of vigilance.

● The committees of vigilance are authorized to requisition private property for public use.

● All males 18 to 56 years old will be registered and subject to military duty.

● In the absence of males called to military duty, the committees of public safety will appoint one man for every five families. That man will be responsible for the care and safety of those five families.

March 26, 1836

BEASON'S CROSSING ON THE COLORADO RIVER — The Texas Army today began an agonizing retreat from this strategic position on the east bank of the Colorado River, despite pleas from officers and men to stand and fight.

Gen. Sam Houston, commanding a force of about 1,400 men, ordered the army to leave campfires burning and to begin pulling out of prepared positions at dusk.

Houston hoped to march about six miles tonight and then to cover about 30 miles tomorrow. That march would bring him to the former Anglo capital of San Felipe on the Brazos River.

For five days, Texas soldiers have been anticipating a battle with a force of 1,200 Mexican troops under Gen. Joaquin Ramirez y Sesma, who have camped across the rain-swollen Colorado.

Texas military sources explained that intelligence reports indicated that Sesma's taskforce was one of four which were threatening to encircle Houston's troops.

"We can't risk a battle here. There are 1,500 men 40 miles downriver under (Gen. Jose Urrea) and 750 above us at Bastrop, with 1,200 in front of us and another column moving up to reinforce them, we could whip Sesma and still be boxed in," one military source explained.

News of the defeat and capitulation of Col. James Fannin's force reached the Texas camp yesterday. Houston attempted to suppress the news and had the courier arrested. He was released today as news of Fannin's defeat at Coleto Creek swept through the ranks.

More than 200 men sought furloughs to take care of their families before the retreat started. Houston's effective fighting force is expected to drop from about 1,400 men to fewer than 1,200 before he reaches San Felipe.

The retreat is expected to set off a panic among civilians in the heavily populated area between the Colorado and Brazos rivers. Houston ordered his rear guard to make sure no settlers are left in the path of the advancing Mexican troops.

March 27, 1836

GOLIAD — Nearly 400 Texas prisoners today were executed by the Mexican Army on the orders of Supreme Commander Gen. Antonio Lopez de Santa Anna.

About 350 men were marched out of the fortress of La Bahia, where they had been imprisoned, and split into four groups. Each group was marched between two lines of Mexican troops armed with loaded muskets.

When the men had been marched about a mile from the fort, they were halted and one file of Mexican guards passed through to the other side. A quick order was given and the guards opened fire from point-blank range.

The men had been told that they were being taken to boats for passage to New Orleans.

There was no time for resistance. Several men yelled out, "Hurrah for Texas," before being shot down in one volley.

Following the volley, the Mexicans fell upon the wounded with bayonets and swords. Mexican cavalry had been deployed behind the execution sites to help cut off any survivors.

Despite the precautions taken by the execution parties, Mexican sources indicated that at least 30 Texans were able to escape the massacre by running to the San Antonio River or by playing dead until they had a chance to make a run for it.

Hundreds of Mexican cavalry and infantry troops tonight are combing the woods and river area for survivors.

After the execution parties returned, the 50 wounded Texans kept at La Bahia were dragged out of the hospital and into the courtyard, where they were shot and stabbed to death.

The commander of the Texas troops, Col. James W. Fannin, was executed separately. He was taken to a small courtyard outside the church, blindfolded and shot in the head.

About 30 Texas prisoners who possess skills needed by the Mexican Army were spared. These included doctors, mechanics, blacksmiths and engineers.

March 28, 1836

GOLIAD — This stunned town today attempted to proceed with business as usual one day after the slaughter of about 400 Texas Army prisoners.

The alcalde of Goliad was ordered to help provide labor for the soldiers who were gathering up the dead Texans.

A huge funeral pyre blazing about one-half mile from town gave off a sickening smell of burning flesh.

All Texas dead are being thrown on the pyre, with layers of wood between layers of bodies. The blaze can be seen for miles.

Mexican troops continued to search for survivors. Several were found hiding near the San Antonio River and were shot and thrown on the pyre.

After the massacre, it was revealed that a number of Mexican soldiers and civilians took dangerous chances hiding Texans from the execution squads.

Apparently, any Texan who was able to stay in town or in La Bahia is no longer subject to execution. The remaining Texans, numbering more than 30, have been put to work on various projects by the Mexican Army. The four doctors and several aides who were spared have been ordered to go under guard to San Antonio to help care for hundreds of Mexican soldiers wounded in the battle of the Alamo.

Mexican military sources revealed that Gen. Jose Urrea, the commander of the Mexican division whose troops captured the men, had pleaded with Santa Anna to spare their lives.

The Texans had surrendered under terms they thought called for their parole to New Orleans after an agreement never to bear arms against Mexico again.

"If those men had known they were going to be shot down like dogs, they would have fought to the end," Urrea told aides.

After a direct order from Santa Anna to execute the Texans, Urrea refused to take part and left for Victoria. The execution was carried out by officers on his staff.

March 29, 1836

SAN FELIPE — The Texas Army today began a retreat from this one-time capital of Anglo settlers, despite loud complaints from soldiers and the refusal of two officers to move their companies.

Gen. Sam Houston ordered the retreat of the approximately 1,200 men under his command from San Felipe Groce's Plantation, about 20 miles upstream on the Brazos River.

The order to retreat was greeted with loud complaints from many soldiers, who called out to the commander in chief to stand and fight.

Two company commanders, Capt. Mosely Baker and Capt. Wiley Martin refused to order their men to fall into line as the retreat began.

Residents of the town, like almost all Texas residents west of the Brazos, have fled east toward the United States border on the Sabine River.

The army has been in a rebellious mood since Houston ordered a retreat from the Colorado River on March 26. That move left the populated farming area between the Colorado and Brazos rivers undefended and set off a panic among civilians which is being called the "Runaway Scrape."

More than 200 men deserted the army during the 35-mile retreat from the Colorado to San Felipe, most of them to take care of their families now in the path of the Mexican Army.

The Mexicans have been waging a war of destruction, burning and wrecking as much as they can of Anglo houses, buildings, ferries, crops and mills.

The Mexican dictator, Gen. Antonio Lopez de Santa Anna, has declared the fighting a "war of racial extermination" although no reports have been verified that Anglo civilians have been killed by Mexican soldiers.

Sources close to Houston said he understood the frustration of his troops, but that he commanded the only effective fighting force left in Texas and he could not risk being caught between two or more of the four advancing Mexican columns.

Houston chose to ignore the actions of Baker and Martin. Instead, he ordered Baker to take his company and move to the east side of the Brazos to guard all possible crossing areas. Martin was ordered 20 miles downstream to the Fort Bend area to guard river crossings there.

Both officers complied, taking a total of more than 200 men with them.

Houston was left with fewer than 1,000 under his immediate command.

Houston told his officers that he wanted to move to Groce's because there was a good supply of corn there to feed the troops and the steamboat Yellow Stone was there and could be used to cross the Brazos, if needed.

Sources close to Houston pointed out that the move continued to keep the main part of the Texas Army between the Mexican forces and the U.S. border.

March 30, 1836

HARRISBURG — President David G. Burnet today issued a proclamation to the people of Texas urging them to aid in the war effort and threatening all citizens who refuse to fight or give assistance to the army with the loss of their citizenship and property.

In his proclamation, Burnet stated:

"Fellow citizens,

"You country demands your aid. The enemy is pressing upon us; families, the wives and children of your neighbors are driven from their firesides and compelled to take shelter in woods and forests, while the enemy gathers confidence and audacity from every disaster we encounter.

"Under these painful circumstances . . . too many citizens are lingering in idleness and lethargy at home or ingloriously flying before the enemy.

"Is it possible that the free citizens of Texas, the descendants of the heroes of 1776 can take panic at the approach of the paltry minions of a despot who threatens to desolate our beautiful country?

"Let every man able to shoulder a rifle or wield a sabre join the army. Soon, your families will be safe and our country cleaned from the pollution of the enemy.

"The blood of the martyrs of the freedom, the heroes of the Alamo, call aloud for vengeance. The minions of despotism, the panderers of priestly ambition, are waging a merciless war of extermination upon us. Humanity itself demands a severe retribution. We must teach these ruffian tyrants a lesson.

"All persons who shall leave the country for the purpose of evading a participation in the present struggle, shall refuse to participate in it or shall give aid or assistance to the enemy, shall forfeit all rights to citizenship and such lands as they may hold in the Republic."

Texas government sources said Burnet is desperate to stop the escalating movement of civilians towards the U.S. border. The civilian flight, termed the "Runaway Scrape" by many observers, is said to be adversely affecting the movements of the Texas Army and inhibiting men from joining Gen. Sam Houston's force.

March 31, 1836

GROCE'S PLANTATION — After marching for three days through an almost constant rain, a weary Texas Army today moved into quarters near this imposing plantation on the west bank of the Brazos River.

Gen. Sam Houston led about 900 men into camp at the plantation, using the buildings to house a portion of the force.

The army moved to Groce's from San Felipe, 20 miles downstream. Houston left more than 200 men to cover the major crossing points of the rain-swollen Brazos from San Felipe to Fort Bend, 60 miles downstream from Groce's.

Sources close to Houston said the commander wanted to place his troops in a location with a plentiful supply of food and free from the possibility of a surprise encircling maneuver.

Groce's is the largest plantation in Texas. Owned by Jared Groce, the plantation has more than 100 slaves and large quantities of food and other supplies. A complete blacksmith shop is at the plantation, as well as supplies of clothing, lead and powder.

Equally important, according to sources close to Houston is the steamboat Yellow Stone which is at Groce's. The sturdy boat has been requisitioned by the Texas government.

Houston has told his staff that the Yellow Stone gives him an edge in mobility, allowing him to move up or down the Brazos or to cross over to the east bank, depending on the military situation.

The main part of the Texas camp is located in a grove of trees on elevated ground on the west bank, safe from the rising waters of the Brazos. The location is practically an island and almost immune from frontal attack.

Houston has told aides he intends to use the time he bought by retreating to Groce's to whip his ragtag army of farmers and frontiersmen into an army capable of carrying out the complex maneuvers necessary in modern military engagements. He has ordered his officers to drill the men as much as possible.

April 1, 1836

WASHINGTON, D.C. — The top Mexican diplomat in the United States today flatly rejected any claims for payments of debts incurred by the rebel government of Texas.

Manuel E. de Gorotiza, the extraordinary envoy and minister plenipotentiary of the Mexican Republic to the United States, said he had delivered instructions from his government to the State Department.

The instructions included the following statement:

"In conformity with instruction given me by my government and with the view of refuting misrepresentations and removing every pretense for future complaints, the Mexican government declares it will never recognize, in any manner whatever, the debts which those persons that have been or may still be at the head of the revolted Texans may have contracted or might contract hereafter.

"The Mexican government also declares that it will neither recognize any alienation of national property or lands in Texas, made, promised or agreed to, by the said persons, or in their name, either under the title of sale, engagement, donation or compensation or in any other shape, as the Mexcian government considers them, from this moment, should there by any, as null and of no value."

Sources at the State Department said the statement indicated that the Mexicans think that they may experience legal problems because of the commitments made by the self-proclaimed Texas Republic.

The sources said the Mexicans are eager to avoid legal problems with Americans, many of whom have given money and other aid to the rebellious Texans and who have received guarantees of repayment in cash or public lands.

The Texas Republic is financing its revolution mainly through loans and contributions from Americans.

April 2, 1836

HARRISBURG — The president of the Republic of Texas today issued orders to crack down on slave traders.

In a proclamation to the people, President David G. Burnet reminded citizens that the newly approved Constitution of the Republic provides that the importation or admission of Africans or Negroes into Texas except from the United States "is forever prohibited and declared to be piracy."

"Whereas the African slave trade is equally revolting to the best feelings of our nature and to the benign principles of the Christian faith, is equally destructive to national morals and to individual humanity and whereas the most enlightened and powerful nations of Christendom are exerting both their moral influence and physical force to suppress that odious and abominable traffic, it is the duty of Texas to contribute in all practical and legitimate means to the prevention in its own jurisdiction of a trade so atrocious and disreputable," Burnet commented.

Burnet ordered all Texas Navy and Army officers to enforce the prohibitions against the slave trade and to arrest any person caught in the act of slave trading.

Burnet also authorized the seizing of any property or ship which is used by slave traders.

Sources close to the government said Texas officials are eager to gain favor with foreign governments, principally the United States and Great Britain, and believe a strong anti-slave-trade policy will help relations.

The sources pointed out that Burnet, a deeply religious man, is personally opposed to slavery and especially to the importation of African slaves.

April 3, 1836

MATAMOROS, Mexico — A Mexican warship was damaged and a U.S. merchant ship seized today in naval action just off this Gulf Coast port.

The Invincible, a 120-ton brig that is the fastest ship in the Texas Navy, engaged the Mexican Navy brig Bravo off the sandbar of the Rio Grande.

According to Mexican naval sources, the Bravo was enforcing the strict embargo placed on the port of Matamoros by military authorities. Only ships carrying supplies for the Mexican Army in Texas are allowed to leave port and they are escorted by Mexican warships.

The Bravo was awaiting the commerical ship Correo Segundo when the Invincible appeared.

In crossing the bar to determine what ship the Invincible was, the Bravo lost its rudder.

Instead of attacking the helpless ship, the commander of the Invincible, Capt. Jeremiah Brown, raised the U.S. flag and sent an officer on board the Bravo dressed as an American officer.

The Mexicans responded by dispatching one of their officers, Lt. Thomas Thompson. The Englishman recognized the ploy and was thrown into irons, as was the Texas officer sent onto the Bravo.

While this action was going on, the U.S. merchant ship Pocket was spotted heading for port.

The Invincible gave the Bravo a broadside, then captured the Pocket.

Texas naval sources said the Pocket contained a false manifest and secret orders to help transport reinforcements to the Mexican Army in Texas. In addition, hidden military supplies were reported discovered on board.

The Invincible put a prize crew on board the Pocket and immediately sailed for Matagorda to deliver the seized supplies to military authorities and to make contact with other elements of the far-ranging Texas Navy.

April 4, 1836

ARMY HEADQUARTERS ON THE BRAZOS RIVER — A Texas soldier sentenced to be executed today for dereliction of duty was spared by order of the commander in chief.

Pvt. Arthur Scales was under sentence of death for falling asleep at his guard post two nights ago.

The officers in Scales' company, including Capt. Amasa Turner, Lt. John Miller and Lt. W.W. Summers, petitioned Gen. Sam Houston for leniency in the case.

Scales, a new recruit, is 18 years old and has no military experience.

Houston had ordered Scales shot after discovering him asleep at his post. Houston has issued strict orders that one-third of the army must remain on guard duty at all times and anyone caught away from his post or unable to perform his duty is subject to harsh military punishment.

The petition delivered to Houston stated:

"Scales is very penitent and has made a promise of a faithful performance of his duty as a soldier in the future for his term of service if he could be pardoned for his present offence. He wishes his officers to intercede for him and your petitioners believe him sincere.

"Your petitioners would therefore most earnestly pray you to reprieve and pardon the condemned."

Houston scribbled a note on the petition, which read, "The commander in chief has ordered this petition to be granted."

Sources close to Houston said he had no intention of executing the youth, but that he is determined to whip the army into a fighting force and that requires a sense of discipline being instilled in farmers and frontiersmen.

April 5, 1836

NATCHITOCHES, La. — The commanding general of U.S. troops massed on the Texas border today issued orders to commanders at key posts to prevent both Texans and Mexicans from crossing the boundary in arms.

Gen. Edmund P. Gaines, who has made his headquarters at Fort Jessup near Natchitoches since being ordered to the border by President Andrew Jackson, issued the order to commanders of Fort Gibson and Fort Towson in Arkansas.

Troops along the Sabine River, which is the boundary line between the former Mexican province of Texas and the United States, have been on an increased alert for the past several weeks.

Gaines ordered all troops guarding the border to keep Indians living in the United States from joining disturbances in Texas.

Gaines has vowed to crush any Indian uprising in either the United States or Texas. He has warned Indian leaders that he will not allow a bloodletting in Texas which might spill over into the United States.

He has sent patrols into Texas and is continuing to mass regular and militia troops at a half-dozen forts along the border.

April 6, 1836

NACOGDOCHES — A committee of leading citizens of Nacogdoches today urged Texas' government to move to this East Texas center of Anglo power.

In a message to President David G. Burnet, the committee, headed by Jesse Benton, John T. Mason, Frost Thorn and Henry Raguet, urged Burnet to move government offices and personnel to Nacogdoches.

The Texas government has recently moved from Washington-on-the-Brazos to Harrisburg to escape the advancing Mexican Army. Work has been speeded up on fortifying Galveston Island in case the government is forced to fall back from Harrisburg.

In the message to Burnet, the committee said:

"The citizens of this section of the country, in conjunction with many in the military service, have strongly expressed the opinion that under the present emergency, the most eligible place for the government is Nacogdoches.

"No place in the country is more healthy at all seasons and none can afford better accommodations nor more ample supplies."

The message went on to point out that moving the government to Nacogdoches would ensure certain and speedy communication with the United States.

The message stated:

"It appears to us that in the progress of the war, you may be cut off from communication with the army. That they (the army) must rally in the woodlands is obvious and in so doing they approach us and become more remote from your present position."

The Nacogdoches businessmen promised the government a cordial reception and as much credit as possible if the government is removed to the far East Texas city.

April 7, 1836

HARRISBURG — Texas officials are fortifying the eastern part of Galveston Island and preparing it for a last-ditch defense in case the Mexican Army continues its drive across the newly-declared republic.

President David G. Burnet today issued instructions to Stephen Richardson to take responsibility for delivering the lumber the government will require to fortify the island.

In a dispatch to Richardson, Burnet wrote:

"The government accepts your proposition to supply lumber from the sawmill on Chocolate Bayou and you are hereby authorized to take general charge and control of that portion of the public service connected with the furnishing of supplies required at Galveston. While you are so employed, you will be exempt from other public duties."

Burnet also authorized Francis Moore to supply a large number of cattle for the population and garrison of Galveston.

Texas military sources said that using Galveston Island as a final fallback position for the government has been under consideration since the general retreat of the army began one month ago.

There are several pieces of large-caliber artillery on the island, and several companies of militia. In addition, the four combat ships of the Texas Navy control the approaches to the island.

Sources here said many refugees already have crossed over from the mainland to the island. It is estimated that more than 1,000 refugees are now on the island.

April 8, 1836

EAST BANK OF THE BRAZOS NEAR SAN FELIPE — The first Texan to fall in combat since the conclusion of the Goliad campaign was killed today in a holding action on the banks of the Brazos River.

Pvt. John Bricker was hit in the head by a small copper ball, probably fired from two cannons raking his company's position on the east bank of the Brazos.

Bricker was part of a 95-man company under Capt. Mosely Baker which is attempting to slow the advance of the Mexican Army. The company has dug trenches near the Brazos River ford close to San Felipe and has endured more than 48 hours of continual musket and artillery fire.

The company is opposite San Felipe and 1,500 Mexican troops under Gen. Juaquin Ramirez y Sesma.

San Felipe, once a thriving center of Anglo power and the capital of Stephen F. Austin's colony, is now a smoldering heap of ashes. It is unclear whether retreating Texans or Mexican advance parties set the fire, which completely gutted the town that had been home to 1,500.

Sharpshooters from Baker's company have accounted for several Mexican casualties and have thus far prevented Mexican troops from crossing the river.

Mexican troops have been attempting to build flatboats to cross the river, but the fire from Baker's entrenched riflemen has thwarted their efforts. Sesma has raked the Texans' positions with fire from two cannons and hundreds of muskets.

The main Texas army, under Gen. Sam Houston, retreated two days ago in the direction of Groce's Plantation, about 20 miles downriver from San Felipe.

Baker's unit was one of two dispatched to hold key fording areas. Capt. Wiley Martin's company was dispatched to hold the Fort Bend crossing.

April 9, 1836

HARRISBURG — A pair of cannons dubbed the "Twin Sisters" arrived here today, providing the Texas forces defending the Brazos River with their only artillery.

The two brass six-pounders were provided by the people of Cincinnati. Money was raised in the Ohio city early this year to purchase the artillery, which arrived recently by merchant ship.

In order to circumvent the United States neutrality laws, the artillery had been shipped as "hollow ware."

At one time the Texas Army possessed more than 30 pieces of artillery, but all the ordnance was lost when the Mexicans captured the Alamo and Col. Fannin's command at Coleto Creek.

There are several pieces of large-caliber artillery defending coastal positions, mostly on Galveston Island, but they are too large to be of use to a mobile army.

The two six-pounders will be forwarded to Houston's command at Groce's Plantation. Lt. Col. James Neill, a veteran officer who at one time commanded the San Antonio garrison, is expected to be put in charge of a new company being formed to handle the artillery.

April 10, 1836

LYNCHBURG — More than 5,000 refugees today crammed into an emergency camp near this small community by the San Jacinto River.

The refugees were part of what is being called "the Runaway Scrape," but the human toll of suffering belies the humorous tone of the name.

Almost the whole Anglo population of Texas between the Colorado and Trinity rivers is fleeing toward the Sabine River and United States territory or making its way to Galveston Island, where the Texas government plans to make its last stand.

The refugees are fleeing from a four-pronged Mexican invasion which has been called a "war of racial extermination" by the Mexican dictator, Gen. Antonio Lopez de Santa Anna.

The exodus of civilians was orderly until news reached the settlements of the murder of Col. James F. Fannin and 400 prisoners who had surrendered near Goliad on March 20. Since then a panic has set in and almost the whole population has headed for safer territory.

Huge logjams have developed at the crossings of the main rivers. All the rivers are up because of unusually heavy spring rains, which have also made the roads almost impassable.

Lynch's Ferry provides transportation across the San Jacinto River for all people coming from the lower coast toward the Nacogdoches area near the U.S. border.

The president of the Republic of Texas, David G. Burnet, rode to Lynchburg to examine the situation following numerous complaints about the operator of the ferry, Nathaniel Lynch.

Lynch had been accused of refusing passage to anyone who could not afford the toll. Burnet is reported to have told Lynch that if he refused passage to anyone because of lack of ability to pay, then Burnet would order the ferry seized by government agents and pressed into service to aid the refugees. Burnet added there would be no compensation for Lynch.

Immediately after their meeting, Lynch announced a new policy of allowing any resident of Texas who was without funds to use the ferry free of charge.

Refugees at the ferry said that large cotton planters from the Brazoria and Columbia area were holding up movement on the ferry by insisting that all their slaves be transported before late-arriving refugees.

"It takes about three days to get across," one refugee estimated.

April 11, 1836

ON BOARD THE YELLOW STONE — The captain of the steamboat Yellow Stone today reported his vessel ready to help the Texas Army.

The steamboat has played a major part in Sam Houston's planning, according to Texas military sources.

Houston, who is in command of more than 1,300 men in camp at Groce's Plantation on the west bank of the Brazos River, has been planning to use the boat to transport troops across the river or downstream. He has told aides the Yellow Stone gives him the mobility that the Mexicans lack.

In a report to Gen. Sam Houston, the commander of the Texas Army, Capt. James E. Ross stated:

"I think the cotton we have on board is necessary to protect the boat and engine — if we have to pass the enemy's cannon — I can transport 500 men with cotton

---

enough to protect the boat from any damage from the enemies' fire. If you wish the cotton landed please instruct me.

"I can cross all the baggage without moving the cotton. I have four cords of wood on board and everything is ready to 'go ahead.' "

April 12, 1836

FORT BEND — The president and commanding general of Mexico today personally leaped from ambush and wrestled a slave to seize control of a crucial Brazos River ferry boat.

Gen. Antonio Lopez de Santa Anna led 600 men down the west bank of the Brazos River to Thompson's Ferry near Fort Bend. Arriving with the advance guard, Santa Anna hid in the underbrush on the river bank while one of his officers tried to lure a black slave into bringing the ferry across the rain-swollen river.

Gen. Juan Almonte used his excellent command of the English language to call out to the slave, who was the only man operating the ferry. Almonte said he was a Texas soldier and needed to get to the east bank of the river.

The slave apparently believed Almonte and began hauling the ferry to the west bank.

When he was close to the shore, Santa Anna was the first man to leap aboard and wrestle the slave until help arrived, according to witnesses at the scene.

Once the ferry was in Mexican hands, troops began moving to the east bank of the river.

A company of Texas soldiers under Capt. Wiley Martin had been defending crossing points in the Fort Bend area. When word reached Martin that large numbers of Mexican troops were on the east bank of the river, he ordered a retreat toward the main Texas force under Gen. Sam Houston.

Houston has held a position at Groce's Plantation, on the west bank of the Brazos and about 30 miles upstream from Fort Bend.

Several hundred Texas riflemen had succeeded in holding every crossing of the Brazos from San Felipe to Fort Bend for two weeks while Houston concentrates his forces upriver at Groce's. The loss of Thompson's ferry is expected to have a profound effect on the military campaign, according to Mexican military sources.

Mexican sources said Santa Anna ordered several columns containing more than 2,000 men to concentrate at Fort Bend.

April 13, 1836

ARMY HEADQUARTERS ON THE BRAZOS RIVER — Amid growing reports of Indian unrest in far East Texas, the commander in chief of the Texas Army today dispatched a message to the leading chief of the Cherokees.

Gen. Sam Houston wrote to Chief Bowles. While not referring to the reports, Houston reminded Bowles of the treaty between Texans and Cherokees which was signed less than two months ago.

Houston was one of three commissioners who negotiated that treaty with the Cherokees, the most numerous of the tribes in East Texas. The Cherokee land includes territory from the Trinity River to the outskirts of Nacogdoches.

In recent days, reports have been received at army headquarters of Mexican agents attempting to lead a confederation of Indian tribes against Texas settlers.

One report stated that 1,700 Indians, including many Cherokees, were preparing to attack Texans in the Nacogdoches area. U.S. troop movements on the

Sabine River border have been stepped up. The U.S. Army has warned Texas Indians it will intervene if attacks are made on white settlers.

The Cherokees agreed in a Feb. 23 treaty to remain neutral in case of fighting between Mexicans and Texans.

Houston has a special relationship with the Cherokees. As a teen-ager in Tennessee, he lived with Cherokees for three years. From 1829 until 1832, he spent time with the Cherokees in Arkansas and the Indian territory north of Texas.

In his letter to Bowles, Houston commented:

"I am busy and will only say, how da do to you. You will get your land as it was promised in our treaty and you and all my red brothers may rest satisfied that I will always hold you by the hand and look at you as brothers and treat you as such.

"You must give my best compliments to my sister and tell her that I have not worn out the moccasins which she made me and I hope to see her and you and all my relations before they are worn out."

April 14, 1836

GROCE'S PLANTATION — The Texas Army today completed moving across the rain-swollen Brazos River and took up a march southeast, its destination shrouded in mystery.

The force of more than 1,000 men took two days to cross to the east bank of the river from Groce's Plantation.

The steamboat Yellow Stone and a yawl were pressed into service to aid in the troop movement.

Following the completion of the move to the east bank of the river, Gen. Sam Houston ordered the boat downriver to aid in the evacuation of refugees to Galveston Island.

Texas military sources said that large numbers of Mexican troops are known to be about 20 miles down the Brazos.

The Yellow Stone crew piled bales of cotton along the boat's sides to provide protection from expected small arms fire from Mexicans.

Texas military sources indicated that the move of the Yellow Stone was mainly a diversion to keep the Mexicans guessing as to what Houston's plans may be.

Hundreds of civilians on the east bank of the Brazos joined in the march, hoping that Houston would order the army to take the left fork of the Harrisburg Road. The route leads away from the known positions of the Mexicans and toward the safety of the United States border.

Houston's officers are urging him to take the right fork and move toward the enemy. They have told Houston that his continued refusal to offer battle may result in his ouster as commander of the army.

Houston refused to comment on his plans, saying that he keeps his own counsel and seeks no one's advice.

April 15, 1836

HARRISBURG — A Mexican patrol, led by the army's general, early today entered this deserted temporary capital of Texas.

In another of the daring moves which have concerned his staff, Gen. Antonio Lopez de Santa Anna led a patrol of 15 dragoons into Harrisburg about 2 a.m. He told his staff he was going to surprise the Texas government before the officials had a chance to flee.

The Mexican patrol barely missed Texas government officials, including President David G. Burnet and members of his cabinet.

Hearing that a Mexican column was closing on the town, the officials had fled a few hours before Santa Anna arrived.

Santa Anna dispatched a patrol of dragoons in an attempt to catch the government officials before they reached the San Jacinto River.

Mexican military sources said the only Texans in the abandoned town were three printers who were trying to finish production of the latest copy of the only newspaper in Texas, the Telegraph and Texas Register.

According to the sources, the printers told Mexican officers that the government had fled to New Washington, which is a small community on a peninsula where San Jacinto Bay joins Galveston Bay. It is located about 20 miles from Harrisburg.

The printers also revealed to their captors that the Texas Army under Gen. Sam Houston had left Groce's Plantation on the Brazos River and were about 50 miles northwest of Harrisburg. The printers said they believe Houston was going to San Jacinto, where he hoped to control the ferry over the San Jacinto River to the town of Lynchburg. They believed Houston intended to use the ferry to retreat to the Trinity River, about 20 miles from Harrisburg.

Santa Anna ordered the press of the newspaper thrown into Buffalo Bayou and the town of Harrisburg burned.

April 16, 1836

ON THE HARRISBURG ROAD — In a dramatic scene, Gen. Sam Houston today ordered the retreating Texas Army onto the Harrisburg Road, assuring a showdown battle with a nearby Mexican column.

The Texas soldiers had become increasingly frustrated at Houston's refusal to offer battle. There was open talk of deposing the former governor of Tennessee as commander in chief if he did not order the army to take the road to Harrisburg.

The Texas Army crossed the Brazos River on the steamboat Yellow Stone two days ago. It had made its way on muddy roads in the bayou country near the San Jacinto River until it reached a crossroads.

One fork of the road led to Nacogdoches; the other to Harrisburg. A Mexican column, reportedly under the personal command of Gen. Antonio Lopez de Santa Anna was known to be in the Harrisburg area.

The Texas column included hundreds of civilians, as well as a fighting force of more than a 1,000 men.

Houston ordered Capt. Wiley Martin's company of about 100 men to take the Nacogdoches Road and guard the civilians. He then ordered the main column, including two recently delivered pieces of artillery, to turn right.

A loud cheer went up among the ranks as the news swept the column that Houston was going to fight the Mexicans.

Sources closest to Houston said he was carrying out his long-standing strategy of waiting until the Mexican invasion force had split up to forage for supplies and then defeating them in detail.

"If the reports we have of Santa Anna being with the column in Harrisburg are right, that's just added gravy. We may be able to end this war with one battle," one jubilant Houston aide explained.

April 17, 1836

NEW WASHINGTON — The president of the Texas Republic today barely escaped from a patrol of Mexican dragoons, who were stopped from firing at the fleeing chief executive by their commanding officer's fear of shooting a woman.

Interim President David G. Burnet, his wife and several aides were fleeing from this Galveston Bay community in a rowboat when a Mexican cavalry patrol arrived on shore within a few yards of the craft.

The troops deployed to fire a volley at the boat. Burnet stood up in order to shield his wife, but Col. Juan Almonte hurriedly rode up and ordered his men to hold their fire.

Almonte told his men he would not allow them to fire into a boat which contained a lady.

"I am not in the business of waging war on women or children," Almonte explained.

The rowboat made its way a half-mile out into the bay, where it was picked up by the Texas Navy ship Flash. The ship transported the Burnet party to Galveston Island, which is being fortified as a last redoubt for the Texas government.

Burnet's party was one of several which recently fled the temporary capital of Harrisburg because of Mexican Army advances. Burnet led his group to Lynchburg, where they crossed the San Jacinto River on a ferry and made their way to New Washington.

Burnet was arranging transportation to the Flash when a messenger galloped up on a horse saying the Mexicans were only minutes behind him.

The party hurried their departure, but were only a few yards offshore when the Mexicans arrived.

Following the failure to capture the president, Almonte ordered New Washington burned. Late tonight, smoldering ashes were all that remained of the once prosperous community.

April 18, 1836

ON BOARD THE YELLOW STONE — The steamboat Yellow Stone today ran a gamut of musket-firing soldiers as it steamed past Mexican positions on the Brazos River.

The 130-ton steamboat had been used by the Texas Army to transport men and equipment from Groce's Plantation on the west bank to the east bank of the Brazos.

Following its use by the army, the Yellow Stone was released from service. It picked up refugees along the banks of the Brazos until it arrived near Fort Bend between San Felipe and Columbia.

Mexican troops are occupying the west bank of the river there and, upon hearing the sounds of the steamboat, hundreds of troops rushed to the shore. Some stared in amazement. Few Mexican troops have ever seen a steamboat, according to Yellow Stone officers.

The boat's crew had lined the Yellow Stone with cotton bales to protect it from enemy fire. The bales protected the crew and critical parts of the boat.

Seeing the rifle fire having no effect on the boat, several cavalrymen attempted to lasso the Yellow Stone by throwing lariats around its smokestack. The lasso attempts failed.

April 19, 1836

HARRISBURG — A grim and determined Texas Army today marched away from the ashes of this former temporary capital of the new republic, determined to do battle with the Mexican Army.

The army, under the command of Gen. Sam Houston, passed through the ruins of the town that had been looted and burned by Mexican troops several days ago.

Texas military sources said Houston had positive information that the Mexican president and supreme commander, Gen. Antonio Lopez de Santa Anna, was in charge of a division of troops which had moved to New Washington.

"They are crossing the Buffalo Bayou, into San Jacinto area; that's really a swamp. There's only one or two ways in or out. This is what we have been waiting for," one staff officer explained.

Houston has been maneuvering cautiously, despite the urgings of many officers to stand and fight the numerically superior Mexican force.

With about 1,200 troops under his command, Houston has been waiting for the 6,000-man Mexican Army to split into smaller units to forage for supplies, according to his aides.

Yesterday, scouts Deaf Smith and Henry Karnes captured a Mexican courier with messages from Mexico City to Santa Anna.

The scouts had to call on officers to save the courier from being lynched when he was brought into camp. The messages were carried in a leather saddlebag stamped with the name "William Barret Travis."

The courier said he obtained the saddle bag when he passed through San Antonio after the battle of the Alamo.

Travis was the commander of the 188-man garrison that was wiped out in the Alamo battle March 6.

"That messenger was invaluable. He made it certain that Santa Anna, himself, is with a force about as large as our own. And if we play this right, we can get him pinned against the bayou," one Houston aide explained.

April 20, 1836

SAN JACINTO — The first clash of the main Texas and Mexican armies occurred today on a plain between two wooded bayous.

At least 12 Mexicans and two Texans were killed or wounded in a series of cavalry skirmishes and long-range rifle fire.

Texas military sources confirmed that a force of about 900 elite cavalry and infantry soldiers under the direct command of the president and supreme commander of Mexico, Gen. Antonio Lopez de Santa Anna, was deployed with its back to a swamp. The Mexicans are eight miles from New Washington, the latest Texas town they have put to the torch.

Opposing them is the Texas Army. Texan sources said that about 250 men, mostly men suffering from an outbreak of measles, have been left at a camp outside Harrisburg, giving Sam Houston command of nearly 1,000 effective fighting men.

"A general engagement is expected tomorrow," one Texas military source said tonight, adding that it was believed about 500 Mexican reinforcements would arrive at Santa Anna's position sometime in the morning.

When asked why he didn't press the attack before Santa Anna was reinforced, Houston replied, "Why take two bites out of the same cherry?"

Houston aides said the general was concerned over reinforcements arriving in his rear at a critical time in the battle and it was more important to get the whole Mexican fighting force in front of him. Sources said the only other source of Mexican reinforcement would be about 2,500 troops massed on the Brazos River about two days' march away.

In today's action, a Texas cavalry patrol under Col. Sidney Sherman intercepted a Mexican cavalry patrol and killed four of the enemy after a running fight that stopped just short of New Washington. No Texans were lost in the fight.

The main Mexican force advanced eight miles from New Washington until making contact with a skirmish line of Texas infantry in the plain between two bayous.

The Texans had moved their two six-pounder artillery pieces (the Twin Sisters) out on the plain, and the Mexicans responded by moving their single piece of artillery, a 12-pounder, into range.

An artillery duel commenced in which one Texan was gravely wounded. Long-range rifle fire killed or wounded several Mexican soldiers.

The Mexicans withdrew their infantry, and the 60-man Texas cavalry unit, under Sherman, made a bold charge in an attempt to capture the Mexican artillery.

About 50 Mexican cavalry troopers intervened and a short battle ensued in which several Texans and Mexicans were unhorsed.

A private in the cavalry, Mirabeau Lamar, rescued two dismounted Texans, including Secretary of War Thomas J. Rusk. He shot one Mexican cavalryman dead and crossed swords with another, wounding and dismounting him.

Lamar's individual action took place in full view of both armies. Following his delivery of Rusk to safety, Lamar rode back into musket range and made a sweeping bow and sword salute to the Mexican lines.

Following the action, Houston appointed Lamar a colonel and commander of the cavalry.

Houston was reportedly upset over Sherman's attempt to bring on a general engagement. Houston has told his aides that tomorrow will be the decisive day.

April 21, 1836

SAN JACINTO — In one of the most lopsided victories in military history, a Texas Army of 900 men today destroyed a Mexican force nearly twice as large in a battle that lasted 18 minutes.

About 700 Mexicans were killed, and another 730 captured. Scores more drowned in Buffalo Bayou trying to flee a slaughter that was carried on by revenge-seeking Texans hours after the Mexicans had ceased organized resistance. Texas casualties were two dead and 17 wounded, including several who are not expected to live.

Under the command of Gen. Sam Houston, the Texas Army swept across a mile of open prairie and poured into the camp of the president of Mexico and supreme commander, Gen. Antonio Lopez de Santa Anna.

The 1,500 men under Santa Anna had been alerted early in the day for a general engagement, but stood down in the early afternoon and posted only a normal guard.

The Texans moved silently toward the camp and were obscured by tall prairie grass. The left flank was guarded by Texas cavalry shielded by clumps of trees. The right flank also moved into the cover of bunches of trees before hitting the left flank of the Mexican camp. The center of the Texas line contained the First Regiment under Col. Edward Burleson and a 30-man artillery contingent who pulled two six-pounders across the prairie.

When the Texas Army was within 200 yards, the alarm was sounded in the Mexican camp. The Texas line started moving at a steady trot while a three-man band struck up a popular and somewhat naughty song, "Will You Come to the Bower I Have Shaded for You?"

The Mexicans had fortified their camp with a breastwork of boxes, cowhide bags filled with dirt and other camp material.

The Texas cannons were about 10 yards in front of the infantry line. They got off several rounds which blew wide gaps in the breastworks.

Mexican troops began firing at the Texans from 200 yards, with little effect. The Texans held their fire until they were less than 40 yards from the breastworks, then ripped off a volley which knocked back defending troops. They then broke into a wild charge, yelling, "Remember the Alamo" and "Remember Goliad."

In a few seconds they were across the breastworks and falling on Mexicans with Bowie knives and clubbed rifles. Others reloaded and discharged rifles and shotguns at point-blank range.

Several Mexican officers tried to rally troops. Gen. Manuel Castrillon was seen on top of an ammunition box, trying to rally troops to make a stand by the Mexican cannon. He was surrounded by dozens of Texans and ordered to surrender. He reportedly shouted out that he was a Spanish officer and had been in 20 battles and had never surrendered. A dozen Texans shot and killed the general.

The Texans had poured into the camp and overwhelmed resistance in just 18 minutes. About 20 Texans were killed or wounded, including Houston, who had two horses shot out from under him and suffered a painful bullet wound in his ankle. Houston was at the head of the infantry attack column and once was nearly killed by a discharge from a Texas cannon. He was pulled out of the line of fire by an aide.

Once the breastworks had been stormed, the Texans encountered little resistance. Hundreds of Mexicans were shot down or killed, clubbed or stabbed as they attempted to surrender. At one point in the swamps, the bodies of Mexicans who had jumped in the water and were shot from the bank made a bridge over which a few survivors fled.

About 400 Mexican survivors grouped around several ranking Mexican officers, who were able to get their surrender accepted. After about an hour, the killing ceased and other Mexican survivors were allowed to surrender.

Santa Anna, in his tent when the battle started, is reported to have fled on a horse as soon as he saw the Texans overwhelm the defenders at the breastworks.

Just before the general engagement, scout Deaf Smith rode down the lines yelling, "Vince's Bridge is burned; fight for your lives."

It was later revealed that Houston ordered the bridge, the only way in or out of the trap Santa Anna had maneuvered his men into, to be destroyed.

Houston told aides he wanted to make sure no Mexican reinforcements arrived during the battle and he wanted to bag the entire Mexican force in front of him.

The Mexican force had been reinforced early this morning by about 600 men under the command of Gen. Martin Perfecto de Cos, who had marched his men for 12 hours to reach Santa Anna.

It was only after this force had entered the trap that Vince's Bridge was burned.

Hundreds of Texans continued to patrol the battlefield and adjacent territory as night fell, rounding up more prisoners.

The one prisoner Houston wanted remains at large. Santa Anna is believed hiding in the swamps surrounding the battlefield.

"We'll get him," one Houston aide predicted. We have a hundred mounted men in a steadily closing perimeter. Santa Anna will be our prisoner shortly. I only hope we can keep our men from killing him on sight."

Sources close to Houston said the general is counting on capturing Santa Anna to end the war. The sources pointed out that there are still 2,500 Mexican troops within 40 miles of San Jacinto, but that they are now in an exposed position.

"All they need is an order from Santa Anna to justify pulling out of Texas and we are sure Santa Anna will be glad to issue that order to save his own life," a Houston aide explained.

April 22, 1836

SAN JACINTO — Gen. Antonio Lopez de Santa Anna was captured by a Texas patrol today, 24 hours after an army under his command was destroyed in a short and decisive battle on the plains and in the swamps of San Jacinto.

The president and supreme commander of Mexico was marched into camp by a patrol of six Texas cavalrymen. One of the cavalrymen had a captured Mexican lance and kept Santa Anna at a trot by sharp jabs from the weapon.

The Texans were not sure of his identity until many of the 730 Mexican prisoners kept in a makeshift corral saw him and yelled out, "El Presidente, El Presidente."

Santa Anna acknowledged his identity and asked to see the Texas commander, Gen. Sam Houston.

Houston was lying propped up against a tree being treated by a doctor for a bullet wound to the Achilles tendon.

Santa Anna was dressed in slave's clothes he had found in an abandoned house. He still had on red velvet Moroccan slippers and an expensive, gold-laced white shirt under the dingy coat and pants.

As soon as the news of Santa Anna's capture spread through the camp, hundreds of Texans surrounded the Mexican president, many demanding that he be shot or hanged.

The Texans pointed out that he was responsible for the murders of 400 men at Goliad and had ordered no prisoners be taken at the Alamo.

Santa Anna appeared to be in an extremely nervous state. He asked that he be allowed his medication.

Houston ordered the box of opium that had been seized along with Santa Anna's other personal possessions brought to the Mexican president. He also allowed him to change into one of his captured uniforms.

After taking a large dose of opium, Santa Anna seemed to recover his courage and began a discussion with Houston.

He defended his actions in ordering the red flag of no quarter flown before the Alamo as "military necessity." He chose not to address the question of the execution of the 400 Texas prisoners at Goliad.

"The man may consider himself born to no common destiny who has conquered the Napoleon of the West," Santa Anna told Houston.

The Texas commander waved the flattery aside and told Santa Anna that the war was over and that he must issue instructions to the 4,500 Mexican troops remaining in Texas to withdraw to beyond the Rio Grande — the border of the Texas Republic.

Santa Anna agreed and said that it was obvious that Texas could no longer be held by Mexico.

Following the conversation, Texas scouts left for Gen. Vincente Filisola's camp at Fort Bend with orders from Santa Anna to immediately begin a retreat.

"These orders will be obeyed; we are sure of it," one Houston aide said, adding, "This is the end of it. The fighting is over. We are now an independent nation in control of our own destiny."

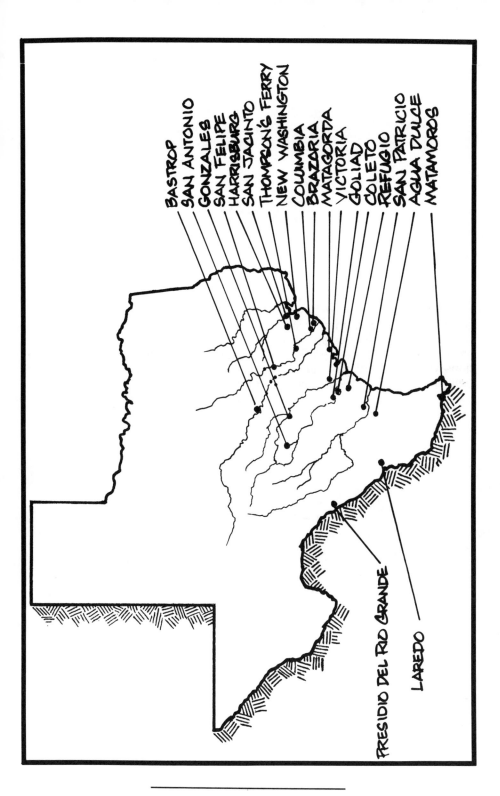

BASTROP
SAN ANTONIO
GONZALES
SAN FELIPE
HARRISBURG
SAN JACINTO
THOMPSON'S FERRY
NEW WASHINGTON
COLUMBIA
BRAZORIA
MATAGORDA
VICTORIA
GOLIAD
COLETO
REFUGIO
SAN PATRICIO
AGUA DULCE
MATAMOROS

PRESIDIO DEL RIO GRANDE
LAREDO

PROFILES

This section contains 17 profiles of people who were involved in the Texas Revolution. The stories are based on numerous materials, including biographies, general histories and primary sources.

In reviewing the lives and motivations of these people, certain conclusions have been made that are not accepted by all historians. Whenever such conclusions were necessary, all available material was taken into consideration and was supplemented by doses of logic and common sense.

Stephen F. Austin

Of Stephen F. Austin, his biographer, Eugene Barker, wrote, "Without him there is no reason to believe that Texas would differ today from the Mexican states south of the Rio Grande."

Without this one man, the state of Texas might well be just another Nuevo Leon, Coahuila or Tamaulipas. It boggles the mind, but it might have been — except for Austin.

For Texas to fall within the orbit of the Anglo world, there had to be an Anglo colony planted in the heart of the province, one that would grow, prosper and draw other Anglos like a magnet. Then, and only then, would it be possible to talk about a separate existence for an Anglo-dominated Texas.

But how to begin? Spanish and later Mexican authorities were suspicious to the point of paranoia about the intentions of the United States and the western push of American frontiersmen.

It would take a man of strong intellect, unquestioned loyalty and honor. A man who was bilingual and who could understand the Hispanic habit of dealing with the indirect. A man capable of great dreams that would excite others. Such men were almost non-existent on the rough-and-tumble western frontier, but Austin was one of them.

Stephen Fuller Austin was born in Virginia on Nov. 3, 1793. He grew up in Potosi, Missouri when that state was still a Spanish province. He distinguished himself at Transylvania University in Lexington, Ky.

His young manhood was crowded with responsibility. He was an officer in a militia battalion, represented his district six years in the territorial legislature of Missouri (after that area was brought into the United States through the Louisiana Purchase) and was part of several of his father's business ventures.

His father, Moses Austin, was also a dreamer of great dreams. He, however, was also something of a loser. He made two fortunes and lost both in land investments and banking. He was one of thousands of small businessmen wiped out by the banking failure and the resulting Panic of 1819.

Moses had one trump card left, arrangements he had carefully made over the years with Spanish authorities that would allow him to start an Anglo colony in Texas.

At first, his son thought it just another of his father's dreams. But it was passionately believed by Moses. Father communicated that passion to son. In 1820, on his dying bed, Moses exacted a promise from Stephen to pursue the dream of an Anglo Texas. Stephen upheld that promise to his dying day.

Land was what fueled that dream, cheap land that could be had on the credit of a man's good name. In the United States, the financial collapse of 1819 had ruined many a good man. The cheapest land available in the United States sold for $1.25 an acre — cash. The banking collapse had resulted in the drying up of almost all land credit.

In Texas, if Austin could pull the right strings in Mexico City, rich farm land would be available in his colony for 12.5 cents an acre — with easy credit terms.

Now, there was a chance for folks to start anew. If a man had faith in himself and his family, was willing to face hardships and dangers, was willing to die if necessary to build an inheritance for his sons, then Texas would be the place to go. A man could buy 10 times as much land, improve it and reasonably expect that, with a continuing arrival of immigrants, he could sell his holdings at an enormous profit.

First, Austin had to steer himself and his colony through the mazes of Hispanic politics. Mexico had revolted from Spain since Moses Austin had received permission for his colony. There were new officials to deal with, new political realities to face. Austin managed it all.

He won the right to settle 300 families (the Old Three Hundred) on lands between the Brazos and Colorado rivers. Later, his grant was extended and he was responsible for bringing 1,500 families to Texas.

He was responsible for much more than that. Until 1827, he was virtually the czar of Texas, making laws, running the militia, signing treaties with Indians and deciding who could settle in his colony and who could not.

Despite his business background and his emphasis on the economy of Texas, Austin was never good at making money. He was good at trusting men who used their connections with him to make fortunes — men such as the land agent Baron de Bastrop and Austin's personal secretary, Samuel Williams. Both these acquaintances made a tidy profit off every land transaction while Austin was not even meeting his own expenses.

Austin was hurt by being too close to these and other men whose actions came under criticism. His name was unfairly tarnished time and time again, while his deeds were given short shrift.

But there were a half-dozen times when he held the fate of Texas in his hands, when a wrong move would have meant the extinction of Anglos in the province. At these critical times, he never failed to do the right, smart and prudent thing.

First, there was the premature cry of revolution from Hayden Edwards in Nacogdoches in 1827. Austin sent his own militia to help put down that minor tempest.

Then there were Mexican Army officers whose job it was to report on the growing Anglo influence in Texas. Time and time again, Austin headed off action that would have been ruinous to the young colony.

When the Mexicans in 1830 passed a law prohibiting further Anglo immigration, Austin managed to get his and another colony exempted. Still, it was getting serious.

Texas colonization could be said to have been one giant land speculation and Austin knew better than anyone else that stemming immigration meant that land prices would not rise and the reason for immigration — to make a secure fortune — would be in jeopardy.

Austin began to work behind the scenes, but Texas was filling up with action-oriented men. Against Austin's advice, they called a convention in 1833 to draw up a list of complaints. They selected Austin to carry their demands to Mexico City.

He arrived in the Mexican capital in July 1833. He got nowhere, became frustrated and made one of the few diplomatic mistakes in his life. He wrote a letter to town officials in San Antonio in haste and in anger. He suggested San Antonians take the lead in forming a state government. They were aghast at this piece of treason from the hands of the respected Estaban Austin (as he always signed his name to correspondence with Mexicans). They turned the letter over to authorities and Austin was arrested.

For 18 months, he languished in a dungeon and under house arrest. His health, never strong, was rapidly being destroyed. Still, he wrote to his friends and begged them not to make a fuss about his imprisonment. "Be quiet, and for God's sake hold no more conventions," he said.

Lawyers won his release in July 1835.

By now, all Texas was consumed with the excitement of the coming showdown with Mexico. Rumors spread about an occupation army on the march. Poised on the precipice, Texans sought out Austin for leadership. Once again, his word would set the course. If he said fight, Texans would be the hammer. If he said wait, Texans would be the anvil.

On Sept. 8, 1835, in the most important speech of his life, almost every leader in Texas gathered in Brazoria to hear what Austin would advise.

"War is our only recourse," this man of peace told the crowd. He urged unity and the calling of a general convention. In just a few minutes of oration, Austin had united Texans at a time when disunity would have meant disaster.

After the fighting started, there was such disorganization and disputed claims to leadership that Austin was called upon to command the army. In this as in all things he tried, he did a good job. Although not a brilliant strategist, he was able to keep the army supplied and in some state of organization until other, better qualified officers, could take over.

He continued to serve Texas, although the major players were now relative newcomers like Sam Houston, William Travis and James Fannin.

Finally, while working hard as the first secretary of state in the new Republic of Texas in 1836, he took ill for the last time.

Austin died at 43 in a two-room shack, on a rough pallet laid on a dirt floor. He didn't own the shack or the pallet.

Two weeks before he died, we wrote a letter that seemed to sum up his life. A group of volunteers from Kentucky had complained that he had treated them inhospitably. He was mortified and hurt as he wrote:

"For I do not merit it. I have no house, not a roof in all Texas that I can call my own. The only one I had was burned at San Felipe during the late invasion of the enemy.

"I make my home where the business of the country calls me. I have no farm, no cotton plantation, no income, no money, no comforts. I have spent the prime of my life and worn out my constitution in trying to colonize this country.

"All my wealth is prospective and contingent upon the events of the future. My health and strength and time have gone to the service of Texas, and I am therefore not ashamed of my present poverty."

Austin died a poor man, but he had dreamed a great dream and lived to see it come true, a wealth that few men will know.

Ben Milam

The success of the Texas Revolution was a near thing.

There were a dozen times when the whole thing could have fallen apart, when the fragile alliances of bickering clans could have brought down what passed for a government in San Felipe, when the centralists in Mexico could have made one gesture to the Peace Party majority of Anglo settlers, when the "army" could have decided it was time to go home and plant crops.

The closest it came to coming apart was Dec. 4, 1835, on a cold and rainy day in the Texas Army camp about a mile from San Antonio.

The unifying dream of driving the Mexican Army out of Texas had brought together the fighting men of Texas. The only Mexican troops left in Texas were in San Antonio.

A decision had been reached that day to end the siege of San Antonio, to retire the soldiers to winter quarters and to give up the dream until the spring.

That spring would never have come.

A huge army (by 1836 standards) was being readied by Mexico's dictator, Antonio Lopez de Santa Anna, to march on Texans in the spring of 1836. With a base of operations in San Antonio secure and the Anglo militia dispersed, it wouldn't have been a fight.

It would have been a massacre, the kind of blood-letting Santa Anna had in mind when he called the campaign a "war of racial extermination."

But on Dec. 4, 1835, none of that was known or even suspected. What was known was that the season of northers was upon the ill-clad and ill-fed 500-man Texas Army besieging a Mexican force more than twice as large in San Antonio. The officers wanted to pull out, but the men had come to fight.

At that one climactic moment, Ben Milam became larger than life.

A 47-year-old adventurer, schemer, land investor, military officer and man's man, Milam knew his macho psychology.

He didn't explain to the troops who were all gathered on the parade ground that he had recently escaped from a Mexican jail and knew what was heading their way. He didn't appeal to any vain glory.

He just looked them in the eye and asked:

"Who will go into Bexar with old Ben Milam?"

All at once, the fight had been put back into the Texas Army. In less than a week, 400 Texans captured San Antonio from 1,600 Mexicans.

One man, Milam, held the army together at a time when dispersal would have meant disaster. He seemed to be a man arriving at his one place in time where he could be everything he had failed to be in his checkered career.

Milam was, bascially, a loser. Not a little loser, but a schemer of great schemes which never seemed to come through. He once owned 21 gold and silver mines and not one earned a profit.

Benjamin Rush Milam was born in 1788 in Frankfort, Ky. He spent the first 24 years of his life in the Kentucky wilderness, sharpening his skills and instinct for survival.

Milam decided to seek his fortune as a trader. He and some partners bought a load of flour and took it down the Mississippi River to New Orleans.

With typical Milam luck, the bottom of the flour market had just dropped out. Milam suggested they sell the flour in Venezuela where flour prices were rumored to be high. Their ship ran into a hurricane and wiped out Milam's first venture into the world of the wheeler-dealers.

Milam's skill as a scout and rifleman caught the attention of filibusters and adventurers who were hanging around the fringes of the dying Spanish empire in America.

Milam became best friends with the most legendary filibuster, James Long, and took part in attempts by Long and Mexican revolutionary figures to oust the Spanish from Texas.

The Spanish drove Long from Texas, but Milam was able to hang on. He became a trader with the Comanche Indians and lived with them for months at a time.

He became involved in Mexican politics. He and Long were together in Mexico City in 1821, a hectic year during which the country went from the rule of a Spanish viceroy, to the rule of a president, to the rule of a self-proclaimed emperor, to the rule of a self-proclaimed president.

Long was shot from ambush and Milam was thrown into prison when he tried to find the killer. It wasn't his first time in a Mexican jail and it wouldn't be his last.

Like most of the major players in the Texas Revolution drama, Milam was a Mason. He was able to use his Masonic connections to escape from many prisons.

Somehow bouncing back into favor with the government, Milam was given a commission in the Mexican Army and was allowed to make several land deals in Texas.

He became an agent for Gen. Arthur G. Wavell's land grant on the Red River. Milam threw himself into the project and helped bring hundreds of families to the area along the Red River. Then confusion: The land in the grant was ruled to be in Arkansas and U.S. authorities told Milam his deals weren't worth a hill of pinto beans to them.

He was given an empressario (land developer) grant himself, but couldn't get enough families to make any money off the deal.

But, he kept trying and occasionally would put together something that would work, like his idea to navigate the Red River with a small steamer.

By all accounts, Milam was actually just trying to take care of business in March 1835 when he traveled to the Texas-Coahuila provincial capital of Monclova.

He was trying to straighten out some of those land claim titles that were dogging him. When the governor of the province asked to ride along with him, he agreed. Only later did he find out the governor was on the run from Santa Anna's brother-in-law, Gen. Martin Perfecto de Cos, and about 2,000 soldiers. There had been a falling out between officials in Saltillo and Monclova over where the state capital should be. The side Milam was backing lost.

Milam and the governor were arrested and moved from prison to prison before winding up in a Monterrey dungeon.

Milam was as good at getting out of tight spots as getting into them, and, within a few months, he had escaped.

He traveled over 270 miles of deserts and valleys and, incredibly, arrived in a clump of trees, near the San Antonio River, one mile from Goliad, at the precise time that a Texas raiding party passed that spot on its way to hit the big Mexican fortress of La Bahia.

At first, there was some confusion and drawn weapons. Then the Texans realized the stranger was Ben Milam, a man whose exploits and bad luck had already made him something of a legend.

Milam joined the group and used his language skills to convince the 25-man garrison that they must surrender or the Texans, whom he could barely restrain, would surely kill them. They surrendered without a fight and were sent scurrying off to Mexico.

Milam moved on to the army which was surrounding San Antonio. Stephen F. Austin used him as the 1836 version of the CIA, sending him on long scouting patrols, often into Mexico, to see what information he could find or trouble he could stir up.

He returned from one of these patrols Dec. 4 and realized that he must act to save Texas. And he must do it right.

He did.

Milam and Frank Johnson led two columns into San Antonio Dec. 5. Instead of fighting it out in the open where cannons could rake them, the way Mexican officers thought they should have fought, the Texans improvised a new way of taking a town.

They would seize a house and then knock a hole in the wall to the next house, never exposing themselves to fire from sharpsooters on rooftops or cannons at street barricades.

Under Milam's directions, his column moved steadily toward the flanks of the Military Square fortifications. Using superior rifle skills, the Texans were picking off the Mexicans at the barricades like squirrels flushed from trees.

For three days, Milam was everything he always knew he could be. He was everywhere, directing his men, providing a flow of ammunition, keeping contact with the second column.

In the afternoon of the third day, with victory in sight, Milam decided to confer with Johnson. He stepped into the courtyard of the Juan Martin Veramendi house in downtown San Antonio. He died instantly from a bullet to the head.

He was mourned, buried with full Masonic rites and his soldiers added his name to their battle cry as they steadily drove the Mexicans back toward the Alamo and eventual defeat.

Milam is usually listed as a "near great" by Texas historians. That is a euphemism for a loser. But Milam's experiences teach us one thing: Even a loser can have a day when he shines as a star in heaven.

Juan Seguin

Two days after the siege of the Alamo began on Feb. 23, 1836, the commander of the Texas garrison asked Capt. Juan Seguin to slip through the lines and deliver an urgent plea for reinforcements to Texans 70 miles away.

Later, there were times when Seguin wished that he had never been asked to deliver that message; times when he longed for the security and respect of martyrdom; times when we wished he had stayed in the Alamo and died with his friends and comrades.

Seguin was a victim of the ugliest after-effects of the Texas Revolution — the racial hatred fed by war and its horrors.

When Gen. Antonio Lopez de Santa Anna ordered the execution of more than 400 Anglo prisoners of war at Goliad, he also killed the hopes of many prominent Texas-Mexicans that they would find equality and acceptance in the newly-forged republic.

The racial undertones of the revolution, never far from the surface, bubbled over and, in one of the tragic ironies of the times, burned the life of one of the most courageous and capable fighters for Texas freedom.

Seguin was born into a prominent and wealthy Texas-Mexican family. His father was the alcalde of San Antonio in 1821, when Stephen F. Austin first appeared on the scene. Alcalde Seguin's help and encouragement were key reasons Austin was able to bring Anglo families to Texas to settle in his colony.

A liberal like his father, Juan Seguin entered politics. In 1834, at age 28, he was appointed political chief of the San Antonio district. Like his father, he sided with Anglo colonists in demanding more self government.

He also became an early opponent of the dictatorial policies of Mexico's president, Antonio Lopez de Santa Anna.

When fighting broke out in October 1835 between the Mexican Army and the colonists, Seguin saw the issue as freedom vs. tyranny, not as Mexican vs. Anglo. He threw his fate and fortune on the side of freedom, recruited 65 fellow Texas-Mexicans and rode off to join the Texas Army.

So distinguished was Seguin's conduct in the December 1835 victory over the Mexican garrison in San Antonio, he won a commission as a captain of cavalry in the regular Texas Army.

Seguin was one of 25 men who rode into the Alamo with Col. William Travis three weeks before the siege began.

Travis put great faith in Seguin, whom he recognized as a man of honor and courage, like himself. When, acting as commander of the Alamo, he needed a crucial message carried to the Texas commander in Gonzales, Travis turned to Seguin.

At first, Seguin refused. He believed it was important for as many Texas-Mexicans to share whatever fate had in store for the Alamo garrison. Even then, Seguin was looking to the future and to the fate of his people — the Mexicans who would live with Anglos in a post war Texas.

But Travis' needs were of the present and they were critical. Seguin knew the terrain, could slip through enemy lines and was the best horseman in the fort. He was the one to go.

He was on his way back to the Alamo on March 6, when the fortress finally fell. Travis, six Mexican-Texans and 180 other comrades lay dead, their place in history secure. Their problems were over, but Seguin's were only just beginning.

But there was a war to be fought, martyrs to be avenged and no one was a better fighter or avenger than Seguin. The Texas commander in chief, Sam Houston, gave Seguin the most difficult assignments he had.

Seguin brought up the rear, behind the long, agonizing retreat of the Texas Army from Gonzales to San Jacinto. His job was to make sure all civilians were out of the way of the Mexican Army.

At San Jacinto, he and his company of Texas-Mexicans were singled out for praise by Houston for their efficiency and gallantry.

After the war, Seguin continued in the regular army. He was detailed to ride into San Antonio, find the remains of garrison's soldiers, whose bodies had been burned by order of Santa Anna, and give them a Christian burial.

He spoke the oration at the small ceremony which followed.

A life of service to Texas seemed in store of Seguin. He was elected to the Senate of the republic in 1838 and was twice elected mayor of San Antonio.

Then it all fell apart. San Antonio was swarming with newcomers who were envious of the wealth and position of prominent Mexican-Texans.

They started dark intrigues, spread vile gossip, nurtured the spark of racial hatred lit by the atrocities carried out by the Mexican Army.

Rumors spread that Seguin was plotting with Santa Anna for the Mexicans to retake Texas. Eventually, Seguin had to flee for his life to Mexico.

In order to live in Mexico, Santa Anna ordered Seguin to take part in a probing attack on Texas. In 1842, Seguin found himself fighting in San Antonio with a Mexican force, against Texans.

He had earned the right to live in Mexico, but his heart and his soul never left Texas.

He petitioned Texas authorities to let him return home.

Now, his old comrades in arms rallied to his side. Men he had fought — men like Houston and Mirabeau Lamar — asked that his service during and after the revolution be remembered.

There were only a few men who had stood shoulder to shoulder with Travis at the Alamo and were still alive to tell about it. Seguin was one of those men. Only now did Texas realize what it had allowed to happen to one of its native sons and heroes.

Seguin was allowed to return home. His family was able to reclaim some of its lost lands and fortune. His sons and the sons of their sons would now be allowed to live in honor on the land of their father.

Seguin had always known there was a danger of racial intolerance running amok in Texas. He had fought to prevent it. It was one fight Seguin had lost.

When Seguin died in 1889, he was once again at home, his honor restored and his place in Texas assured.

James B. Bonham

The good die young.

It is the life and death of a man such as James Butler Bonham that gives the old saying poignancy.

Bonham's name is of French origin and was Anglicized when the family moved to England in the 13th century from the original Bonhomme — meaning the good man.

But what is good in a man in certain times is trouble at other times.

Certainly the administrators of South Carolina College did not use the term "good" to describe Bonham in 1827, when he instigated a series of student strikes which led to the dismissal of the entire senior class.

Bonham was good in the sense that he never compromised his admittedly exaggerated sense of honor and duty. His biographers have never found an instance during the dashing South Carolinian's 29 years when he stood for anything but freedom and honor — even if it meant a fight.

Bonham was an excellent example of privileged Southern manhood. Inspired by romantic characters of Sir Walter Scott, taught to trust in his own physical and mental abilities and filled with pride of state, race and clan, such men could be formidable in war and trouble-makers in peace.

Bonham came from a line of rebels and nonconformists, people restless in spirit and independent in thought. After migrating to England, they became part of the yeomanry — the lower middle class peasant stock.

They became Puritans and Nonconformists and moved to the New World in the early 1600s when religious repression intensified in England.

Landing in Massachusetts, the Bonham clan continued to move westward, stopping for a years of planting here, half a generation there, but always pushing west.

James Butler Bonham was born in the Saluda River valley of South Carolina in 1807. His father was a successful farmer and even though he died when James was 8, his estate assured his son an education at the best schools in South Carolina.

His brother Milledge later reflected that James was always talking about Scott's characters. He was, said Milledge, imbued with patriotic impulses, with chivalrous dreams of knights in shining armor and of honor. Above all, honor.

Butler was a handsome man, well over six feet tall, well-proportioned, with dark hair and dark eyes, a magnetic personality, and the ability to draw men and women to his causes.

After an outstanding three years at college (later the University of South Carolina), Bonham agreed to be the point man for complaints from the students: The food was bad; the dormitories and classrooms were seldom heated; the students were forced to attend classes in miserable weather.

The rhetoric escalated. Bonham called a student strike. Every member of the senior class stood by him and all 46 were expelled.

No matter. Honor was not soiled. A year later he passed his law exams and started a promising career in Pendelton.

It was during this period that the first stirrings of armed struggle between the states emerged. In South Carolina, a series of federal tariffs were ordered ignored by the governor, who claimed state's right to nullify any laws it could not live with.

Tempers flared and rhetoric heated up. Gov. James Hamilton used Bonham as one of his key lieutenants. Bonham commanded the militia artillery battery in Charleston, exactly where the first shot would be fired if the dispute led to bloodshed.

It did not and Bonham went back to the day-to-day business of making a living in a town overrun with lawyers.

In 1833, he was defending a woman in a civil action when the opposing lawyer said something which Bonham took to be an insult to his client. He demanded an apology, got none and caned the offending lawyer while they were in court. When the judge objected, he threatened to cane him, too.

That got Bonham three months in jail, but the women of Pendelton considered him their knight in shining armor. His jail cell filled with flowers every day. The women brought him Southern-fried chicken and hot apple pie. Jailers were sternly rebuked if his every wish was not granted. It might have been the best time of his life.

He had won the hearts of every woman in Pendelton, except the one he loved. With his Scottish sense of romance and undying love, that meant only one thing: he must leave town, push on to the west.

But now real war clouds were building to the south. His boyhood friend, William B. Travis, wrote him and urged him to join him in Texas.

"These are stirring times in Texas," Travis wrote, adding that there would probably have to be some fighting before too long.

Bonham started for Texas. En route he stopped at Mobile, Ala., and gave several stirring speeches in favor of aid to Texas. He helped recruit the Mobile Grays and then joined the 40-man fighting force destined to succumb almost to the man in the Goliad massacre.

Bonham reached Texas in December 1835. He joined Travis in San Felipe. Travis was the regular army recruiting officer in town. Bonham was given a commission and helped his friend in the difficult task of convincing resident Texans that they must join the army.

Gen. Sam Houston, the regular army commander, took an interest in the aristocratic South Carolinian who came so highly recommended. Bonham began a series of tasks for Houston, usually as a messenger. His horsemanship and ability to find his way in the wild deserts of western Texas did not go unnoticed.

He was attached to a 30-man force Col. Jim Bowie brought to San Antonio on Jan. 17, 1836. His training as an artillery specialist was put to work getting into working order the 24 captured artillery pieces at the Alamo.

He took part in the preliminary planning for the defense of San Antonio, during which it was agreed that the 156 men then in the garrison would have to give up the town and try to hold out in the Alamo fortress until help arrived.

But supplies were low, ammunition limited and the Alamo too big to be adequately manned by so few. As disturbing reports of Mexican military movement across the Rio Grande reached Travis, he sent out urgent appeals for reinforcements.

He sent Bonham to Goliad on Feb 18. There Col. James Fannin had 500 troops, well-equipped and eager for a fight, mostly new arrivals from the United States.

Bonham pleaded with Fannin, but Goliad's commander insisted that his orders were to stand fast. He was convinced the Mexican Army would make its main thrust toward his position.

Bonham rode back to San Antonio in a dark mood. But, the sound of cannons shook off lethargy. He raced to the top of a hill and saw hundreds of Mexican cavalrymen moving into town. He raced into the shelter of the Alamo walls, along with the startled garrison, who had been partying the night before in San Antonio and were nearly caught by surprise.

For four days, Mexican troops poured into San Antonio and surrounded the Alamo. Their trenches inched forward daily; their cannons tore at the limestone walls. The garrison waited for reinforcements.

Travis had sent several messengers urging immediate help. None had been heard from.

Even though he needed Bonham's help with the big guns, Travis turned to his boyhood friend and asked him to try once more to get through to Goliad and get Fannin moving.

Bonham, one of the best horsemen and swordsmen in the fort, made it through the lines. But Fannin insisted that he could not move. This time his reason was that Mexican troops were moving on Goliad. He needed every man to defend his position. Besides, he told Bonham, there was no chance for the garrison at the Alamo. Better to stay here and rejoin his old comrades in the Mobile Grays. An attempt to return to the Alamo was certain death, Fannin said.

Bonham got up, looked Fannin in the eye, spat on the ground and said that the surrounded men should be told that no help would be coming.

"I will report the result of my mission to Travis or die in the attempt."

Bonham got through the lines again. He returned to the Alamo on March 3.

By then the garrison had grown to 188 with the arrival of 32 men from Gonzales.

Using Bonham's information, and maybe some inspiration from Sir Walter Scott, Travis drew his immortal line in the dirt with his sword. It was a gesture straight from Scott, but it worked well in cementing the garrison. Every man but one crossed over, signifying his determination to hold the post or die trying.

They died trying. Every one of them.

Bonham commanded the main artillery position of three 12-pounders on top of the church.

He had 11 artillerymen and several sharpshooters under his command. Together, they took a fearful toll of Mexicans during the final assault March 6.

The church was the last bastion to fall and Bonham was one of the last defenders to die. His body, riddled by musket balls, was found lying over a cannon.

Jim Bowie

Jim Bowie broke into a spasmodic cough and doubled over. He pushed himself up on his deathbed, back propped against the wall.

He had two loaded pistols and one of the knives that bore his name. Jim Bowie would not die alone.

The 40-year-old adventurer, knife-fighter, land speculator, slave trader, and larger-than-life figure on the frontier had made his peace with God hours before. He could hear Mexican soldiers inside the chapel, the last holdout of the Alamo garrison. There was fighting and killing among men cursing in two languages. Soon, they would be knocking down the door to his small room.

It looked like the boys might be holding them off. Stopped them twice, but on the third charge, there were just too many Mexican soldiers. If only he hadn't gotten so sick after the siege started.

So it all came down to this moment. A life of high adventure, bold romance, great dreams all about to end. Bowie would have laughed if he had known that 150 years later historians would still be arguing over how he met his death.

Born in Logan County, Ky., in 1796, James Bowie was the eighth of 10 children, four of whom died young. A respiratory illness resided in the genes of the family. It was respiratory failure that put him on the bed in the Alamo chapel and would have killed him if the Mexicans hadn't.

But Bowie was never weak. He grew up fast and strong in the Kentucky and Louisiana back country.

At age 18, he had cleared his first tract of land and started the first of the many legends which would follow and magnify his accomplishments throughout his life — he had ridden his first alligator.

It was really simple, he later explained to friends. The trick was to get on the gator's back and at the same time grasp his upper jaw firmly while gouging thumbs into his eyes.

Bowie and his older brothers Rezin and John operated on the fringes of the filibuster set which were hanging around no-man's land between Louisiana and Spanish Texas. They sold horses to the top filibuster, James Long, and through him struck up a business relationship with Jean Lafitte, who had recently moved his base of operations to Galveston Island.

The Bowies bought African slaves at $1 a pound (average $140 per slave) and smuggled them through no-man's land into Louisiana where they were sold on the average for $1,000 — a tidy profit.

The Bowie brothers carried five knives each during these trips. They could throw five knives on target at 20 yards for every pistol shot they could get off. Such accuracy tended to reduce the chances of escape attempts by the slaves.

Then came a series of shady land deals in Arkansas and the emergence of Jim Bowie's fame as a knife-fighter.

In 1827, the bad blood which had been building over land disputes boiled over in the Sandbar Duel near Natchez, Miss.

Jim Bowie was acting as one of four seconds for one duelist. Bowie's archenemy, Norris Wright, was a second for the other duelist.

Both duelists fired their pistols harmlessly into the air to satisfy honor, then shook hands — their disagreement was not worth looking down the barrel of a loaded pistol.

Then a melee broke loose as Wright and a friend rushed Bowie with cane swords. Bowie's reflexes were faster. He whipped out his knife and slashed one opponent in the abdomen clear to the backbone, then stabbed Wright, "twisting the knife to cut his heart strings," he later explained.

The knife Bowie used in the fight was something new to the frontier. Designed by Rezin Bowie from Jim's specifications, it became the overnight sensation of the Southwest. It was called, naturally, the Bowie knife.

It looked like a short butcher knife and was forged from the best steel. It differed from other knives by having more curve on the blade near the point, by having a heavier handle, often made of horn, and by having handle, blade and guards all so well balanced that the knife could be thrown a maximum distance with deadly effect.

Until the arrival of the repeating pistol, it was the preferred sidearm of the frontier, being quicker and more reliable than a single-shot pistol.

The knife was both economical and practical for skinning, cutting up meat, eating, hammering and, of course, fighting.

Fighting was what Bowie did best. If he ever lost a fight, no one remembered it.

Bowie traveled to Texas in 1828, but didn't stop at the Anglo settlements along the Brazos River. He went on to San Antonio.

He was attracted to the richest and most beautiful young woman in town, Ursula Maria de Veramendi. Two years later, he married the 18-year-old beauty and took her to New Orleans on a honeymoon.

Using San Antonio as a base, Bowie plunged into Texas intrigues, land specula-tion and fortune seeking.

He usually found fighting along the way, like the time he and a dozen associates held up in a clump of trees and shot it out with 150 Caddo Indians near the present-day town of Menard. He had been searching for the fabled wealth of the lost San Saba silver mines when the Indians found him and his party.

But the need to take such wild chances was growing less each day. His various ventures in the United States were earning a tidy profit and he had married into the richest Mexican-Texan family. He was an accepted member of top society in Mexico and Texas. Only his craving for adventure pushed him on, but now Ur-sula and his two children were holding him back. He was learning what it meant to be a family man.

A terrible cholera epidemic swept Texas in the summer of 1833. Several thou-sand Anglo colonists and Mexican-Texans died of the disease. Fearing for the health of his beloved family, he sent them to the drier climate of Monclova in nor-thern Mexico.

He was on an extended trip east in September 1833 when his wife, their two in-fants, his father-in-law and mother-in-law died. The cholera plague had struck Monclova.

Popular history has it that Bowie lost control after he learned of his family's fate and began drinking himself to death.

While there is no doubt he deeply loved his wife and children and mourned their loss, the facts don't back up a collapse of character.

He was on the go in 1834, traveling from San Antonio through Mexico and to New Orleans. There were more dubious land deals, more money-making schemes and, probably, more drinking than usual.

But Bowie was at his best when the Texas Revolution began in October 1835. He rushed to San Antonio and became one of Stephen F. Austin's trusted officers. He led the troops who won the critical battles of Concepcion and the Grass Fight.

Gen. Sam Houston trusted him, too. He called on Bowie for crucial assignments. In January, he sent him to San Antonio to blow up the Alamo and remove its artillery. Houston wanted no Texans trapped inside forts.

But Bowie knew better than Houston of the almost mystical importance of San Antonio and the Alamo.

After sizing up the situation (Houston had given him wide discretion in carrying out his orders), Bowie wrote to the commander:

"I would rather die in these ditches than give them up to the enemy."

Bowie stayed on at the Alamo and shared command for a time with Lt. Col. William B. Travis — a bit of a stuffed shirt, but a fighting man like himself.

With Bowie's help the garrison scraped up enough supplies to make a stand in the Alamo. On Feb. 23, 1836, the vanguard of a 6,000-man Mexican army march-ed into Main Plaza in San Antonio. The siege had begun.

The next day an illness variously described as tuberculosis, pneumonia, typhoid fever, typhoid-pneumonia and "a disease of a peculiar nature," put Bowie on a bed for the remainder of the 13-day siege.

But there was the heart of a giant beating in that coughing, heaving chest on that cold morning of March 6 when the door to his room began to splinter open from pounding by musket butts.

Bowie braced himself against the wall, determined to die as he had lived — weapon in hand, smeared in the blood of his opponents.

The Mexicans were lucky they met only a shadow of the man in that room, for the evidence is compelling that he put up the best fight he could.

The first two Mexicans into the room were shot dead. Another one or two died from last-gasp, wide-arching knife thrusts. It must have been a bloody scene, because the Mexican soldiers went out of control after mortally wounding Bowie.

A dozen soldiers thrust bayonets into him and carried him, still breathing, into the plaza, where his body was burned with the rest of the 188-man garrison.

Flesh burns, but legends such as Bowie's are indestructible. His place is assured in history as the ultimate masculine model — the kind of man you want by your side when there is fighting to be done.

James W. Fannin

In the roll call of Texas Revolution heroes, James W. Fannin is always last.

Instead of his name being called out with the resonance of Travis or Bowie, it is whispered in an embarrassed tone.

Why?

Fannin fought as hard as any other Texas soldier. He offered all his worldly goods to be sold to buy arms for the revolution. He accepted the most dangerous assignments and carried out his orders to the best of his ability.

He gave his life for Texas.

But fate was not kind to the illegitimate son of a Georgia plantation owner. He was not given the chance to make a command decision such as Travis to stand, to fight and to die drenched in blood and glory at the Alamo.

Instead, he was caught up in the confused politics and conflicting orders of a governor and council who refused to recognize each other's authority.

Fannin was sent to Goliad to organize an attack upon Matamoros. At Goliad, decisions were not black and white as they were in San Antonio.

Almost daily, Fannin received contradictory orders: Proceed with the invasion of Mexico; fortify the old bastion at La Bahia; send reinforcements to the Alamo; make no retrograde movement; don't risk too much in battle; and on and on.

This was not the glory of combat that Fannin had dreamed of as a cadet at West Point. It was the harsh reality of an army floundering without a working government to support it. It would ultimately lead to the deaths of 500 brave men and the worst military atrocity ever committed on the North American continent.

James Walker Fannin Jr., the son of Dr. Isham Fannin, was born in 1804 in Georgia. He was adopted by his maternal grandfather, James W. Walker, and raised on a plantation near Marion. On July 1, 1819, he entered the U.S. Military Academy at West Point under the name of James F. Walker, but withdrew from school in November 1821 following an argument with a fellow cadet.

He returned to Georgia, married Minerva Fort and had two daughters. In the autumn of 1834, he and his family moved to Texas and settled at Velasco. He bought a small plantation, but his letters confirm that he was primarily engaged in slave trading.

Fannin became an agitator for the Texas Revolution and worked to recruit officers of the U.S. Army to come to Texas to help lead an army that was not yet formed.

His military training at West Point and in the Georgia militia were invaluable in the opening stages of the conflict.

He commanded a company (the Brazos Guards) at the opening battle of the revolution at Gonzales on Oct. 2.

Stephen F. Austin, the commander of the Texas Army, put great trust in Fannin and considered him a capable and loyal officer. He entrusted Fannin and James Bowie with the crucial task of scouting the San Antonio area to find a place for the army to camp.

Fannin and Bowie led 90 men, who were surrounded by 400 Mexicans. On the morning of Oct. 28, the two officers, through cool leadership and sound military maneuvering, crushed the Mexican force, killing 67 and wounding almost that many. Only one Texan was killed.

Fannin led a series of patrols which constantly harassed the Mexicans besieged in San Antonio and denied them supplies.

Fannin received an honorable discharge from the Volunteer Army on Nov. 22 (Texas maintained two separate armies, the volunteers and the regulars). Shortly afterwards, the commander of the regular Texas Army, Gen. Sam Houston, named Fannin inspector general.

On Dec. 7, he was promoted to colonel and given added responsibilities for recruitment and obtaining equipment.

Fannin proved to be an excellent recruiter. Many of the men he would later lead to their deaths came to Texas because of his efforts.

On Jan. 6, 1836, the council appointed Fannin to organize an attack upon Matamoros. In this, as in almost all other orders, the council was hopelessly confused. It had previously ordered Col. Frank Johnson to organize the expedition. He refused, then changed his mind and accepted. James Grant also received orders to mount an expedition against Matamoros. No one told Fannin, who proceeded to gather men and equipment on the far frontier.

Meanwhile, Houston was trying to shoot down the plan to invade Mexico. He rode to Refugio, where Johnson's men were being formed and talked most of them out of the idea. The situation was deteriorating into a military version of slapstick comedy. Fannin did the best thing he could think of and ordered all troops who would answer to his command to withdraw to Goliad.

There, he began to rebuild the imposing fortress of La Bahia, renaming it Fort Defiance. More troops poured in from the United States through the nearby port of

Copano Bay. There were fighting forces with fierce names and brimming with pride such as the Alabama Red Rovers, the New Orleans Greys, the Kentucky Mustangs — men eager for glory and adventure, men destined to be executed like common criminals.

Meanwhile, Grant and Johnson led separate companies totaling about 100 men to gather horses in the semi-desert area west of the Nueces. They were both still attempting to keep alive the hope of an attack upon Mexico.

By mid-February, Fannin had received enough intelligence to convince him that a major Mexican advance upon both Goliad and San Antonio was being launched. With dwindling supplies and no support from colonists, Fannin asked for permission to withdraw his forces and was told not to retreat without orders.

A series of disasters befell the army. The commands of Johnson and Grant were wiped out in fighting at Agua Dulce and San Patricio by the advance units of a 2,000-man army under the command of Gen. Jose Urrea.

Next, came word that Texans in the Alamo were surrounded by 6,000 Mexicans. Travis sent word to Fannin pleading for help.

Because Fannin did not send reinforcements, he has been criticized for 150 years, his name dragged through the mud by men who had no concept of his problems.

Fannin tried to organize a relief force. He had 420 men under his command in late February, almost all volunteers from the United States. He organized 320 into a relief force, but they were a pathetic sight.

Capt. John Brooks, Fannin's aide-de-camp, described the force in a letter to his father.

"Most of the men were nearly naked and entirely destitute of shoes. As horses were not available, oxen were used to draw the artillery and baggage wagons. It was at best a forlorn hope. I frankly confess that without the interposition of Providence we cannot rationally anticipate any other result to our Quixotic expedition than total defeat."

Breakdowns in baggage trains and news that Urrea was closing fast on Goliad prompted Fannin to retire again to Fort Defiance.

He grew increasingly bitter at the failure of Texans to come to his aid or even supply the army with food.

On March 14, after hearing that the Alamo had fallen, Houston sent Fannin orders to blow up his fortifications and retreat.

But, on the same day, urgent pleas came from colonists in Refugio asking protection while they evacuated their families. Now, at this most critical time, Fannin allowed his concern over civilians who should have left long ago to interfere with sound military judgment. He split his forces and sent troops to Refugio.

He waited four critical days for their return. Finally, with Urrea's cavalry on the outskirts of Goliad, he ordered a retreat.

Nine miles from Goliad, near Coleto Creek, one mile from a wooded area which would have afforded his riflemen the protection they needed to beat off any Mexican attack, he was surrounded by an enemy force six times as strong as his 250 men.

The men who had come to Texas so eager for combat put up a good fight. They formed a square and shot down 250 Mexicans before nightfall. But they were without water and Mexican cannons raked their position. Nine of Fannin's men died and 60 were wounded, including Fannin.

Fannin was faced with a terrible choice: Allow the unwounded men to make for the woods and safety and abandon the wounded, or see what terms the Mexicans would offer.

The next morning Urrea met with Fannin and told him (although Mexican historians dispute the actual wording of the discussion) that if the Texans would surrender, they would be paroled to New Orleans.

Fannin was too concerned with the welfare of his wounded to listen to warnings that Mexicans had already executed many Texans and that their word was worthless.

He surrendered. One day later, 150 men who had fought at Refugio and escaped after running out of ammunition were captured at Victoria.

The 400 prisoners were taken back to La Bahia. One week later, on the orders of Gen. Antonio Lopez de Santa Anna, they were marched out in four separate groups.

Before they were marched out, they were told they were going to be taken to ships to transport them to New Orleans, as promised.

After marching about a half-mile, the groups were stopped. A few realized what was going to happen seconds before they were shot. One group yelled out, "Hurrah, for Texas" before musket volleys silenced them.

In the confusion, several prisoners escaped by running to the river and swimming through musket fire. They lived to tell the story of the atrocity.

The wounded had been left at La Bahia. They were dragged into the courtyard where they were shot or stabbed to death.

Fannin was the last to die. He had heard the volleys, knew what had happened to his men and had no wish to live any longer. He was taken to a small courtyard just outside the fort's church. He gave a Mexican officer a $5 gold coin and his watch and asked that he keep the coin and send the watch to his family. He asked that he be shot in the breast so he could have a decent burial.

The Mexican officer kept the watch and gold piece for himself and shot Fannin in the head. His body was thrown on the huge pyre where the bodies of the rest of his men were burning.

Just before he began his final retreat, Fannin penned these words to a close friend.

"I have not so much confidence in the people of Texas as I once had. They have been called on and entreated to fly to arms and to prevent what has now been done.

"I have but three citizens in the ranks and although I have called on them for six weeks, not one arrived and no assistance in bringing me provisions; even Texas refused me.

"I feel too indignant to say more about them. If I was honorably out of their service, I would never re-enter it. But I must now play a bold game. I will go the whole hog. If I am lost be the censure on the right head and my wife and my children and children's children curse the sluggards forever."

Davy Crockett

Davy Crockett died fighting at the Alamo.

He did not surrender. He did not ask for quarter. He did not beg for his life.

He died fighting back-to-back with two of his Tennessee comrades. Before they had finished, a pile of dead enemies, estimated at between 14 and 24, lay around them.

The evidence for this is undeniable. The only Anglo survivor of the siege, Susanna Dickinson, passed by his body minutes after the battle ended and described the scene. Gen. Antonio Lopez de Santa Anna had his cook, who had seen Crockett many times in Washington, D.C., identify the body. The cook later described the aftermath of Crockett's death scene. Other Mexican accounts confirm that his death was a valiant and vengeful one.

But, for 170 years, something about Crockett has inspired his admirers to embellish his accomplishments and his detractors to sully his reputation.

Such effort is waged now by revisionist and sloppy historians eager to make a name by claiming spurious proof that Crockett tried to surrender after the Mexicans broke into the Alamo.

It didn't happen that way. It couldn't. Davy Crockett never surrendered to anyone or anything in his whole life. Surrender wasn't part of his colorful vocabulary.

Crockett has been described as the personification of the American frontier experience and the Alamo has been described as the climax of that same experience.

Call it destiny or call it luck but it is from fusions of great men and overwhelming events that enduring legends are made.

Crockett had the same type of upbringing as most first generation Trans-Appalachian Anglo Celts. By the time he was 9, he was expected to use a rifle to bring home something for the pot if he wanted to eat. His formal schooling consisted of six months at an academy where he worked to pay for tuition and board.

His kind never expected to get anything for nothing except the freedom to run their own lives. The result was probably the toughest, most self-reliant, most combative generation in American history and Crockett was the epitome of that generation.

David Crockett, the son of John and Rebecca Hawkins Crockett, was born in 1786 in northeastern Tennessee.

His father was a soldier in the American Revolution and a wanderer, moving ever westward, looking for land, a new beginning and financial security.

He found disputed land titles, dogging creditors and an insensitive government. His father's experience made an indelible mark on Davy's conscience. He would later advocate political and economic theories that would have put him to the left of mainstream American politics a century later.

His father's mounting debts forced him to put a 12-year-old Davy to work herding cattle to Virginia. Upon his return, he had a falling out with his father and left home for three years. After a brief reunion, he left home for good.

In 1806, he married Polly Finley, who could trace her ancestry back to Macbeth, but who had none of Mrs. Macbeth's ability to guide her husband.

Crockett had inherited the wanderlust from his father. He moved Peggy and their rapidly growing family several times, always westward, until they were living in an area near the Alabama border where land titles were insecure and tempers were short.

He fought in the Creek Indian Wars under Gen. Andrew Jackson. He admired Jackson at the time. Later, he would be one of Old Hickory's most bitter opponents.

During this period, Crockett demonstrated a pattern of life he would follow to his grave. Once the crops were in and the family was snug for the winter, he would wander into the woods, either to search out a new piece of land for his family or to hunt and trap. One year he killed 105 bears.

During one of these outings, his wife died. He returned to a sad home of three small children with no mother.

He rectified the situation by quickly courting and marrying a widow, Elizabeth Patton. With her two children and, eventually five of their own, the Crocketts were never lonely for the sound of small feet in the log cabin.

Bad luck haunted Crockett all his life. He attempted to go into business with borrowed money but suffered a setback when a gristmill and distillery he built burned down.

He attempted to recoup his losses by producing 30,000 pipe staves to float down the Mississippi River to New Orleans. The flatboat they were loaded in sank along with his dreams.

The unsettled nature of the area Crockett was living in gave him his first taste of real politics. He was asked to run for magistrate. He knew nothing about the job but, after an easy election victory, began on the job training.

Crockett's fame as a marksman and his ability to entertain crowds with tall tales and hilarious yarns made him a natural for the 1821 version of the rubber chicken circuit. Soon, he was elected to the state legislature.

He consistently introduced and supported bills designed for the relief of the settlers in the western part of Tennessee. They needed credit but Jackson, his one-time commander and now political powerhouse, was opposed to either more legislation to open bank credit or to spending public money for internal improvements. Crockett broke with Jackson and would later be used by Jackson's much more powerful Whig opponents in an effort to discredit the president. The two became bitter enemies.

But, Crockett was able to hold his constituency together for two terms in the U.S. House of Representatives. Jackson's Whig enemies supported a national tour for Crockett and attempted to use him to show that Jackson did not have the hearts of the westerners as he claimed.

Jackson finally had enough and ordered his well-oiled political machine to dump the fiery-tongued radical from west Tennessee.

Crockett was defeated for re-election in 1835 and told his constituents that, "They could go to hell; he was going to Texas."

Texas was the frontier at that time. It was where a man could gain title to land without having to have cash in his hand. It was where all of what he had fought for was coming to pass.

It was to be the 50-year-old Crockett's final frontier.

He gathered together a few friends, kissed his wife goodbye and set off for Nacogdoches.

On the way, he did a little exploring in the Red River area and wrote home that he was in fine spirits because it was obvious Texas was the place where he would finally make his fortune.

But first there was the matter of a revolution to be fought.

Crockett signed up in the Texas Army in January in Nacogdoches to ensure his right to a bounty of nearly 5,000 acres of land. Then he led his band, now grown to about a dozen frontiersmen, to San Antonio.

He arrived two weeks before the Mexican Army and was warmly greeted by the officers and men of the increasingly threatened and isolated garrison.

Lt. Col. William Travis offered him a commission as an officer, but in a moving speech to soldiers and civilians in Main Plaza, Crockett asked only to serve as a high private. He did agree to command his dozen comrades.

When the siege began Feb. 23, 1836, he asked Travis, "Here I am Colonel. Assign us to some place and me and my Tennessee boys will defend it all right."

Travis assigned Crockett's sharpshooters to one of the most critical areas to defend — the low wall and stockade that extended from the end of the barracks on the south side of the fortress to the corner of the church.

And it was at that spot that Crockett and the rest of his squad were found after the battle. Their bodies had been mutilated by repeated stabbings and point blank musket shots, but the spot was also littered with Mexican dead. They had defended their assigned spot until it was too late to retreat and had met their deaths fighting back-to-back with Bowie knifes and rifle butts.

He gave the doomed men of the Alamo many a light-hearted moment during the siege with his tall tales and wry sense of humor. He provided an example for other, perhaps frightened fighters, and he exacted a terrible toll on the Mexican Army.

William Barret Travis

William Barret Travis appealed to the men of Texas for help two times during his life.

The first time the Texans came, saved him from a military prison, and in the process drove occupying Mexican troops from East Texas.

The second time, the Texans did not come — not in the numbers needed — and the result was the death of 188 Alamo defenders.

If the first appeal and its consequences are sometimes lost in the confusing politics and military maneuvering of Texas history, the second is burned into the soul of the state.

Sam Houston was eventually to become the hero of the revolution, but Travis was to become first on its list of martyrs. It would be Travis whom historians identify as having the most profound impact on the Texas character.

It was his cool courage, grace under pressure, commitment to freedom and gritty determination to hold his post that have been perpetuated in Texas lore and legend. If Texans seem to fight harder, show more ability to withstand pressure and are more willing to die for their convictions, it might well be that it is because somewhere in their psyche a voice is saying to them, "You wouldn't want to let Travis down."

Historian Joe Frantz has described the Travis phenomenon better than any other writer:

"For a brief tragic fortnight, William Barret Travis was all that is noble and exalted in mankind and it is good fortune for the Texas tradition that he chose his fortnight of grandeur in a Texas setting.

"In a world that sometimes has to fabricate its heroes, the hero that is Travis is genuine. His story is magnificent and inspiring in its unvarnished details and no embroidery of fine writing can improve upon the bare facts of elementary loyalty to a cause that he displayed in the siege of the Alamo."

Texas was a sparsely populated Spanish subprovince just beginning to stir with revolutionary spirit when Travis was born in 1809 into a modestly successful farming family in Saluda County, S.C.

When he was 9 years old, his family moved to a farm in Sparta, Ala., where young William began to show signs of extraordinary abilities. He completed school, studied law and passed his bar examination before he was 20.

But Alabama was awash with lawyers and, to make ends meet, he took a job teaching at a local academy. He soon found himself in love with his most beautiful pupil, Rosanna E. Cato, daughter of a local farmer.

Travis was a handsome man, 6 feet tall, with red hair and blue-grey eyes (the Mexicans would later describe them as "killer's eyes").

Rosanna also felt herself moved by the relationship and on Oct. 26, 1828, Travis married his 17-year-old love.

Like many other great men of Texas revolutionary history, Travis seemed plagued by trouble with women. The marriage was not a happy one. After three years, Travis left for Texas without a pregnant Rosanna and his 2-year-old son.

Rosanna visited Travis four years later and asked that he either renew the marriage or give her her freedom. But it was too late for Travis to turn back. It was September 1835. Travis had less than six months to live.

Eventually, Rosanna petitioned and received from the Alabama Legislature a divorce decree.

She left Charles Edward Travis in his father's custody after their dramatic last meeting at an inn in San Felipe.

By the time Rosanna journeyed to Texas for one last attempt to salvage her marriage, her husband had become the most wanted Anglo in Texas. He was considered a radical leader of the trouble-seeking War Party and his bold actions had caused him to fall out of favor with a majority of established colonists.

Travis began his revolutionary career several months after he arrived in Texas in 1831 and settled in the official port of entry of Anahuac.

He became a close friend and associate of two more radical War Party members, Patrick Jack and Robert (Three-Legged Willie) Williamson. About this time, the Mexican government decided to tighten up on customs collections. George Fisher, a Serbian adventurer and former U.S. citizen, was named customs collector and John Davis Bradburn, Kentucky renegade, was placed in command of the Anahuac garrison.

The trio of Travis, Jack and Williamson took an instant dislike to the garrison and its political and military leaders. When it became clear that these officials were determined to actually collect customs duties, they became disliked by all of Anglo Texas.

The trio agitated against the garrison, then played a series of practical jokes on Bradburn and Fisher. Eventually, the officials had enough and threw Travis and Jack into jail.

Travis slipped out appeals for help.

Alarm spread up the Brazos River valley. Williamson helped raise a force of nearly 200 men to free the prisoners.

The relief force decided to bring a cannon from Brazoria to help in persuading the Mexicans to release their friends.

A Mexican fort at Velasco guarded the approach to Brazoria. The Mexicans refused to let the Texans pass; a battle ensued and 50 Mexicans and 15 Texans were killed or wounded. The garrison surrendered and left for Mexico.

Travis and Jack were released. A few weeks later, another battle erupted in Nacogdoches when the Mexican garrison commander, fearful of a uprising by East Texas Anglos, ordered them to surrender their arms. Another sharp engagement, followed by a surrender of the Mexican troops, meant that East Texas was free of all occupation troops.

During the next three years, Travis moved to the center of the Anglo-American colony in San Felipe. He established himself as a lawyer of considerable skill and handled more than 1,000 cases during his short career.

He was also something of a social blade, and kept a diary which listed a number of romantic conquests. He read extensively and was especially fond of the great historical romances of Sir Walter Scott, which were full of themes about honor, duty, undying love and destiny.

Travis put aside his romantic wanderings in 1834 when he discovered the woman he was sure was his true love, Rebecca Cummings.

He planned to marry Rebecca as soon as his divorce was final, but war intervened.

Meanwhile, another garrison was established at Anahuac and more disputes over tariffs began. Travis and a company of men disarmed the garrison without a shot being fired.

This time, Texans did not act as one. Many older residents thought Travis' action rash and certain to cause retribution. Several towns held public meetings and sent messages to Mexican authorities apologizing for the actions of Travis.

But when Mexican officials demanded that Travis and six other radical leaders be turned over to them, the die was cast. It went without saying that no Anglo Texan would allow fellow colonists to be turned over to the uncertainties of Mexican justice.

War followed. Travis joined the regular army and rose to the rank of lieutenant colonel in the cavalry.

On Feb. 23, 1836, he found himself with Jim Bowie in joint command of the 150 Texans guarding San Antonio.

On that date the first elements of a 6,000-man invasion force headed by Gen. Antonio Lopez de Santa Anna arrived and the Texans retired to the Alamo to await reinforcements.

The next day, Bowie became bed-ridden and Travis took over sole command of the fort.

Travis was determined to stop the Mexicans in San Antonio. If they were allowed to have that city as a base of operations, they would be able to destroy all that Anglo settlers had made out of a wilderness.

Travis now showed his natural calling as a leader. He struck just the cord of camaraderie and call to duty that the garrison needed to sustain itself as thousands of Mexicans slowly encircled them.

On March 1, 32 more Anglos from Gonzales arrived to bring the total fighting force in the Alamo to 189.

On March 5, when it was obvious that no more help would reach them in time, Travis immortalized himself and the garrison with a gesture straight out of a Scott novel.

He ordered all the men except the guard to assemble in the courtyard, drew a line in the dirt with a sword and asked all those who would fight to the death to cross over. All but one did and that man, Louis Rose, would later feel obligated to tell the story of the line despite the fact that it branded him as a coward.

Now pledged together to hold their post or die, the garrison awaited the end of the siege.

It came early the next morning, when thousands of Mexicans rushed the walls of the fort and for six hours were engaged in one of the most brutal battles in American history.

Travis had planned the defense of the post. His men knew what to do. When the alarm sounded, Travis rushed to his post by a cannon on the north wall. He is known to have yelled but one order to his men, "Here come the Mexicans, boys. Give 'em hell."

He was shot in the forehead during the third and last charge. He fell back, then picked up his sword. A Mexican colonel entered a breach in the wall, saw Travis holding his ground and started to plunge his sword into him. With life oozing from his wound, Travis still had his fighting instinct. He drove his sword home first. Together, the two men fell dead by the ramparts.

It was an ending Sir Walter Scott could not have improved.

Susanna Dickinson

Of the images from the Alamo none is more poignant than that of Susanna Dickinson, with babe in arms, being led across the blood-splattered, body-strewn plaza for a face-to-face meeting with the man who ordered the attack that killed her husband and every member of the garrison.

The 21-year-old mother had seen and heard the screaming, yelling, cursing and killing of that incredibly savage six hours. And yet, she was able to hold up under the grief and stress of the moment. Her spirit remained intact and she found the courage to stand up to the dictator of Mexico in a fight for her baby.

It is a moment that Texas women can look at with pride. What happened to Susanna after the Alamo must be viewed with compassion and understanding. A part of Susanna must have died with her husband, Capt. Almeron Dickinson, and the rest of the 188-man garrison who all called her a friend.

Susanna was born in 1814 into Western Tennessee frontier family. She was not taught to read and write, because there were no public schools. Frontier families spent money to educate their sons. Mothers were supposed to teach daughters everything they would need to know to run a household.

Her mother must have taught her well, because in hard times Susanna would always fall back on her cooking talents. She ran a successful series of boardinghouses.

Susanna was a beauty — a dark-haired, passionate, intense woman with a full figure and an ability to move men in her direction.

Almeron was nearly 30 years old, with bulging muscles from blacksmithing and a sensible outlook on life when he crossed paths with the 15-year-old beauty.

He courted her for a time but during a lovers' spat he became engaged to one of Susanna's best friends.

On the wedding day, Almeron rode to the home of Susanna's family to escort the teen-ager to his wedding. She was to be a bridesmaid.

Sometime during the journey, the old flame became a blazing love again. They forgot about the wedding and headed off to a new life. The next day they became man and wife.

Two years later, the couple scrawled GTT (Gone to Texas) on their cabin and headed for the far frontier of Gonzales.

Almeron and Susanna were greeted warmly in Green DeWitt's small colony. Almeron had talents sorely needed on the frontier. He was a blacksmith, gunsmith and mechanic. In addition, he had served as an artilleryman in the regular U.S. Army.

Susanna had talents, too, although she never did learn to read or write. She could cook up delicious cornbread, greens and pork dinners and soon took in a boarder to help make ends meet.

She seemed to make friends with everyone who came into her life, Mexican or Anglo, male or female. The political chief of the area, Ramon Musquiz, and his wife came to know Susanna and always stayed with her and Almeron while on official business. Later, after the fall of the Alamo, the Musquizes would prove their loyalty.

By the fall of 1835, the couple was thriving. The crops were good, the land increasing in value and they had a new addition to the family, Angelina Elizabeth Dickinson, born in December 1834.

But the war clouds building in the south were blowing straight for their cozy cabin. In October 1835, the first shot of the Texas Revolution was fired near their home as Mexicans and Texans fought over control of a cannon manned by Almeron. The Texans won and the Mexicans retreated to San Antonio.

Almeron commanded the cannon, a crudely mounted six-pounder dubbed "the flying artillery." In less than two weeks a hastily formed Texas Army was besieging San Antonio while the women of Gonzales, Susanna included, kept the home fires burning.

But the kind of trouble which would plague Susanna all her life broke out several weeks after the men of Gonzales marched off to war. In sketchy reports from one of the few men left in town, it appears that a violent riot broke out in or around Susanna's house. A company of soldiers from the bayou country on the Louisiana border broke into her cabin and beat up one man who attempted to oust them. Susanna fled to a neighbor for safety.

As soon as the Texans drove the Mexican Army out of San Antonio, Almeron sent for his wife and child. They were probably the garrison's only Anglo family members living in the Alamo or San Antonio.

Susanna moved in with her friends, the Musquizes. She cooked and did washing for a number of the Texas troops during the 10-week lull before the arrival of Gen. Antonio Lopez de Santa Anna and 6,000 Mexican soldiers.

On the day the leading elements of the Mexican Army arrived outside San Antonio, Almeron leaped on a horse and raced to the Musquiz house.

"Give me the baby; jump up behind me, and ask no questions," he shouted.

Susanna and Almeron rode into the Alamo as the garrison quickly mustered in the mission's plaza. It was the beginning of a 13-day siege.

During those 13 days, Susanna was kept busy cooking, mending clothes, wrapping bandages and tending to the sick, including Jim Bowie. She became close to a number of the members of the garrison. David Crockett took a special liking to the sturdy, beautiful frontier woman.

Because Susanna never learned to write and because she only reluctantly talked about her experiences in the Alamo, many historians have failed to explore the wealth of knowledge she had about those glorious but confused events.

But study of the records she did leave gives a clear picture of what conditions were like during the siege and the terrible final day when the bastion fell.

Susanna was called on to give a number of depositions for people seeking land due them because a family member fought at the Alamo. Susanna was the only Anglo survivor and was interviewed about a number of men. It is through such interviews that the one-time discarded story of William B. Travis' line in the dirt can be verified.

Susanna's testimony also makes it perfectly clear that Crockett died fighting and was not taken prisoner and executed as revisionist historians would have one believe.

On March 6, the Mexicans attacked in overwhelming numbers, but for several hours were beaten back by superior marksmanship and the firepower of 21 cannons. Susanna recalled that it was only after early attempts had been defeated that she took her baby into the powder magazine in the chapel to await the outcome of the battle.

During the lull between the second and final charge of the Mexicans, Crockett sought her out in the chapel.

"He fell on his knees and gave himself to Jesus," Susanna recalled.

During the final assault, Almeron, who was commanding three cannons on top of the chapel that housed Susanna and Angelina, dashed into her room and cried out, "Good God, Sue, the Mexicans are inside the fort. If you are spared, love our child."

He drew his sword, returned to his post and was never seen again by his wife.

In the final, agonizing moments of the battle Galba Fuqua, a 16-year-old gunner ran into her room. He tried to speak, but his jaw had been shattered. He tried to hold it together with his hands, then gestured pitifully and headed back to his post. Later three unarmed Texans were bayoneted in front of her. She saw Mexican soldiers break into Bowie's room and heard the shooting and cursing as the old fighter took several enemies with him.

Then it was over. She recalled that the stillness was worse than the cannonade. An English officer in the Mexican Army called her by name and she was taken to a personal meeting with Santa Anna.

While crossing the plaza, she saw Crockett's body, mutilated and surrounded by dead Mexicans he and his Tennesseans killed in their final stand.

There were still shots ringing out as Mexican troops fired into the dead bodies of the defenders. A stray bullet hit Susanna in the calf. She grimaced but limped on.

Santa Anna questioned her, but seemed drawn to Angelina. He asked Susanna to let him adopt her beautiful baby. He pointed out that he could give Angelina a much better life than Susanna could hope to provide.

Susanna looked at her baby, innocently playing with a ring that Travis had given her just a day before, and defiantly shook her head.

"My baby stays with me," she said to the man who was absolute ruler over millions.

Her courage affected Santa Anna. He later told aides he had made up his mind to keep the child until the mother showed such courage.

Susanna, Angelina and two black slaves were sent to Gonzales to tell all colonists what had happened at the Alamo.

Susanna accomplished that task and then was caught up in the "Runaway Scrape" as thousands of Texans fled before the Mexican Army.

In 1837, she was married again, the first of three bad marriages which lasted only a short time. She charged one husband with abusing Angelina, the babe of the Alamo. Another claimed that she left his home and committed numerous acts of adultery.

In 1849, in front of 1,500 people crowded on the banks of Buffalo Bayou in Houston, she was baptized by one of the most famous Baptist preachers in Texas history, Dr. Rufus C. Burleson.

After the baptism, Burleson said Susanna's change was so complete as to be observed by her neighbors.

"During all my pastorate in Houston, and especially during the cholera epidemic, she was a zealous co-laborer of mine in every good work," Burleson wrote.

Burleson admitted that Susanna would occasionally backslide, but, "Whenever she did wrong, especially in giving way to passion, she would confess and weep over it," Burleson explained.

In 1857, she apparently found the peace of mind she had lost at the Alamo and married another blacksmith, Joseph Hanning.

They moved to Austin and Susanna settled into old age, always honored and hounded for her Alamo role.

During the last years of her life, she was asked to come to San Antonio to help save the Alamo from destruction. It was being used as a warehouse at the time.

With reporters in tow, she walked through time, pointing out where heroes had died.

"My God. This was a hospital room. Fifteen Texans were murdered in this room and now it is full of garbage," she told a reporter.

Her efforts helped save the Alamo and turn it into the shrine it is today.

On Oct. 7, 1883, she died at age 68. She was buried in Oakwood Cemetery in Austin.

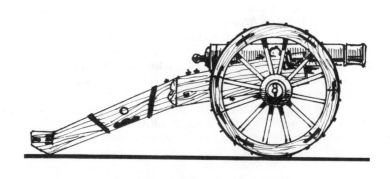

Gen. Santa Anna

The stereotype of Antonio Lopez de Santa Anna is well known, both in the United States and in Mexico.

He is viewed as an ego-centered, merciless ruler, who gave away huge chunks of his nation to secure his freedom and to gain personal wealth; a womanizer; opium addict; and, as someone thoroughly lacking in honor.

Santa Anna is held in contempt by mainstream Mexican historians, who refuse to give him any positive marks for the 20 years he ruled the country.

In America, he is viewed much like Richard Nixon after his resignation of the presidency. Commentators lined up to call Nixon a politician who appealed to the dark side of the American character.

Santa Anna has enjoyed no respite from relentless character defamation despite the passage of 13 decades since he held the reins of power in Mexico.

There is only one way for a politician to remain on the top rung of power for 20 years. He must know his constituency better than they know themselves and be able to tap into the character of his people, to speak to their innermost hopes and fears. And he must put on a good show.

Santa Anna did all those things and more. He understood the Mexican people and how to exercise the power of his position. He was ridiculed when he was out of office, but worshiped when he resumed leadership of the nation. He was deposed as ruler 10 times and brought back to power nine times. He never asked for his old job back. He waited until the Mexican power structure decided that, like him or not, he was the only man who could curb chaos and prevent the mob from seizing control.

Like the French leader he worshiped, the self-styled Napoleon of the West knew how to play to the masses while protecting the privileged status of the large landowners, the army and the Church.

He held his nation together (at least the part south of the Rio Grande and California) during one crisis after another, each one capable of breaking apart the Mexican union of states.

His methods were sometimes cruel, often brilliant and always showmanlike.

But, he was playing with a losing hand. Mexico had been ripped apart by 12 years of war with Spain in order to gain independence. The infrastructure of the nation was wrecked, especially the all-important silver and gold mines that were much more vital to the nation's economy than oil is to present-day Texas.

When Spain left, it bequeathed no educated and self-reliant middle class, no tradition of self-rule, no sense of a special mission for its former colony.

But it did leave the pride of the Mexican people, a pride some historians insist that Spain did not succeed in breaking. Since long before the Aztecs came to power, the land was dominated by the Valley of Mexico and driven by the will of a people who knew they were part of La Raza — the race, the culture, the tradition, the ancient heritage. La Raza predated the Spaniards and absorbed the Spanish language and values into the collective culture.

Santa Anna was born in Jalapa in 1795 into a well-to-do Creole family (of Mexican-born Spanish blood-line) and received a soldier's education.

As a young cadet, he took part in a bloody repression of revolutionaries in Texas. In San Antonio, he witnessed how his first mentor, Gen. Joaquin de Arrendondo, dealt with rebellious residents of Texas. More than 800 were shot, hanged or hacked to death, many after surrendering. Included in the rebel army were a number of Anglo-American adventurers. He was not impressed by this new breed. They died as easily as Mexican-Texans.

Santa Anna fought in the Royal Spanish Army south of the Rio Grande as it destroyed the mob armies of Father Hidalgo and survived the early response to the "Grito" (cry for freedom).

But revolution was in the air, both in the New World and in the Old World. Spain was racked by revolt. A liberal king, who was under the influence of reform-minded enthusiasts of Napoleonic France, assumed the throne.

The power structure of Mexico was threatened. Reforms could mean a reduction in the domination of Mexican life by the army and clergy. Large landowners began to worry about how far this idea of more individual rights would go. The stage was set for another revolution in Mexico; this time the rebels were the landlords, Army officers and bishops. It was a revolution to preserve the status quo.

Santa Anna exercised his uncanny sense of timing and jumped into the rebel camp at just the right moment, when the pendulum was swinging away from the Spanish viceroy. In 1821, Santa Anna, recently promoted by the viceroy to lieutenant colonel, took his troops over to the side of rebel general Augustin de Iturbide. Santa Anna's move put the final nail in the coffin of Spanish Mexico. Within weeks after Santa Anna's switch in loyalty, Iturbide declared Mexico independent by an edict called the Plan of Iguala. The plan was full of platitudes about a fraternal union of all Mexicans. In reality, it guaranteed that those who had power would keep it.

But Iturbide overplayed his hand and declared himself emperor. That was just the opening 24-year-old Santa Anna needed. He declared Iturbide an "imperialist reactionary" and proceeded to precipitate another rebellion. Iturbide was banished and executed when he attempted a return to power.

Santa Anna displayed his political genius when he refused to take absolute power. He preferred to operate in the background while a three-man regency attempted to implement unpopular reforms.

The regency drew up the Constitution of 1824 under whose flag 188 Texans would die 12 years later attempting to hold back Santa Anna's army at the Alamo. It used the United States Constitution as a model. It was doomed from the start and Santa Anna knew it. The Mexican people had no understanding nor desire for the type of government practiced in the United States of the North.

Santa Anna waited patiently for the right time to make his next move up the ladder of power. Four years later, he recruited a popular politician, Vincente Guerrero, as a front man for another palace revolt.

Guerrero was proclaimed president by a submissive congress, but the Mexican establishment knew that the tall, good-looking, 31-year-old general from Jalapa was the power behind the president. Nine months later, Guerrero's vice-president, Gen. Anastasio Bustamante, seized power.

Santa Anna sensed his destiny was at hand. He retired to his villa and waited until the nation demanded an end to Bustamante's tyranny.

Santa Anna accepted the draft and rallied most of the army to his banner. The fighting was over quickly. This time Santa Anna assumed the Number One position.

Santa Anna had achieved his goal of absolute power two years before the first shot was fired in the Texas Revolution. The confrontation between Mexicans and Anglo-Americans was inherited by Santa Anna, but he did nothing to head it off. In fact, he seems to have decided that a showdown with Anglos was inevitable and the sooner the better, before more inroads were made in traditional Hispanic territory by the land-grabbing, democratic-government-demanding Anglos.

Santa Anna was too shrewd a politician and too good a soldier not to know that he was playing what eventually must be a losing hand. Anglos were pouring over the border into Texas with their long rifles and fierce determination to rule their own destiny. Mexico would have to marshal the resources of the entire nation to fight the newcomers in a land distant from the population centers of Mexico. Santa Anna was determined that such an effort would ensure another generation of Mexican rule in Texas. That meant a war of racial extermination — the destruction of everything Anglo, the killing of every Anglo who dared to bear arms against Mexico. It was a Moorish tradition Spain had added to La Raza — subjugation through terror.

Santa Anna proved his military abilities by pushing an army of 8,000 men on a winter march into Texas. His orders to kill all who opposed his troops were carried out. Hundreds of Texans and American volunteers were slain, more by treachery than in battle. But Santa Anna's hand finally played out in the swamps of San Jacinto.

His division was destroyed, and he was captured. He ordered all remaining troops to retire south of the Rio Grande. He has been cursed for that order by Mexican patriots ever since, despite the fact that a retreat was the only way to save the remaining Mexican troops.

Santa Anna was held in Texas for six months. He signed a treaty that did nothing more than acknowledge the obvious fact that Mexico's days in Texas were finished.

He was cursed at home until a French invasion in 1838 gave him the opportunity to regain his name. He lost a leg, but regained the dictatorship.

In 1848, after he had fought and lost to invading American troops, his past caught up with him in a dramatic scene.

Santa Anna had negotiated a surrender with American officers outside Mexico City. He was traveling by carriage to another exile. A regiment of Texas Rangers — the sons, brothers, cousins and friends of many of the men he had ordered murdered — discovered his route and lined both sides of the road.

American officers on the scene described Santa Anna's reaction upon seeing his old enemies. He turned pale, then pulled himself together, sat straight in a soldier's pose and stared directly ahead. He thought he was going to his death. The Rangers had come to kill him, but American officers rode down the mounted lines, appealing to the men.

"Don't shoot him, boys. He deserves to be shot, but we have given our word. The honor of Texas is at stake," they cried.

The Rangers stared holes through their hated enemy as he passed, but kept their guns holstered.

The honor of Texas was secure and Santa Anna lived to regain power two more times. After many years of intrigue and scheming, he died in obscurity in Mexico City, June 1876.

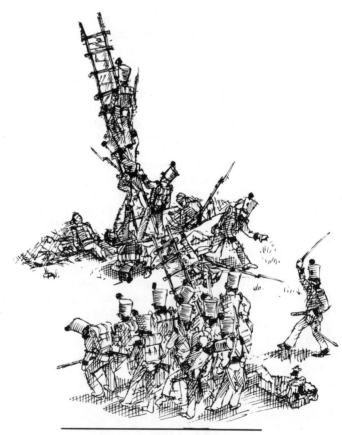

Sam Houston

On the day after the battle of San Jacinto, the victorious general lay under an oak tree, grimacing as a doctor probed his wounded foot for bone fragments.

Sam Houston occupied his mind during the painful procedure by twisting a garland out of wild magnolia leaves.

The 43-year-old general was preparing the garland for 17-year-old Nacogdoches beauty Anna Raguet. He enclosed a note with his handiwork:

"To Miss Anna Raguet,

"These are the laurels I send you from the battlefield of San Jacinto.

"Thine, Houston."

Many months before Houston conquered Antonio Lopez de Santa Anna, he was himself conquered by the widely acclaimed charms of Miss Raguet.

The third of six children and eldest daughter of Houston's friends, Henry and Marcia Ann Raguet, Anna was 15 when she returned home from an exclusive finishing school in Philadelphia to rejoin her family in Nacogdoches.

When she returned home, she met Houston, a newcomer to Texas, who spent a great deal of time at the Raguet household.

Raguet was the richest man in Nacogdoches and was a key contact for Houston, who had arrived in Texas in 1832 and was attempting to set up a law practice in the Redlands area.

Miss Raguet had attended the finishing school for four years. She had become an able linguist with a command of Spanish, French and German. She was also a talented performer on the French harp and reflected a social grace and maturity beyond her years.

Houston fell in love with her.

But, the former Tennessee governor had experienced problems with women in the past and didn't want to move too fast with his new romantic interest.

When Houston was a teen-ager growing up in the backwoods of Tennessee, he ran away from home and lived for three years with the Cherokee Indians. During this time he had his first experiences with women. He seems never to have fully appreciated the differences in the ways Indian and Anglo women felt they should be treated.

When he returned to white society, he used the first money he earned to buy gaily colored cloth for his Cherokee girlfriends.

After serving as a regular army officer and working as a lawyer, prosecuting attorney and major general in the Tennessee militia, Houston plunged into national politics.

That was good enough background to qualify him for two terms as a congressman in Washington, D.C., where he willingly served the interests of his mentor, Andrew Jackson.

Jackson arranged for him to get the inside track to the Tennessee governorship, and he was elected to that office in 1829.

It was widely assumed that this protege of Jackson's was on a presidential tract — serve two terms as Tennessee governor, one term as senator, then follow Jackson into the White House.

Houston easily won the first-term governorship and was preparing to embark on a campaign trail to a second-term victory when trouble struck and derailed his political express.

In January 1829, the 36-year-old governor married a shy 18-year-old, Eliza Allen. Four months later, his new wife left him to return to her parents.

Houston came apart. He began drinking heavily, refused to pay any attention to his job as governor and, within a few weeks, resigned from office.

He left Tennessee on a riverboat bound for Arkansas. Rumors spread quickly, but their attributions were deliberated carefully.

Houston's final words before departing were that what had happened between his wife and himself was his fault and if he heard of anyone saying anything derogatory about Eliza, he would return and kill that person.

A threat like that from a proven fighting man, 6-foot-4 inches and 220 pounds of muscle, was enough to make the bravest man weigh his words carefully.

There were many theories as to why the marriage broke up. Eliza was brought up in a wealthy, sheltered environment, while Houston preferred personal habits picked up from the Indians. He was accustomed to going nude at home, and such behavior shocked his young wife, who had been pushed into the marriage for political reasons.

She was widely rumored to have preferred a suitor her own age. Houston is supposed to have found this out and had his pride permanently pierced.

Houston spent a few years in and out of Cherokee land. He married a Cherokee woman named Tiana, but left her when he decided to remake his career in Texas.

He was always more successful with Indian women. Tiana sent him a pair of moccasins to wear during his campaign against the invading Mexican Army.

But Anna Raguet was the burning love of his life.

On the night before he left for the General Convention which would declare

Texas an independent nation and appoint Houston commander in chief of the armed forces, he was feted by the Nacogdoches establishment at a formal party at the Raguets.

He sat opposite Miss Raguet, his back to an open door — something a careful frontiersman never did.

Miss Raguet saw a movement, but her fears were laughed away until she grabbed the hand of a Mexican who attempted to assassinate Houston with a knife. The man was quickly subdued, escorted to jail and summarily hanged.

Houston now owed his life to the woman of his dreams.

Before he left for Washington-on-the-Brazos, the dark-eyed, dark-haired beauty offered to prepare a scabbard for his sword fashioned from a red sash she had been saving.

For that deed, he promised her laurels from his victories. Indeed, he sent a message to Miss Raguet before officially informing the Texas government of his victory at San Jacinto.

After he assumed the presidency of the Texas Republic in October 1836, he often wrote Miss Raguet two or more letters a day. But they were stilted and showed his insecurity with affairs of the heart. He never built up the nerve to ask her to marry him.

Eventually, her interest turned to the man Houston dispatched to deliver his laurels — Robert Anderson Irion.

She eloped with Irion in March 1840 and settled down to a happy domestic life.

Two months later, Houston, then 47 years old, visited a friend in Alabama. In one week he had met, courted and married his friend's daughter, 20-year-old Margaret Lea.

The new Mrs. Houston was an ardent Baptist and is generally credited with curbing many of her husband's excesses. He cut down on his drinking after his final marriage, although he was known to backslide occasionally.

Through his wife's influence, he joined the Baptist Church.

The couple had eight children. Mrs. Houston spent most of her time running the family businesses, including two large farms and numerous investments.

It was a marriage on the rebound which worked well enough. At age 52, Houston still displayed a sense of humor. After the birth of his first son, he wrote a friend:

"You have, I doubt not, heard that my wife controls me and has reformed me. This is pretty true, and I tell her that I am willing that she should have the full benefit of my character.

"But she gets all the credit for my good actions, and I have to endure all the censure of my bad ones. Thus, you see, that I am bankrupt in all good reputation. Well, so long as a good name remains in the family, I will be satisfied."

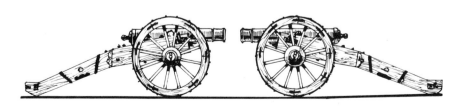

Robert Potter

The life of Robert Potter, one of the founding fathers of the Texas Republic, can best be described as somewhere between colorful and bizarre.

Many of his contemporaries said he had the hottest temper, used the most powerful rhetoric, had the most damning past, was the most dangerous ladies' man and subscribed to the most radical politics of his era.

Of all of the heavyweights who make up the pantheon of Texas heroes, he is the only one who carries a supernatural legend with him.

He is more famous in his native North Carolina than in Texas, where he lived for only seven years before being murdered in an episode that spawned an East Texas folk song still heard in the Caddo Lake area.

North Carolinians recognize him as the man responsible for a peculiar Carolinian word, potterize, which means to castrate.

Potter was the only sitting representative of the U. S. Congress to ever be convicted of castrating a man.

Potter was born in 1800 into a prosperous Oxford, N.C., farming family. At the age of 15, he joined the navy and served five years as a midshipman.

Like most details of Potter's life, his departure from the navy is shrouded in rumor and mystery. He used his time aboard ship to further his education and physical prowess. He became an excellent fencer and, reportedly, was asked to resign after killing a fellow officer in a duel.

Potter returned to North Carolina and completed law study, taking a bar exam in 1823.

Nothing in Potter's life came easy and practically nothing came without a fight. In 1824, he decided to enter politics and began one of the wildest careers in North Carolina's history of elective offices.

A series of insults and counter-insults between Potter and a conservative incumbent, Jesse Bynum, led to such violence that the state legislature suspended the election and the county of Halifax went without representation for two years.

Potter won the legislature seat in 1826 and was re-elected in 1828. In 1829, he was elected to the U.S. House of Representatives.

Potter's politics, considered radical for the times, terrified many of the established powers in North Carolina.

Among other things, he advocated free education, a much-feared issue in the South, and was a strong advocate of the rights of free blacks. A rumor campaign alleged that he had purchased the votes of about 300 free blacks in Halifax County.

He was a Jacksonian Democrat who moved far to the left of the president. He urged the sale of public lands to provide money for river and harbor improvement. His liberal economic views of how to get a stagnant economy moving again were, in many respects, a century ahead of his time. Many of his ideas can be found in Franklin Roosevelt's New Deal policies of the 1930s.

An early populist with solid backing from the working class, Potter appeared headed for a more powerful political position when his temper struck.

For some time, Potter had feared that his wife, Isabella, had been having affairs with two different men, one a 55-year-old minister and the other a 17-year-old youth.

Upon seeing the minister in a buggy riding away from his house at an unusual time, Potter hailed him and engaged him in conversation until he was able to loop a rope around the man's neck. In seconds, the minister was hogtied and expertly castrated with a Bowie knife. The future secretary of the Texas Republic Navy then gave emergency medical treatment to keep the man alive.

Potter rode on to the home of the youth, who was similarly surprised and maimed.

The father of the maimed youth took a shot at Potter and missed. Others threatened retribution but Potter's constituency rallied around him.

From the window of his jail cell, he whipped up such emotion among hundreds of onlookers that he was moved out of the county.

Potter conducted his own defense in his trial and claimed innocence.

He cited the sanctity of the marriage bed as his defense. The working class stayed by his side during the trial. He was sentenced to six months in jail and fined $1,000 for maiming the youth. The other offense was never brought to trial.

Potter had resigned from the U.S. House of Representatives when arrested. He won his old seat back in the state legislature in the next election.

Historians are in agreement that his enemies, unable to beat him at the polls, trumped up card-cheating charges against Potter and he was expelled from the state legislature in 1835.

Potter than became a GTT man — Gone to Texas.

He arrived in Nacogdoches in July 1835 as war clouds blew in from the west. He enrolled in a militia unit under the command of Thomas Jefferson Rusk and threw himself into the financing of the Texas Revolution, raising funds and supplies for the successful siege and storming of San Antonio.

Drawn to the turbulent politics of the time, Potter was nominated to represent Nacogdoches in the General Convention. He was one of the signers of the Texas Declaration of Independence and helped to write the Republic's Constitution.

A close ally of Interim President David G. Burnet, Potter was given the awesome task of stopping any Mexican invasion by sea. He was made secretary of the navy and commander of the defenses at Galveston Island.

Potter proved to be an excellent choice for navy secretary. While much of the initial work of bringing together a fleet of fighting ships had already been accomplished, Potter made sure the Texas Navy was supplied and directed.

Under his leadership, the Navy seized control of the Texas Gulf, captured a number of Mexican ships and kept open the supply lines to New Orleans. The Texans' command of the sea prevented Gen. Antonio Lopez de Santa Anna from boarding a ship for Mexico before the battle of San Jacinto.

During the mad flight of refugees to escape Santa Anna's army, Potter came upon a group of civilians bogged down in a quagmire. Included in the group was Mrs. Harriett Page. She had picked up her two children and started running when she heard a false alarm that the Mexicans were near her farm outside Velasco.

When Potter saw her she had on her best clothes, a mud-splattered black soaked dress, white crepe shawl and velvet-trimmed black hat with white satin ribbons. She looked vulnerable and confused.

Potter, always the gallant knight, dismounted and offered to let the woman ride with him.

Their lives were forever linked after that ride to a boat destined for Galveston Island.

Mrs. Page, it turned out, had a husband in Sam Houston's army, but had vowed never to live with him again because of his loathsome and drunken ways. Instead, she took up residence with Potter.

Whether or not she ever got a divorce is uncertain, but Harriet and Robert considered themselves married from that day forward and did go through a legal ceremony some years later.

After his tour of duty as navy secretary, Potter became one of the most powerful members of the Republic's legislature. He moved to Potter's Point, on Caddo Lake near the San Jacinto River.

Potter was a Moderator in the Regulator-Moderator conflicts in East Texas. The Moderators were opposed to the vigilante tactics the Regulators used in imposing their will on residents of no-man's land in far East Texas, including Potter's Point.

One morning in March 1842, a group of Regulators surrounded Potter's house. Harriet tried to get him to stay in the house and shoot it out, but Potter thought his chances were better if he made for the lake and swam out of harm's way.

He raced through a hail of gunfire to the lake, while Harriet searched in vain for matches to light the small cannon Potter kept for home defense.

He dived in and swam as far as he could. When he broke surface, he was shot through the head.

A Regulator turned to Harriet and said, "How do you like your pretty Bobby now?"

Harriet and friends searched for two days on the lake before finding the body. She found the matches in Potter's pocket.

Potter is still remembered in the wilds of backwoods East Texas through a folk song and a legend.

It is said that Harriet returns to Caddo Lake every year, usually in March and her ghostly form can be seen searching the lake for the body of her lost love.

Thomas Jefferson Rusk

When a tired, despondent and emotionally spent 56-year-old Thomas Jefferson Rusk picked up his shotgun and took a final walk around his farm before blowing his brains out, he joined a long and tragic line of Texans who have taken their own lives.

Suicide has hung over the spirit of Texas like a black shroud waiting for a body still burning with life.

Psycho-historians have not neglected this side of the Texas character. They have identified a number of forms of suicide in the land called Texas, ranging from political, to salvation from torture, to personal, to collective, to racial.

The principal author of the Texas Declaration of Independence stabbed himself in the stomach with a Bowie knife and bled to death.

Two candidates for president in the 1836 Texas Republic elections committed suicide, one by jumping out of a rowboat in Galveston Bay; the other with a pistol.

The first chief justice of the Texas Supreme Court and the last president of the Republic used firearms to end their lives.

During the 40 years that Texas was a frontier on fire with Indian raids and counter-raids, it was expected that any man or woman caught in the middle of an Indian fight would save the last bullet for himself or herself — especially herself. Women who allowed themselves to be taken into captivity rather than perish at their own hands were often considered cowards.

Although it is still a hotly debated topic, some historians believe that the decision of the 188-man Alamo garrison to stay and fight a Mexican Army 30 times its size was a form of collective suicide, symbolized and ritualized by William B. Travis's immortal line drawn in the dirt. Those who stepped over agreed to the suicide pact (so the theory goes). All but one did. And they kept the pact to the last man.

But the most unusual and, in its unrelentingly tragic nature, the most heart-tearing episode of suicide in Texas history would seem to be the fate of the Crancahua Indians.

For hundreds of years, these mellow cousins to the cannibalistic Karankawas, roamed the coast from South Padre to Galveston Island, subsisting on the easy fishing and enjoying the sun and surf that now draw millions of visitors a year.

They were considered to be quite a formidable people in their prime. In 1817, the tribe could field more than 300 fighting warriors and they were of the unusually large and athletic Karankawa stock.

They were a proud people. No one, not even the feared Comanches, challenged them.

One day, while a group of Crancahuas was visiting Galveston Island, a group of Jean Lafitte's pirates surprised them and made off with one of their most beautiful maidens.

The Crancahuas retaliated by killing four of the buccaneers. Lafitte exacted revenge by raising 200 men, equipping them with modern firearms and several cannons, and battling the Indians. After three days of carnage, the Crancahuas were finished as a major fighting force in Texas.

The survivors fled to what is now modern-day Houston, where the resident Indians continued to harass them until they were forced to push on.

For 30 years the Crancahuas attempted to find a new place to call home, but they were scorned and driven out by Anglos, Mexicans and other Indians.

Having lost all self-respect, they stooped to stealing and in 1846 were accused of killing a deputy sheriff near Gonzales. They fled down the Guadalupe River, past Goliad and Corpus Christi. Making their way down Padre Island, they halted at an old tribal gathering spot.

The men held a council and decided that they could not allow another generation of Crancahuas to suffer their humiliation. That night, they killed the 40 remaining women and children in the tribe.

Then the men, about 15 or 20 in number, sat down, stared out at the pounding surf of Padre and starved to death, determined to end the existence of their race.

Historians have assembled the evidence tracing their movements and decline since the Lafitte encounters, but the decision to stop their seed for eternity remains one of the most stunning in history.

Psycho-historians have several theories to explain rarely discussed aspects of suicide in Texas history.

Texas was a land of beginnings. But that meant throwing it all together for one last chance. Men who were losers in love, cards, the stock market or running a store could find one last chance in Texas, where the long arm of bill collectors from the United States could not reach.

But to fail in Texas meant the end for many men.

It is the dark side of the wheeler-dealer image that Texas is famous for. When the wheeler-dealer goes flat and the deals turn sour, he may choose his own way to close out his hand.

Guns, too, play their part in the recurring tragedy. Texans have always been more familiar with and better at using guns than people from any other state. A gun to many Texans was a friend, a companion, a life-saver. It seemed natural to be a life-ender as well.

Suicide in early Texas did not carry the onus it does today. While not ritualized like the Japanese, it was accepted and no one thought less of the deceased because he might have taken his own life.

Certainly that is true of Rusk.

Rusk was one of the handful of men who made Texas' independence and eventual statehood a reality. He did everything asked of him and more. While never receiving the glory heaped upon Sam Houston, his close friend, Rusk played just as vital a role in Texas history.

He came to Texas in 1835. He was 33 years old and was chasing several business partners who had swindled him out of his savings in a phony land scheme. Unable to return to his family in Georgia or to his native South Carolina because of debts, he decided to stake his future on Texas.

Like many Texas patriots, he was a powerfully built man, towering well over 6 feet tall and well-proportioned; he was every bit as awesome a man as Houston.

Rusk had the ability to moderate differences. He was the link between the War Party and the Peace Party. Both sides respected him.

Only once was he ever known to have a personal clash with a Texas politician.

In Washington-on-the-Brazos, with the Mexican Army only days away and the Convention desperately trying to finish the job of writing a Constitution for the new Republic, discussions were continually held up by Secretary of the Navy Robert Potter.

Finally, Rusk put his Bowie knife on Potter's throat and asked him if he was going to shut up or did he want the cutting to start.

Discussions ended almost immediately and the convention adjourned shortly before the arrival of the Mexicans.

Rusk was named secretary of war. He kept the government from firing Houston when the general showed a preference for retreating rather than fighting. Houston was biding his time and Rusk knew it. Rusk was sent as the government's personal representative to the army. Many officers begged him to sack Houston and take command himself.

He refused. He stayed by his friend and fought as a private at San Jacinto.

After the victory and capture of Gen. Jose Antonio Lopez de Santa Anna, it was Rusk who played the hardest role of all. He took command of the army, which was bent on revenge, and held the troops in check, calmly following the thousands of retreating Mexican soldiers as they headed for the Rio Grande.

As he passed through Goliad, Rusk ordered a formal burial for the 400 victims of the massacre at La Bahia.

In his oratory, he sounded the feelings of a generation of Texans:

"(This group) nobly threw themselves between the people of Texas and the legions of Santa Anna. There, unaided by reinforcements and far from help and hope, they battled bravely . . . Surrounded on an open prairie they were induced under the sacred promise of receiving the treatment usual to prisoners of war, to surrender . . . . They were marched from yonder fort a week later (and executed).

"Our tribute of respect is due to them; it is due to the mothers, sisters and wives who weep their untimely end and we mingle our tears with theirs."

Rusk was destined to serve again as an army field commander and secretary of war. Six times he led the forces of Texas in battle and six times he won.

When Texas became a state in the Union, he and Houston were elected senators. He is credited with doing most of the work, while Houston positioned himself for a possible presidential bid.

He was elected president pro-tem in the Senate after his third election.

But he never recovered from his wife's death a year before his own.

The last business act he performed was to order a tombstone for his wife's grave inscribed, "Blessed are the pure in heart for they shall see God."

Later that day, he announced he was going hunting, picked up his shotgun and took a walk in the woods. He never returned.

The Holland family

The wresting of Texas from the wilderness and the fight to gain independence was, for the most part, carried out by average people caught up in large-than-average events.

Typical of the pioneers who were to forge a new republic were the Hollands.

The Francis Holland family, including four sons and two daughters, along with a brother, cousin and their wives and children, moved into Texas in 1823.

The father was a veteran of the War of 1812 and always seemed to find himself on the cutting edge of the frontier.

The Hollands were among the first in Stephen F. Austin's colony. Francis Holland became a fairly successful farmer and minor politician, although his heart remained in the woods where he had earned his reputation as a hunter and Indian-fighter.

Three of his sons became caught up in the early stages of dissatisfaction with Mexican rule. (His fourth son suffered from severe curvature of the spine and was an invalid.)

After a cholera epidemic in 1834 killed the mother, father and fourth son, the Holland boys drifted toward the war faction of the colonists and were among the troops that besieged the Mexicans in San Antonio in October 1835.

None of the sons married.

Soon after the storming of San Antonio, James, the eldest son, became ill with pneumonia. The youngest son, Frank, took him home to Hollandale (present-day Navasota).

Two months later, Tapley, the only Holland left at the Alamo, bought a portion of immortality by being the first man to cross the line Col. William Travis had drawn in the dirt of the Alamo. To cross it meant a fight to the death in the trenches of the besieged Alamo. A total of 188 crossed over; one did not.

Twenty-four-year-old Tapley — a close friend of Travis — jumped over, saying, "Here's one life for Texas."

Two days later, Tapley and the rest of the garrison were dead. Two months later, James Holland died of his illness.

The only Holland brother left at that point was Frank, the youngest and by some accounts the most like his father. He was a haunted man — haunted by the deaths in his family, haunted by the fact that he was not at Tapley's side at the supreme moment.

Frank decided to keep fighting after San Jacinto. He had joined the Ranging Company of Riflemen (later shortened to Texas Rangers) shortly after he took his brother home and was on duty guarding against Indian attacks when the climactic battles of the Texas Revolution took place. He stayed with the Rangers and, for two years, fought Indians, Mexican military incursions and outlaws.

In 1838, he was assigned with two other Rangers to guard a party of surveyors working its way up the Trinity River basin. Near present-day Corsicana, they were attacked by 300 Kickapoo Indians.

The Rangers organized a defense, and the surveyors and their party fell back. Frank was killed. The last of the Holland brothers was dead.

Six months later, a Ranger patrol re-entered the territory and buried Frank's remains.

James died during the civilian retreat from Santa Anna's Army of Occupation. His grave, if he had one, is unknown. Tapley's body was burned along with the other defenders of the Alamo by order of Santa Anna.

Because of the nature of Indian-fighting in the 1830s and to prevent desecration of his remains, the Rangers who buried Frank did not mark his grave. None of the sons of Francis Holland lie under the ground the family fought so hard to attain.

But if one is driving along Texas Highway 105 half-way between Navasota and Anderson, stop at the Ten Mile Creek Bridge. This is the heart of Holland's tract of land, where he intended his sons to raise their families and be buried. You might feel a slight chill. This is land that was purchased at a high price.

Gen. Vicente Filisola

Gen. Antonio Lopez de Santa Anna lost the war in Texas, but Gen. Vicente Filisola saved the army.

If it had not been for the cool professionalism of Filisola, most of the 4,500 Mexican soldiers remaining in the Army of Operations after the battle at San Jacinto would have perished or been made prisoners.

The destruction of the entire Mexican Army in Texas would have been a blow to the national pride of a nation of 8 million, an insult which could only be avenged with another major attack upon Texas.

Instead, because of the sound decisions of Santa Anna's second in command after the disaster at San Jacinto, a tacit understanding was reached with Texas officers. The 2,500 Mexican soldiers massed on the west bank of the Brazos River would be allowed to retreat, picking up an additional 2,000 men scattered in garrisons throughout the new republic. They would not be molested as they endured a heart-breaking and arduous retreat beyond the Rio Grande.

The remainder of the Army of Operations was already dead or dying in poorly staffed and pathetically equipped military hospitals.

The upshot of Filisola's decision was that an undeclared border war was carried on throughout the nine-year existence of the Texas Republic, but no major military moves were made by Mexico against its former province.

Instead of being hailed as a hero who saved the lives of thousands of brave men, Filisola was denounced by other officers because of his actions. He was called a traitor and worse — a foreign mercenary who acted out of cowardice.

That probably hurt Filisola more than any other cut, for he considered himself a loyal Mexican citizen, and his courage had been tested in scores of battles.

Filisola was an example of a type of soldier who made up a significant percentage of Mexican and South American armies during the 1830s. He was an Italian who got his military training in the Napoleonic Wars that tore Europe apart for 20 years. When the blood-letting finally stopped after Waterloo, thousands of hardened veterans began looking for other places to ply their trade.

The New World, with its seething intrigues and dying empires, was tailor-made for these soldiers of fortune. They flocked to Mexico, Central and South America. Many went to the United States and some even took up residence in Texas.

During the siege of the Alamo, there were veterans of Waterloo on both sides of the walls.

Only five of the top 20 officers in the Army of Operations in Texas were native-born Mexicans. The others included Spaniards, Frenchmen, Italians, Germans, Cubans and Englishmen. Many junior officers were also Europeans or Cubans. There were even a sprinkling of Americans in the pay of the Mexicans, mostly in the navy, which was almost wholly staffed by foreign officers.

The best sharpshooter in the Mexican Army in Texas was an expatriate from Kentucky.

Filisola was one of the best of the lot. He appears to have been a man ideally suited to be second in command. A modern corporation would recognize his type and ability in an instant. He was the kind of man to carry out the instructions of the leader. He kept the organization together, took care of the details, could be counted on to fill in as Number One in an emergency, but always knew his place.

Filisola was born in Ravello, Italy, in 1789. He emigrated at an early age to Spain, where he joined the army in 1804 at the age of 15. He moved steadily through the ranks. By 1808, he had risen to the rank of first sergeant. Two years later, he became an officer when he was promoted to second lieutenant because of the valor and cool conduct he had shown in more than 20 battles.

Such was his reputation and status when he arrived in Mexico (New Spain at the time) in 1811. He was part of the royal army charged with putting down the mushrooming revolt in the New World provinces.

He continued to advance in rank while proving his professionalism. He was a man of detail who was trained by experts.

Filisola became a confidante of Agustin de Iturbide's, a brilliant but unpredictable soldier and politician who would eventually succeed in overthrowing the viceroy, declaring Mexico an independent nation and proclaiming himself emperor.

Filisola rose to the rank of brigadier general supporting Iturbide, but realized there was no future in backing a losing hand. Mexico had not thrown off the rule of the king of Spain in order to place itself under a erratic emperor.

Before he made the final break with the emperor, however, Filisola succeeded in one of the most remarkable military campaigns in the Western Hemisphere. With an army eventually reduced to only 700 men, he conquered Central America (for a brief time a part of the greater Mexican Union) and occupied the city of San Salvador.

While Filisola was conquering Central America, Antonio Lopez de Santa Anna was conquering Mexico. Santa Anna deposed the emperor in 1823 and settled in for a period of 30 years during which he was to become the dominant political and military figure in Mexico.

One of Santa Anna's strengths was his ability to recognize and promote men of ability. He succeeded in recruiting Filisola to his cause. Filisola was primarily a professional and considered it no breach of honor to switch sides as long as he served the current ruler of Mexico and did the best he could for the army and for his adopted country.

Santa Anna gave Filisola a series of increasingly important military assignments. He served as major general of the cavalry of the army which Santa Anna commanded in his much-hailed victory over invading Spaniards in 1829 at Tampico. It was Filisola who pulled the outflanked Santa Anna's chestnuts out of the fire on that occasion. Seven years later, he would be two days' march away from preventing an again over-extended Santa Anna from being overwhelmed by another enemy army — this one made up of Texans.

By 1833, Santa Anna had put Filisola in the hottest spot in the army — commander of the eastern provinces with specific orders to monitor Texas and crush any attempt at rebellion.

Filisola made his headquarters at Matamoros, ran an efficient command and impressed Texas political powerhouse Stephen F. Austin as a man of principle. He might have been a moderating influence in the increasingly bitter confrontation between Anglo colonists and Mexican rulers if he had not been struck down by a nearly fatal bout with pneumonia. He retired from the army late in 1833 and took up residence in Mexico City.

But tough talk in Texas soon turned to shooting. After a Mexican patrol was fired upon at Gonzales in October 1835, word was rushed back to Santa Anna, who knew that it would take an all-out effort of the Mexican nation to keep the rebellious province from breaking away from the motherland.

Santa Anna assembled the best troops and officers. He knew who he wanted for his second in command. Filisola climbed out of his sickbed and answered Santa Anna's call with enthusiasm.

While Santa Anna made the major moves in bringing together an army of nearly 10,000, it was Filisola who provided the expertise necessary to keep such a force in fighting trim. Filisola made sure supplies arrived at the right place at the right time. Filisola made sure that what medical services were available were in place. Filisola handled the daily problems that plagued any such undertaking (and this was a major task for the resources available to Mexico in 1835-36).

Filisola did not arrive in San Antonio until three days after the storming of the Alamo. While Santa Anna raced to the head of the advancing Mexican Army, Filisola followed in the rear, keeping the army supplied and moving.

While at Fort Bend on April 23, Filisola learned of the destruction of the entire command under Santa Anna and of the capture of his commander in chief and more than 600 Mexican soldiers.

He had repeatedly warned Santa Anna about overextending the army in hostile territory. Now, he was faced with a rapidly growing Texas Army (there were many hundreds of Texas fighting men crossing the Sabine after escorting their families to safety, in addition to at least 1,000 volunteers from the United States within a few days' march of Texas).

Filisola also knew of the danger posed by three Texan steamboats. With these boats Texans could move up the Colorado and fall on him from the rear. His troops, already on limited rations, were at the mercy of the Texans. They could be easily surrounded and cut to pieces.

Santa Anna communicated with Filisola and revealed to him that he had signed a treaty giving Texas its freedom. He ordered Filisola to retreat beyond the Rio Grande.

Filisola carried out the painful withdrawal over rain-swollen rivers in a professional manner. He lost only one piece of artillery and left no troops to fall into the Texans hands.

For his efforts, he was hounded the rest of his life with demands to know why he did not continue to fight instead of run away.

He wrote several literate works defending his action. He remained a patriot of Mexico to the end. When the U.S. Army invaded Mexico in 1846, he was again called out of retirement by Santa Anna and given command of one of three divisions formed to resist the invasion. He performed well, as usual, but it was another losing war.

In 1850, his weakened lungs collapsed and he died in Mexico City. The cloud still hung over his head. As far as Mexican historians are concerned, it remains over his head today.

William Goyens

By almost any standard, William Goyens was a successful businessman and respected civic leader in Nacogdoches in the 1830s.

He was a talented craftsman and started his career in the East Texas center of commerce as a gunsmith, blacksmith and wagon maker.

He wisely invested his earnings in a hotel and a freight-hauling business, and used income from those ventures to buy some of the richest farming land in Texas. He eventually owned more than 12,000 acres and six slaves.

Goyens was a free black, one of several of his race who played important but almost forgotten roles in the Texas Revolution.

In the heady days of 1835 and 1836, when colonists were in the throes of revolution and nation-building, Goyens was called upon to negotiate with Cherokee Indians.

Goyens traded with the Cherokees and knew their language. He counted among his friends the two most powerful chiefs of the tribe, Bowles and Big Mush.

In September 1835, with war clouds rising in the west and settlers fearing a second front against the Cherokees, Goyens was asked by some of the most powerful men in Texas, including his personal friend Sam Houston, to use his influence and pacify the Indians.

Goyens was born into a free black family in North Carolina in 1794. Like a number of free blacks in the South, he moved to Texas to seek refuge from racial persecution.

He arrived in Nacogdoches in 1820. Noted for his sharp wit and sound business judgment, he soon counted community leaders among his friends.

In 1832, at the age of 38, he married the widow Mary Sibley, a white woman from Georgia.

Mrs. Sibley's two brothers traveled to Nacogdoches to check on their sister. After meeting Goyens, they satisfied themselves that Mrs. Sibley was in good hands.

Goyens' increasing wealth brought him animosity and jealousy. Several attempts were made to force him into slavery and seize his property, but he always defeated such moves by buying the best legal talent in Texas to defend his rights.

While he kept slaves, he was active in supporting the anti-slavery movement and entertained leading abolitionists in his comfortable two-story home.

Despite his best efforts, he could not stop the inevitable confrontation between the Cherokees and Texans. The Indians were defeated at the battle of the Neches in 1839 and driven from the republic.

When legislators in the republic bowed to pressure from slave interests and passed a bill in 1840 that required "all free persons of color" to leave Texas, Goyens' friends rallied to his side.

A petition to exempt Goyens was signed by 54 citizens of Nacogdoches including Thomas Jefferson Rusk, the republic's secretary of war. Houston also intervened on his behalf. The Legislature approved the petition and Goyens was able to live his life as a rich and respected member of the community.

When he died in 1858, he was the biggest landowner in Nacogdoches and Angelina counties. Historians believe most of his holdings were lost to rightful heirs by spurious claims against his estate.

Erastus 'Deaf' Smith

If Hollywood ever decides to make an authentic movie about the Texas Revolution, it should focus on the character of Erastus "Deaf" Smith.

If there was one soldier who managed to be where the action was, and who could come closer to saying he won the war singlehandedly, it was Smith — a man who would today be classified as severely handicapped.

Smith was born in Dutchess County, New York, in 1787 into a frontier family accustomed to rough times and hard fighting. From infancy, Smith suffered from a severe hearing loss, probably exceeding 70 percent, and weak lungs.

Smith's father took the family west, attracted by cheap land and fertile soil.

Young Smith grew up in Mississippi, and was lured in 1817 to Texas by one of the many schemes of adventurers who dreamed of carving an empire out of the decaying Spanish province.

That scheme fell through, but Smith discovered that the climate of western Texas did wonders for his consumption (tuberculosis). He returned in 1821 to make the province his home.

Smith started out his Texas career by driving a herd of muley (hornless) cattle from Velasco to San Antonio and took up residence on a range below Mission San Jose.

The Spanish residents of the area were soon calling him "El Sordo" (the deaf one). He came to know every mile of the area as he roamed the woods alone.

Smith became renowned as a buffalo hunter and Indian scout. He found that living in the open and eating wild meat improved his once-puny health. He became a strong advocate of eating skunk meat as a cure for consumption.

The 35-year-old bachelor married Guadalupe Ruiz Duran, a Spanish widow with three children, and built his new family a house in La Villita section of San Antonio. Soon, he began adding children of his own to the household.

Like a number of early Texans, Smith was free of the prevailing racial prejudice in the United States. He became best friends with a free black, Hendrick Arnold, who became his partner in buffalo hunting and, eventually, his son-in-law.

Although he was destined to die in poverty, Smith always had a yearning to make a big financial killing, such as discovering a silver mine. He was a friend of Jim Bowie and was talked into accompanying Bowie and 10 others in a search for the fabled lost San Saba silver mine.

The group never found the riches they sought, but they did find 150 Caddo Indians who considered them trespassers.

The result was one of the most famous Indian fights in Texas history. Near the present-day site of the town of Menard, the Bowie party took cover in a clump of trees and held off the Indians for 14 hours. When the Caddos withdrew, 50 of the warriors had died. One of the silver-mine seekers was killed.

That was enough for Smith's wife, who laid down the law to Deaf — no more crazy expeditions with Jim Bowie.

Proficient in the Spanish language, married into an established Texas-Mexican family and free of the vices of most Anglos, Smith became a favorite of the Hispanic community.

He was as much Mexican as Anglo and when war clouds started blowing toward San Antonio in 1835, Smith was determined to stay neutral.

But then the Mexican Army commander of San Antonio, Gen. Martin Perfecto de Cos, made Smith fighting mad.

Smith was used to traveling back and forth between San Antonio and Anglo Texas. After the town was put under siege by Texans, Smith got the required passport from Mexican officers to allow him through the lines.

One day, while his papers were being checked at a barricade, he noticed a Mexican cavalry patrol riding fast toward him. His sixth sense of danger, enhanced by his near-deafness, warned him that he was betrayed. He pulled his horse around, was struck by a saber from a Mexican officer, but managed to escape to the Texas lines.

Gen. Stephen F. Austin was delighted to accept the services of such a renowned scout. Still furious, Smith arranged for Lupe and the children to be slipped out of town and sent to safety, but he was never one to forget treachery. He vowed to kill Cos. From that day forward, he probably was responsible for more Mexican soldiers killed in the war than any other Texan.

Smith was joined by his son-in-law, Arnold. Together, they made a formidable scouting team and killing squad.

Smith was always on the point, near the spot of maximum danger. He scouted Mission Concepcion for Bowie before the Texans moved into the area.

On Oct. 28, 1835, in the first battle of the revolution to draw an appreciable amount of blood, it was Smith who warned Bowie that 400 Mexicans were attempting to surround his force of 90 Texans. It was Smith, probably the most accurate marksman in Texas, who dropped the first Mexican infantryman at more than 300 yards.

Seven weeks later, Smith and Arnold were chosen to act as scouts for two columns of Texans preparing to assault San Antonio.

Once again, Smith was on the point. He was standing beside the assault commander, Ben Milam, when Milam was fatally shot. Legend has it that it was Smith who stalked and shot the soldier who killed Milam.

Smith was a close associate of Gen. Sam Houston and was with the Texas Army commander when he rode into Gonzales on March 11, 1836, to take command of the force massing there to save the Alamo garrison. But, it was too late.

Smith was in a party of three scouts who found Susanna Dickinson, the only Anglo adult to survive the assault on the Alamo. While another scout rode off to warn Houston, it was Smith who carried Susanna's baby back to Gonzales.

As Houston ordered the army to retreat, civilians half-mad with fear of Mexican racial extermination threats ran for the safety of the Sabine River and U.S. territory.

Smith was in charge of the scout company covering the retreat. He engaged Mexican advance parties at every opportunity and his Kentucky long rifle brought down many of the enemy.

The climax of the revolution was fast approaching when Smith was ordered to capture, instead of kill, Mexican couriers. He was the man who seized a courier with the invaluable news that Gen. Antonio Lopez de Santa Anna had split his forces and was heading for Harrisburg, near Buffalo Bayou, with only one-fifth of his army.

The stage was set for a savage reckoning in a swamp called San Jacinto.

For two days before the battle, Smith dressed as a Mexican and wandered in the enemy camp, pretending to be a deaf and dumb laborer while gathering information.

185

Just before the battle Houston bowed to Smith's urgent plea that he and his six-man scout squad be allowed to burn Vince's Bridge, the only way out of the swamp where the armies faced each other.

With the Texans moving on the Mexican camp in a silent line, Smith rode a lathered horse to the front, yelling, "Vince's bridge is down; fight for your lives."

Then he turned his horse toward the Mexican camp. Many eyewitnesses said Smith killed the first Mexican in the battle — bringing down the bugler who tried desperately to alert the slumbering army.

Smith was everywhere that day. He was mad with revenge. His good friends had been killed at the Alamo and butchered at Goliad. Worse, Mexican officers had called his wife a traitor.

He killed the enemy soldiers with rifle, Bowie knife, saber and bare hands. He was probably out of control, but no one was about to try to stop him.

He searched for Cos and finally found him hiding in the brush. Only Houston's request saved Smith from killing his old nemesis.

After San Jacinto, Smith drew the dangerous duty of taking a message from Santa Anna to Mexican generals still in the field, ordering them to retreat from Texas.

He was the chief scout who trailed the retreating Mexicans all the way to the Rio Grande, pausing only to help bury the charred remains of the butchered prisoners at Goliad.

After the war, he served with the Texas Rangers and distinguished himself in several encounters, but his health was failing. He was 48 years old when the revolution began. He was 50 when he finally died of tuberculosis. Skunk meat couldn't work forever.

After Smith's death, Texas authorities made sure that his beloved wife and family were taken care of. They were given their choice of houses in San Antonio, more than 4,000 acres of land and a $500 a year pension.

This most effective of Texas soldiers would today be denied the right to serve in the armed forces. He would be classified 4-F. Perhaps this is a clue to the reason Texas won its independence against such great odds. No one told a good man he couldn't fight for freedom. Certainly no man would have had the courage to say that to Deaf Smith.

This article was originally published in the June 1983 issue of Infantry Magazine, Fort Benning, Ga.

The strategy of The Alamo defense

It has been said that in time of need a nation draws its strength from heroic stories of its past military accomplishments and that such stories should therefore be preserved and passed on to future generations. The defense of the Alamo by a small group of volunteers in 1836 is one of these stories.

The settlers of Texas, then a province of Mexico, had been denied statehood in September 1835 and were now seeking independence instead. A garrison numbering fewer than 200 men at the abandoned Spanish mission in San Antonio held off a Mexican Army of several thousand for 13 days before dying. In so doing, they gave General Sam Houston, in command of the Texas regulars, the time he needed to prepare to meet that same Mexican army. Theirs is a story of great courage and sacrifice.

Although it is a familiar story, the purely military aspects of the battle have been generally neglected by the various historians who have written about it in the past. To make matters worse, revisionist historians on both sides of the border are now steadily slicing away at the Texans' accomplishments. They would reduce the number of Mexican casualties from more than 2,000 to between 300 and 600, and they even call into question the wisdom of defending the Alamo in the first place.

If, in fact, the Mexican casualty count had been so low, such a question would be quite appropriate. With his striking force scarcely scratched, Mexican General (and dictator) Antonio Lopez de Santa Anna would have run down Houston's army before that hard-pressed commander had had time to whip together a fighting force from raw volunteers.

But these figures, along with many of the other ideas about events during the siege, are not borne out by the facts.

The best Alamo historians still insist that the half-dozen, first-hand accounts of Mexican casualties from figures of authority are accurate, and these accounts put the toll at betweeen 2,000 and 2,500. (Almost fogottten are the 200 to 300 Mexicans killed in forays and ambushes during the 12 days of siege before the final battle.)

As for the wisdom of defending the Alamo, recently released findings, together with some purely military research, reveal that the decision to fight there was not an ill-considered one.

Historians schooled in the politics and personalities of the time think that the mission had become a symbol — one that Santa Anna could ignore only at his own political peril. But in command of the Alamo garrison were Jim Bowie and South Carolina militia officer Col. William Barret Travis, both no-nonsense men who would not have asked their men to die for a mere symbol.

These two men clearly saw San Antonio as the key to the battle in Texas. Bowie had been ordered to blow up the Alamo and remove its guns to Gonzales which lay to the east. He ignored the orders and Travis agreed with his decision. The

Alamo still stood.

Bowie and Travis and the volunteers with them probably decided to stay and defend the Alamo simply because they believed that they could hold off any attack until reinforcements could arrive. (They had no way of knowing that those reinforcements would never come.)

They had several reasons for their confidence. First, the Alamo was easily the best fortified position in the Southwest. In addition, the Texans were well armed — not only with the best artillery battery and best rifles, but also with a comprehensive battle plan.

Most of the garrison had been quartered at the old mission since December 1835 when 300 Texans had forced 1,400 Mexican soldiers under General Martin Perfecto de Cos (Santa Anna's brother-in-law) to surrender. That battle, which had raged in the houses and streets of old San Antonio for five days before ending up at the Alamo, had given the Texans an enormous store of munitions and cannon. Only two Texans had been killed in the fighting, while about 200 of Cos's garrison had been killed and the others (including Cos) sent back across the Rio Grande on parole.

Few Texans had really expected the terms of that parole to be honored. Most believed that Santa Anna, in outrage at the defeat, would throw the biggest and best army he could field at the Alamo, and then at the East Texas settlements, as soon as the spring grasses were abundant enough to provide fodder for the horses. As it turned out, Santa Anna marched earlier than they expected.

ARTILLERY

Even so, there was still plenty of time to turn the garrison's quick-witted frontiersmen into first-rate artillerymen. Led by Almeron Dickinson and James Bonham, a solid cadre of trained gunners welded one of the crack artillery units of the 19th century. These men and others had been trained either by the regular army or the Southern militias in the United States, and they knew their business. Finding 30 cannon at the Alamo in a sorry state of disrepair, they were able to return at least 18 and possibly as many as 22 of them to first-rate condition. The battery was larger than any other from New Orleans to Monterrey, Mexico. By comparison, no more than four field pieces were used by either side in any other battle of the Texas revolution.

The guns ranged from several 4-pounders to a huge 18-pounder, but most of them were the deadly 12-pounder smoothbore cannon. These 12-pounders were ideally suited for firing the homemade brand of shrapnel the Texans had made from chopped-up horseshoes, nails, iron slugs, and other such material. (It can be argued that, with all this artillery, the Alamo had to be defended; the cannon could not have been moved anywhere else with the available transport.)

The Texans were also armed with Kentucky long rifles, which were deadly at 300 yards, and most of these men were sure shots. By comparison, the Mexicans had mostly Brown Bess-type muskets, which could hurl a ball only 100 yards and then with no claim of accuracy. (They fired in volleys and tried to achieve the same type of firepower as an automatic weapon — with no pretense of individual accuracy.)

In addition to as many as six long rifles per sharpshooters, the Texans had hundreds of captured muskets, which had been made into shotguns for close-in firing. The loaded rifles and shotguns lined the walls and redoubts, and there were other weapons as well — pistols, swords, and tomahawks in abundance. More important, for close-in fighting they also had Bowie knives and the quick reflexes to use them effectively, while the Mexican soldiers had only bayonets and little or no training in using them.

Just as important as all of their arms — perhaps even more important — was their battle plan. Although no copy of such a plan exists today, a reconstruction of the events of 6 March 1836 leads to the inevitable conclusion that there was one and that it had been thoroughly communicated to the entire garrison. This battle plan undoubtedly stressed the need to gut the elite assault battalions that Santa Anna would throw against them.

The plan would have had two parts. First, the garrison would stop the Mexicans at the walls if it could. With sharpshooters able to fire six or more times without reloading and with double-loaded shrapnel in every cannon, any attacking force would have to be willing to sacrifice a great many soldiers to get over the wall. The Mexicans had not impressed the Texans with their courage under fire before, and there was every reason to believe that the assaulting troops would break.

If the Mexicans did get over the walls in force, it meant certain death for everyone in the garrison. They all knew that. The second part of the plan, then, would have been to inflict as much damage as possible on the attackers. This second part of the plan called for a number of collapsing perimeters that would always give the defenders a sizable edge when first attacked. Like a deflating balloon, the Alamo's fortifications would literally take the air out of the best troops in the Mexican Army.

To work as well as it did, this plan must have been known by every man in the garrison, and its execution entrusted to every officer and noncommissioned officer; during the battle, there would be no way for a shouted command to be heard and the garrison had no buglers.

So, for all of these valid reasons, the Texans decided to stay in the mission and fight for it, and ultimately for an independent Texas. But their perceptions of their enemy also had to have some bearing on their decision. If 300 Texans could rout a garrison of nearly five times as many Mexican regulars and force them to surrender the very fortress in which the Texans were now housed, what could well-armed and strongly entrenched Texans do to the next batch of Mexicans thrown against them?

FORTIFICATIONS

As the garrison prepared to meet the inevitable all-out assault, a long-forgotten genius of military engineering, Capt. Green Jameson, came forth to supervise the construction of the fortifications. Jameson took the rubble and the crumbling walls of the old mission and, using the materials at hand, turned it into a surprisingly sturdy fortress that fit in perfectly with the battle plans.

The accompanying map, published in 1980 after years of research by the long-time curator of the Alamo Museum, Charles Long (and aided by some lucky digs in downtown San Antonio), illustrates the fortifications and the collapsing perimeter principle.

The discovery of an outer fortification ditch puts to rest the criticism that no defensive measures were taken outside the walls. The deep fosse shown on the map covers the entire south wall and is probably the main reason the supposed "soft spot" of the fortress, the 75-foot stretch of open ground between the chapel and the low barracks, was not taken by storm. Jameson had built up earthworks to cover the ground, and Travis placed Davy Crockett's Tennesseans at this point. He added an artillery unit with four 4-pounders.

Long's research also rebuffs the long-held theory that 12-foot limestone and adobe walls that protected most of the mission were manned by troops firing from shoulder-high earthworks two feet in diameter. The finding that the walls were flat gives an entirely differenct picture of the first stages of the battle. Sharpshooters were not exposed, as had been previously assumed, but were in prone positions atop the walls.

In addition to the six or more loaded long rifles the marksmen would have had by their side, each also would have had a shotgun. These marksmen could fire into the inevitable masses of troops who, having reached the safety of the wall overhang, would no longer be threatened by cannons firing from the mounts cut out of the wall or from the elaborate inner earthworks 10 yards from the walls. Of course, any Texan who stood to unload his shotgun would be an easy target for massed musketry, but he could take two or three attackers with him with a double-load blast.

The main battery of three 12-pounders was located on the roofless second story of the chapel. The best of the garrison's marksmen also manned this last citadel.

It has been said that the Alamo was too big (2.5 acres) for so few men to defend, but events proved that statement inaccurate — thanks, partly, to Santa Anna himself.

Santa Anna was obsessed with Napoleon's tactics but, more a politician than a general, he lacked any real understanding of the methods behind the tactics he copied. He drew up meticulous battle orders, which called for four attacking columns, one from each side. He dictated the number of ladders, axes, picks, bullets, and other gear for each column of about 800 men. A fifth assault battalion marched into battle in true column style behind one of the front columns.

Against such an attack the Texans could use every cannon in the fortress along with enfilading rifle fire. A mass lunge at one wall would have reduced the defenders' initial firepower by at least two-thirds, but Santa Anna could not grasp the simplicity of the tactical situation. Napoleon would have realized that the Texans were in what amounted to a British square and would never have allowed a four-pronged attack on a standing square. Instead, he would have hit it with everything he had at its weakest point — a corner.

But true to what he thought Napoleon would have done, Santa Anna massed his five columns 40 men per rank, 20 ranks deep. Only the first two ranks could use their weapons, and nearly one-third of them were carrying implements with which to scale or break through the wall.

He deployed his cavalry behind the infantry, and it literally sword-whipped many reluctant warriors into the firestorm. Santa Anna made no use of his artillery, which is crucial to a column advance.

On the day of the final assault, Santa Anna further hurt his cause by ordering his men to be in position at 0100 and to lie on the freezing ground for three hours before he gave the signal to attack. As a result, reflexes that should have been at their best in the coming fury were numbed before the attack began.

Thus, incredibly, the finest army Mexico had ever fielded would attack a dug-in enemy whom it outnumbered 30 to 1, but whose firepower was greater than the whole that the attacking army could bring to bear (at least while its officers held their men in rigid column formation). In a six-hour battle, Santa Anna would throw away the best bargaining chip the Mexican nation had — the elite of its army.

During the 12 days of siege before the final assault, the first barrier the Mexicans had to cross was the river. Although it was quite narrow for the most part, it was also quite close to the walls at many points. When the Mexicans tried daylight crossings — either by fording or crossing a bridge south of the Alamo — the Texans could pick them off easily. After taking many losses, they chose to cross at night instead. Then they either dug in or took cover behind some small huts that the Texans had neglected to destroy while they had a chance.

The assault finally came at 0400, 6 March 1936. The Texans held their fire until their cannons could hit the columns at point-blank range. Riflemen poured down a hot and incredibly accurate fire, and few shots missed their mark. (Mexican officers said after the battle that most of the soldiers killed before the walls were shot in the head.)

A second charge met with only slightly more success for the Mexicans. A number of them made it to the wall overhang before withdrawing. The officers and NCO s even formed the troops for a third charge, but it was nearly 0800 before they were ready. Santa Anna ordered his reserve, most of his personal staff and every man in his 6,000-man army who could carry a musket into the fight. Again, some troops made it to the wall, and a number of Texans were killed while firing into them. Travis, the garrison's commander, was mortally wounded in this manner. Shot in the head, he fell back, gathered his final ounce of strength, picked up his sword, and held his ground. A Mexican colonel appeared at a breach in the north wall at this time and plunged his sword into Travis. The dying garrison commander replied in kind, and the two men died together. But Travis' battle plan was just unfolding.

Now painfully aware that this Mexican army was made of sterner stuff than they had expected, the Texans fought frantically to hold the walls. The east and west columns had merged with the north attacking force and created, by confusion, what should have been Santa Anna's plan from the start. Now massed, his troops poured through the breach in the wall. Worse, they wiped out the few defenders at the northwest corner and scaled the wall there, getting in behind that wall's defenders. The Texans began retiring to the earthworks (the second perimeter). Their cannons raked the attackers on the walls, but there was no time to reload. The Mexicans quickly stormed the earthworks and forced the garrison into its third perimeter.

The defenders now formed a huge U-shaped line in the large plaza with the open end pointing toward the long barracks. For 15 minutes the Texans fought with Bowie knives against bayonets. Like the Romans against the massed spears of a phalanx, the frontiersmen again proved the worth of dispersal, speed, and fighting spirit. They dived under the awkwardly thrust bayonets and gutted their opponents or deftly stood aside from the thrust to cut a jugular vein. The Texans kept up this butchery until the number of enemy troops in the plaza became overpowering.

Once again the battle plan worked to perfection as the remaining defenders dashed to the long barracks. The plaza was now packed with Mexican soldiers who were greeted by the most brilliant part of the Alamo inner-defense plan.

A 6-pounder placed on the roof of the long barracks for just this moment pointed down at the mass of infantry and fired two double-load blasts of shrapnel before its three gunners were shot down. One or two other cannon still in the Texans' hands also fired. Although none got off more than two rounds, these inflicted considerable damage. Mexican dead lay everywhere, and dozens more dropped with every volley from concentrated fire from the barracks.

The barracks had a number of separate rooms and had been sandbagged, loopholed, and made ready for use as a redoubt. But the Texans had no monopoly on fighting ability. Several Mexican officers manhandled the captured cannon into position to blast down every door of the barracks. Then, each room was taken by bayonet. (Although these barracks had always been thought of as being two stories high, Long's discoveries prove that the famed place where the bitter last stand took place was only one story high.)

The chapel still defied the assault and its three 12-pounders cut down the first wave of troops directly attacking it. Hundreds of muskets soon found the gunners. The sharpshooters supported the few men who gathered to contest the door to this last bastion. A few shouts, shots, curses, and then silence.

But one more item remained — an old Indian-fighter trick. The last marksman alive on the chapel's second floor played possum — faked death — on the narrow ledge.

With the firing almost over, Santa Anna and his entourage had moved forward. When they were about 500 yards from the walls, a single shot whistled just above the head of the commander in chief, sending him galloping to the rear. Although the marksman's Kentucky long rifle was deadly at 300 yards, a hit at 500 yards would have been adding a good deal of luck to the outcome. But it was a fitting ending and in keeping with the spirit of the garrison.

Only when their battalions were reformed did the senior Mexican officers realize what the Texans had done. Carefully picking their targets, they had killed every officer and NCO they spotted. The Texans were clearly trying to gut the army. And the best way to gut an infantry unit is to shoot for brass and stripes. There was no way of replacing those experienced men and no time to rebuild the shattered formations.

When the Mexican Army next faced a force of Texans with their blood up, the Mexicans stood for only 18 minutes despite a numerical superiority of nearly 2 to 1. The Mexican soldiers who marched with Santa Anna had seen one slaughterhouse and survived. They had no stomach to face another, 1,500 miles from home, in a swamp called San Jacinto. And it was there six weeks later that they met Houston's force and were defeated — all either killed or taken prisoner.

The battle cry in that final contest for Texas independence was "Remember the Alamo." Remembering no doubt gave the Texans strength in their time of need. We should remember, too — remember and preserve for future generations this and other stories of courage and valor and self-sacrifice.

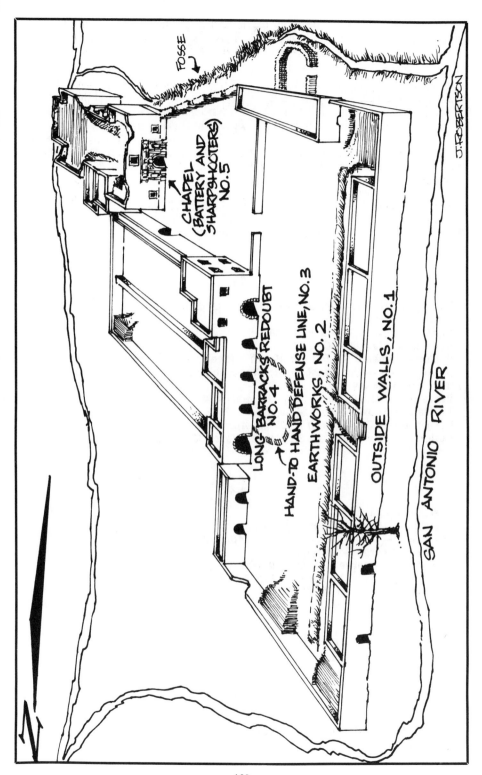

FOSSE

CHAPEL (BATTERY AND SHARPSHOOTERS) NO. 5

LONG BARRACKS REDOUBT NO. 4

HAND-TO-HAND DEFENSE LINE, NO. 3

EARTHWORKS, NO. 2

OUTSIDE WALLS, NO. 1

SAN ANTONIO RIVER

J. ROBERTSON

INDEX

The following listing indexes by dates the daily dispatches of the Texas Revolution found on Pages 1-129 of this book. The dates covered are Sept. 29, 1835, to April 22, 1836.

A

B

C

D

Dickinson, Susanna — *March 6, 13.* (See profile, Pages 161-164)
Dimmit, Philip — *Oct. 21, 22, 23; Nov. 13, 16, 19, 20, 21; Dec. 12, 17, 20, 22; Jan. 16; March 12.*

E

Edwards, Hayden — *Feb. 3, 6.*

F

Fannin, James — *Oct. 23, 28, 29; Nov. 10, 23; Feb. 4, 15; March 9, 11, 14, 18, 19, 20, 23, 24, 26, 27; April 10.* (See profile, Pages 150-153)
Farias, Gomez — *Sept. 29.*
Filisola, Vicente — *Nov. 15; Dec. 18, 19, 24, 28; Jan. 8, 23; March 10; April 22.* (See profile, Pages 179-182)
Flags — *Oct. 12; Dec. 22; Jan. 16.*
Forsyth, John — *Sept. 29; Oct. 27; Jan. 27; Feb. 8, 20.*
Fort Defiance — *March 18, 20.*
Fort Jessup — *Jan. 22; Feb. 22; March 15; April 5.*
Fort Lipantitlan — *Nov. 5, 6, 16, 20.*
Fort Settlement — *Oct. 4.*

G

Gaines, E. P. — *Sept. 29; Jan. 22; Feb. 22; April 5.*
Galveston Island — *Oct. 8; Nov. 29; Dec. 25; Jan. 12, 31; Feb. 10; April 6, 7, 9, 10, 14.*
General Convention — *Feb. 1, 3, 5; March 2, 3, 17.*
General Council — *Oct. 16, 26; Nov. 1, 3, 14, 24, 25, 27; Dec. 11, 30; Jan. 10, 11, 14, 17, 20, 21, 24, 26, 28, 30, 31; Feb. 15, 19; March 2.*
Goliad — *Oct. 2, 5, 9, 10, 13, 14, 21, 22, 23, 24, 30; Nov. 13, 16, 19, 20, 21; Dec. 4, 12, 16, 20, 22, 31; Jan. 5, 16, 19; Feb. 2, 10, 11, 15, 27; March 14, 18, 19, 24, 27, 28; April 21, 22.*
Gomez, Gregorio — *Oct. 20.*
Gonzales — *Sept. 29; Oct. 1, 2, 4, 5, 7, 9, 10, 12, 16, 21, 24, 25, 30; Nov. 4, 17, 24; Dec. 4; March 1, 9, 11, 12, 13, 21.*
Goyens, William — *Oct. 6.* (See profile, Page 183)
Groce's Plantation — *March 29, 31; April 8, 9, 11, 12, 14, 15, 18.*

H

Harrisburg — *Oct. 7; Jan. 4; Feb. 10; March 25, 30; April 2, 6, 7, 9, 14, 15, 16, 17, 19.*
Holland, Tapley — *March 5.* (See profile of Holland family, Pages 177-178)
Hornsby's Station — *Dec. 29.*
Houston, Sam — *Oct. 11; Nov. 23, 30; Dec. 21, 26, 30; Jan. 7, 14, 26, 28; Feb. 2, 3, 12, 15, 21, 25; March 2, 9, 11, 12, 13, 21, 26, 29, 30, 31; April 4, 8, 11, 12, 13, 14, 16, 19, 20, 21, 22.* (See profile, Pages 169-171)

J

Jackson, Andrew — *Sept. 29; Oct. 11, 27; Feb. 8, 9, 22; March 2; April 5.*

K

Kickapoos — *Nov. 12, 18; Feb. 21.*
Kiowas — *Nov. 18; Dec. 29.*

L

La Bahia — *Oct. 10, 13, 14, 21, 22, 24, 30; Nov. 13, 16, 19, 20, 21; Dec. 12, 16, 20, 22, 30; Jan. 5, 16, 19; March 9, 10, 18, 20, 23, 24, 27, 28.*
Lamar, Mirabeau — *April 20.*
Liberty — *Oct. 7; Feb. 1.*

M

McMullen, John — *Jan. 11.*
Martin, Wiley — *March 29; April 8, 12, 16.*
Masons — *Sept. 29; Oct. 3; Dec. 7.*
Matagorda, Mexico — *Sept. 30; Oct. 7, 15; Jan. 12; Feb. 10.*
Matamoras — *Oct. 8; Dec. 3, 31; Jan. 5, 6, 7, 10, 11, 19, 26, 28, 30; Feb. 7, 10, 17, 18, 20; April 3.*
Mexia, Jose Antonio — *Dec. 3, 13, 14, 23; Jan. 25, 27.*
Mexico City — *Sept. 29; Oct. 3, 30; Jan. 12, 25, 27; Feb. 8, 10, 17; March 15.*
Milam, Ben — *Dec. 4, 5, 7, 10.* (See profile, Pages 135-138)
Monclova, Mexico — *Sept. 29.*

N

Nacogdoches — *Oct. 6, 7, 11, 15, 25; Nov. 27; Feb. 1, 3, 6, 12; April 6.*
Neill, James — *Dec. 5, 21, 30; Jan. 6, 10, 14, 24, 26; Feb. 2, 5, 9, 11, 13, 14; March 9; April 9.*
New Orleans — *Oct. 8, 15; Dec. 3, 13, 23, 25, 31; Jan. 9, 13, 15, 18, 20; March 27, 28.*
Newspapers — *Jan. 26; March 22; April 15.*

O

Organic Law — *Nov. 14; Jan. 14.*

P

Parker, Silas M.— *Oct. 17.*
Peace Party — *Sept. 29; Nov. 9; Feb. 1, 3, 19.*

Permanent Council — *Oct. 16, 17; Nov. 27.*
Ponton, Andrew — *Sept. 29; Oct. 1, 2.*
Potter, Robert — *Feb. 3; March 17.* (See profile, Pages 172-174)

R

Refugio — *Dec. 20; Feb. 3, 4, 27; March 14, 16, 18, 23.*
Robertson, George R. — *Dec. 14.*
Robinson, James — *Jan. 11, 14, 17, 21; Feb. 2, 15; March 2.*
Rose, Louis — *March 5.*
Royall, R. R. — *Oct. 26; Nov. 1.*
Runaway Scrape — *March 29, 30; April 10.*
Rusk, Thomas Jefferson — *Feb. 3; March 17; April 20.* (See profile, Pages 174-177)

S

San Antonio — *Sept. 29; Oct. 2, 5, 9, 14, 16, 17, 19, 21, 22, 23, 24; Nov. 2, 4, 8, 9, 10, 17, 23, 24, 26, 28; Dec. 4, 5, 6, 7, 8, 9, 10, 16, 17, 21, 28, 30; Jan. 6, 7, 19, 24, 26, 29; Feb. 2, 5, 9, 11, 13, 14, 15, 16, 23, 24, 25, 26, 28, 29; March 1, 3, 4, 5, 6, 7, 10, 24.*
San Felipe — *Sept. 29; Oct. 2, 4, 7, 11, 13, 16, 17, 18, 25, 26; Nov. 1, 3, 9, 14, 18, 25, 29, 30; Dec. 2, 11, 12, 20; Jan. 10, 11, 14, 17, 20, 21, 28; Feb. 1, 15; March 26, 29; April 8.*
San Jacinto — *April 15, 19, 20, 21, 22.*
San Luis Potosi, Mexico — *Jan. 1, 18, 19, 24, 28; Feb. 10.*
San Patricio — *Nov. 3, 5, 7, 16; Dec. 20; Jan. 19; Feb. 27; March 7.*
Santa Anna — *Sept. 29; Oct. 2, 3, 19, 24, 30; Nov. 3, 15, 20; Dec. 1, 3, 12, 15, 18, 19, 23, 24, 28, 30; Jan. 8, 10, 19, 20, 23, 24, 27; Feb. 2, 8, 11, 23, 26; March 4, 6, 7, 10, 13, 16, 23, 24, 27, 28, 29; April 10, 12, 15, 16, 19, 20, 21, 22.* (See profile, Pages 165-168)
Seguin, Juan — *Oct. 19; Feb. 29.* (See profile, Pages 139-141)
Sesma, Joaquin Ramirez y — *Dec. 1, 18, 19; Jan. 19; Feb. 11; March 4,10,26; April 8.*
Smith, Deaf — *Nov. 26; April 19.* (See profile, Pages 184-186)
Smith, Henry — *Nov. 14, 25; Dec. 23, 30; Jan. 7, 9, 10, 11, 14, 17, 20, 21, 24, 26, 28, 29, 30; Feb. 2, 4, 11, 13, 14, 15, 16, 19; March 2.*
Smithwick, Noah — *Oct. 25, 29; Jan. 3.*

T

Texas Constitution — *March 17.*
Texas Navy — *Nov. 25, 29; Jan. 31; March 8; April 3, 7.*
Texas Rangers — *Oct. 17; Nov. 12, 18, 30; Dec. 29; Jan. 2, 3.*
Tonkawas — *Nov. 12, 18; Dec. 29.*
Tornel, Jose Maria — *Oct. 24, 30; Nov. 15; Feb. 8, 10.*
Travis, William B. — *Sept. 29; Oct. 4; Nov. 8, 9, 17; Jan. 29, 30; Feb. 5, 11, 13, 14, 23, 24, 25, 29; March 1, 3, 5, 6, 11; April 19.* (See profile, Pages 157-160)

U

Ugartechea, Domingo de — *Sept. 29; Oct. 2, 5, 9; Nov. 28; Dec. 8, 10.*
Urrea, Jose — *Dec. 19; Feb. 27; March 7, 10, 14, 16, 18, 19, 20, 23, 24, 26, 28.*

V

Velasco — *Oct. 7.*
Veracruz, Mexico — *Oct. 24; Nov. 15.*
Victoria — *Oct. 10.*
Viesca, Agustin — *Nov. 19, 20; Dec. 3.*

W

Wacos — *Nov. 18; Dec. 29.*
War Party — *Sept. 29; Oct. 3, 4; Nov. 9, 14; Jan. 4; Feb. 1, 3, 11.*
Washington, D.C. — *Sept. 29; Oct. 27; Jan. 22; Feb. 22; April 1.*
Washington-on-the-Brazos — *Oct. 7, 16; Dec. 21, 26; Jan. 7; Feb. 1; March 2, 9, 17; April 6.*
Westover, Ira — *Nov. 5, 6.*
Wharton, William — *Nov. 8, 9, 14; Dec. 25; Jan. 9; Feb. 19.*
Wichitas — *Dec. 29.*